Other works by Dora Pym

Readings from the Literature of Ancient Rome
in English Translation
(Harrap 1922; Hardpress 2013)

Readings from the Literature of Ancient Greece
in English Translation

Alive on Men's Lips: Latin Anthology

The Tragedy of Dido and Aeneas

Outlines for Teaching Greek Reading

Salve per Saecula

Free Writing

Tom Pym: A Portrait

ORIGEN AS APOLOGIST

DORA IVENS

(MRS. T. W. PYM)

VALONIA PRESS

ISBN 978-0-9557105-1-3

British Library Cataloguing in Publication Data:
A catalogue record for this book
is available from the British Library

Typeset in Times New Roman and SP Ionic

Printed and bound in England by
Printondemand-worldwide.com
9 Culley Court, Bakewell Road,
Orton Southgate
Peterborough PE2 6XD

Valonia Press

47 Brittains Lane, Sevenoaks, Kent TN13 2JP

CONTENTS

INTRODUCTION

The author of the thesis contained in this book was Dora Pym, née Ivens (1890-1980). On her death, her papers were given to the archive at Girton College Cambridge, where she had been successively undergraduate, research student and (after a brief interlude at Westfield College, London) lecturer in Classics. However her family retained a carbon copy of *Origen as Apologist*, which came to light recently. I undertook the task of making a digital version, principally for her descendants' interest.

The thesis was largely written in 1914-15, and was submitted for and won Girton's coveted Gamble Prize in 1916. The research topic had been suggested to her by T.R. Glover, an outstanding historian of the early church. However it is clear that her interest was more than academic. At the time when she embarked on her studies, she believed that God was calling her to be a missionary. (In the event the war, plus duty to her mother at home, thwarted this hope. Her overseas service was confined to war work with the YMCA in Calais.) As the final chapter suggests, she saw that Origen's example remains relevant to Christian mission.

Origen (184–254) is a towering figure in church history. "One of the greatest teachers ever known in Christendom," writes G.L. Prestige, "an Abelard without his arrogance, a Newman who never mislaid his disciples. He was the founder of biblical science."[1] Origen made it intellectually respectable to be a Christian in an age when hostile

[1] *Fathers and Heretics*, London: SPCK 1940, 1968, p.43.

propaganda said that Christianity was the faith of the ignorant and the gullible. Studies of Origen tend to focus on his work as a theologian, for he made a significant (if sometimes flawed) contribution to the development of Christian doctrine. However Mrs Pym took as her theme his work as an apologist: and this excited my interest.

I am a pastor, not a scholar. The people I meet, Christian or non-Christian, want to know whether there are good reasons for believing in Jesus as Son of God, and trusting him as Saviour. Today's atmosphere is uncongenial to faith. In the words of A.N. Wilson, "Public discourse assumes that most intelligent people have given up religious belief."[1] In this century-old thesis of a Girton research student I found a lively account of another age in which, as today, Christian faith came under savage intellectual attack; and of one of the defenders who ensured that it emerged triumphant.

Out of all of Origen's prodigious literary output, Mrs Pym focuses on one work: *Contra Celsum*, his rebuttal of an anti-Christian diatribe by the philosopher Celsus. Celsus wrote his *True Word* about a decade before Origen was born. *True Word* is now lost; but its contents can be gathered from Origen's extensive quotations. Scholars agree that Origen is a reliable witness to his opponent: he would have destroyed his own credibility if he had distorted Celsus' words.

In the eighteen hundred years since Celsus and Origen, the battleground has moved. For example: Celsus and Origen argued over theories of cosmogony which are scarcely comprehensible to a general reader today. Cosmogony is still important to philosophy as well as to physics: we wrestle with multiple dimensions, alternative universes, the Big

---

[1] *The Telegraph* London, 29 December 2013.

Bang, and the quantum world. However the shared assumptions of Celsus and Origen are too remote and alien to help us with our contemporary debate.[1]

But other aspects of Celsus' onslaught retain their power to shock. Centuries before Richard Dawkins, Celsus mocks the Judaeo-Christian claim that human beings have a special place in the world of living things. Unlike Dawkins, Celsus felt no need to be polite or respectful towards Jesus of Nazareth. He accuses him bluntly of being a charlatan. He sneers at Jesus' teaching as either wrong or, when right, merely an inferior copy of the inspired words of the philosophers. He regards the story of the resurrection as a reworking of pagan myths. These charges are still made.

Celsus proudly tells us that he has done his homework. He has read the Christians' books; he has attended their meetings; he has spoken to their prophets. Paradoxically, he undermines one of the accusations frequently made today by popular opponents of Christian faith – that the gospels and Jesus as divine Saviour were invented by the later church.[2] Celsus, in the mid-second century, shows us that he had read the gospels[3] and some of the New Testament letters. He confirms that the standard Christian teaching was that Jesus

---

[1] See for example p.127ff below. Celsus is sometimes vague as to which of the ideas he attacked were mainstream ("the great church") and which were sectarian. Origen easily swats attempted criticism of what orthodox Christians did not, in fact, believe: e.g. Contra Celsum VI. 24

[2] For example: "Constantine upgraded Jesus' status almost four centuries [*sic*] *after* Jesus' death… Constantine commissioned and financed a new Bible, which omitted those gospels that spoke of Christ's *human* traits and embellished those gospels that made him godlike." Dan Brown, *The da Vinci Code,* London: Bantam, 2003, pp.316-7.

[3] *vide* numerous quotations from Matthew; and apparent allusions to John (see pp.87, 96 footnotes).

was the Son of God, born of a virgin, who after his baptism was filled with the Spirit, taught a message which differed from the Jewish law and performed miracles; that he was crucified and raised from the dead; and that he offers new life to believers. But although Celsus cites the Christians' preaching, his lack of sympathy makes him miss its point. He is horrified at the idea that God might choose sinners and people of poor moral standing. He scoffs at the notion that bad men could, through the power of God, change their way of life. You may meet Celsus today: a certain type of person who has been through an Alpha or Christianity Explored course, but has rejected the Good News – indeed cannot see why it should be considered good news in the first place.

Origen, when he was first introduced to Celsus' work, reckoned that it needed no refutation. He expected that a Christian reader

> although he has met the book of Celsus, does not need any defence against it at all, but despises everything which is in it, considering, and with good reason, that all its contents deserve contempt from one who believes in Christ through the Spirit that is in him.[1]

As Mrs Pym's essay makes clear, Origen's entire life was based on trust in his risen Lord. His discipleship of Jesus Christ was personal and immediate, and it informed his every thought and action. He considered that Celsus, for all his scholarship, had produced a very shallow book. In taking this view, Origen put his finger on the truest and best form of apologetic. Origen passionately believed that it is not arguments that finally convince anyone to become or remain a Christian: it is encountering Jesus Christ in person.

[1] *Contra Celsum* Introduction, section 6: cf. p.3 below.

Celsus had met people with such attitudes, and they enraged him: "Faith takes possession of their minds first and forces this agreement of theirs about Jesus."[1] It did not help, that the Christians he met evidently included many who really were both uneducated and anti-intellectual. Celsus was right to complain if Christians refused to "give a reason for the hope that was in them".[2] Origen wrote his book to repair this deficiency. He exemplified Paul's statement: "We demolish arguments and every pretension that sets itself up against the knowledge of God, and we take captive every thought and make it obedient to Christ."[3]

Yet at root, Celsus' impatience with apparent fideism is an argument at cross purposes. The word "believe" in English as in Greek and Latin is ambiguous. It includes both a conclusion reached after the study of evidence, and also confidence placed in a person perceived as trustworthy. Both are necessary; but the latter is of more practical importance.

Human beings like to think that their picture of the world is the result of observation and deduction. But in reality, people generally base their lives on an aspiration, a vision of what is possible: often, the example of someone they trust and with whom they wish to identify. They then work out a rationale for the world-view they have embraced. Personal commitment (as it might be to Dawkins, to the lifestyle of Miley Cyrus, or to Jesus) gives us the lens through which we view the world.

The late John Wimber introduced to Christian missiology the terminology of bounded sets and centred sets.[4] Bounded

[1] See p.101.

[2] 1 Peter 3.15.

[3] 2 Corinthians 10.5. This was Origen's clear purpose: cf. p.159 below.

[4] The Vineyard Churches' website expands this idea.

sets define group membership by reference to shared rules and beliefs; centred sets define group membership by reference to shared goals. Churches sometimes act as if they were bounded sets: their evangelism appears to say "Sign up to our doctrinal package". But the church of the New Testament, like growing churches today, functioned as a centred set. It was centred on Jesus. It invited people to worship him, and to see the world his way. New members are added to such a church by following the path *Belonging – Believing – Behaving*. Believing (in the sense of agreeing with the group's doctrine) is important, but it comes second. St Anselm of Canterbury, writing a millennium before Wimber, put it in a slogan: *Credo ut intellegam.*[1] That is to say: placing personal trust in Jesus, and belonging to his people ("credo"), is the foundation for understanding the teachings of faith ("intellegam"). Anselm, like Wimber and Origen and like Christians throughout the ages, recognized that making sense of faith is important: but knowing Christ comes first.

This essay was written when its author was a young woman in her early twenties. I met her as my wife's grandmother, almost sixty years later. She was still the person who may be detected in her scholarship: sharp, insightful, passionate and kind. It was fitting that she chose Origen for her subject: something of the quality of his faith was echoed in her.

The carbon-copy typescript from which this edition was prepared is quite clear to the human eye, but less legible to the Optical Character Recognition program which I used.

---

[1] Proslogion 1. Traditionally rendered "I believe in order that I may understand".

Every page required extensive correction by hand. I do not for a moment suppose that I have caught all the mistakes: be assured that wherever detected they are mine (or the technology's), not Mrs Pym's. I have corrected or footnoted the very few apparent slips by the copyist she employed. I would be glad to be informed[1] of all errors so that I can correct them for subsequent copies.

I have usually retained Mrs Pym's punctuation and her (for the most part) capitalization of pronouns referring to God and to Jesus; and also her citations of the Bible in the Authorized Version. The effect is to make the text seem more dated than is fair to her ideas; but I suppose that readers would rather hear her voice than mine.

Most of us are less comfortable in Greek and Latin than was Mrs Pym. I have supplied in footnotes some translations (mainly sourced from the internet, a very few of my own) of Greek citations in the main text. Translations of her lengthy quotations from Tertullian are by Charles Dodgson, the father of Lewis Carroll.

Paddy Benson — Hereford, February 2014

[1] via archdeacon@hereford.anglican.org

Funde, quaesumus, Domine Deus,
in mentes nostras gloriam tuam[1]

In arduis fidelis[2]

[1] ["Pour, we ask, Lord God, into our minds Thy glory". In an unpublished memoir, Dora Pym records: "A friend had taught me a Latin prayer which she said was on the wall in one of the college Halls at Oxford… I printed this at the beginning of my Origen notebook, so that I might do the research in the best possible way."]

[2] [2] ["In difficulties, faithful", or "When things are hard, stick to it". This, the motto of the Royal Army Medical Corps, was chosen by Dora Ivens as the motto at the head of her thesis when it was submitted.]

CHAPTER I
THE NEED OF APOLOGY

Students born in later days, who stand far enough away from the early history of the Christian Church to see it in perspective, single out a treatise written by one Celsus and called ἀλήθης λόγος[1] as the most able attack made on Christianity by philosophy and paganism, even though it is only preserved fragment by fragment in the work of the man who refuted it. Further, in the refutation itself, the eight books of Origen κατὰ Κέλσου,[2] the experience of later ages has found a defence of the Faith, which does not become obsolete with years but is rather a deep and lasting foundation for Christian apologetic. Therefore, in the effort to read these books with a clear idea of their general setting and the motives of the writers, it is astonishing to find that we must rely on internal evidence and on inference drawn from contemporary history rather than on direct information. It seems almost by chance that the "True Word" survived and was answered and as though the originality of the works had only emerged as history gave a background. The varied controversy about the identity of Celsus and the consequent dispute as to the date of his treatise show that it is impossible to discover anything certain about him and his surroundings beyond what appears in his own words and the statements made about him by Origen. Yet even here it is necessary to remember that Celsus was a Roman and Origen an

[1] ["True Word" – Celsus' (now lost) attack on Christianity – GPB]
[2] ["Against Celsus" Origen's reply, is known in both Greek and Latin ("Contra Celsum") versions – GPB]

Alexandrian, and to make allowances for occasional misunderstanding on Origen's part both of the outlook and meaning of his opponent.

The majority of critics agree in dating the True Word in the latter half of the second century A.D., but the answer of Origen was not written till years after Celsus was dead and then rather unwillingly at the request of a convert, Ambrosius, who came across the book himself and was impressed by the power of its attack. In his introduction Origen states clearly his opinion of the book and his reluctance to reply to it. In the first place, he says that the true answer to false charges against Jesus Christ is not made "by the spoken word, but in the life of those who are His genuine disciples",[1] and this is stronger than any false evidence. "I venture even to say," he continues, "that the apology which you demand from me, subtly weakens both the apology which rests on facts, and the power of Jesus, which shines clearly forth to those who can perceive anything at all. But still, that I may not seem to shirk the task you have laid upon me, I have tried to the best of my ability to suggest by way of answer to each of the statements made by Celsus what seemed to me adapted to refute them, though his arguments have no power to shake one who really believes."[2] Here then is Origen's second reason for not writing an "apology". He does not consider the arguments of Celsus worthy of the name of true philosophy or strong enough to shake the faith of one, who has received and made his own "the love of God in Christ Jesus our Lord."[3] He consents to write however on the supposition that among the

---

[1] Introd. 2

[2] Introd. 3

[3] ib.

crowds of Christians some few may be found, who need his arguments; otherwise Ambrosius would not have sent him the book. "Yet", the introduction ends, "better is he who, although he has met the book of Celsus, does not need any defence against it at all, but despises everything which is in it, considering, and with good reason, that all its contents deserve contempt from one who believes in Christ through the Spirit that is in Him."[1]

Origen is certain that no shock from the wisdom of philosophers can affect those who have experienced even in a slight degree what Paul meant by τὸ ὑπέρεχον τῆς γνώσεως Χριστοῦ:[2] the English translation, "excellency", has lost nowadays the fullness of its meaning and hardly conveys the unique characteristic of "the knowledge of Christ Jesus", which Paul was trying to express – its all-embracing nature, which broke the bounds of human knowledge and passed beyond them: it is this knowledge which sets the knowledge of philosophers in the right proportion, so that it is not an adversary to the Christian but an ally. So Origen makes it clear at the outset for whom he is composing the treatise: "Not for those who are definitely believers has this book been written, but either for those who have tasted not at all the faith which trusts in Christ, or for these who are, to use the word of the Apostle, 'weak in the faith'."[3] This preface is the starting-point for discovering the purpose which Origen had in mind, when he wrote his answer to Celsus, the kind of people who would read it, the terms in which they thought and the surroundings, mental

[1] Introd. 6
[2] ["The excellency of the knowledge of Christ", Phil. 3.8 (KJV) – GPB]
[3] Introd. 6

and spiritual, in which they lived. Circumstances of place and time affect vitally the understanding of any literature that deals with philosophy or religion, but probably most of all they are an indispensable part of the study of apologetic. An apologist states and explains eternal facts to the people of his own race and time; insofar as he makes plain the eternal facts his apologetic is true and effective, and the way to this runs along the lines of thought prevalent in his day, through the use of words and terms which convey a living meaning to his hearers. Therefore, to understand the Apology of Origen both in plan and substance, it is worth while to try to form some ideas about Ambrosius, who thought it necessary, and the unknown "weak in the faith", who were to be strengthened by it.

Their home was Alexandria and their mental outlook was inevitably coloured by the life and thought of a city, which could rival even Rome. Dio Chrysostom summed up the unique position of Alexandria in a picturesque phrase, which might well be the text for any description of the city in the second or third century. "It lies at a kind of clasp of the whole earth and the races, who dwell furthest apart, and like the market-place of a single city, it brings all men together, showing them to one another and making them as far as possible of one race and tribe."[1] Over four hundred years before the days of Dio, Alexander had come and, in the words of Strabo the geographer, "seeing that excellent possibilities there were, resolved to found the city at the harbour."[2] Then Strabo enumerates the advantages of the site: "it was washed by two seas, it possessed a fine harbour,

[1] Or. XXXII para.669. κεῖται… ἐν συνδέσμῳ τινι ὅλης γῆς

[2] Bk XVII p.792

double-sided; the Nile made the Delta rich, and further, kept the climate healthy in summer" when most cities near marshes suffer from their position. It was indeed a site to "clasp the whole world" – a meeting-place for the trade of the East and the trade of the West and therefore also a meeting-place for ideas and thought, a wonderfully cosmopolitan whole.

Diversity and paradox were the dominating features of every side of the city's life. It was a new city with no mythology or ancient legend: it was an historic creation by an historic king, primarily for the advantage of commerce.[1] Therefore, in the eyes of a dweller near the Acropolis, it had all the spaciousness of a modern town. The streets were wide and lined with trees: Deinocrates, the architect, had marked them out at right angles to one another with such mathematical precision that Strabo says the whole city was "cut into strips" by the roads. The buildings were large and stately; the palaces, the temples, the Museum and the Halls of Commerce, rivalling the glory of ancient Tyre, whose "merchants were princes and her traffickers the honourable of the earth". Down from the "Gate of the Sun" ran a wide roadway to the famous harbour, and there stretched miles of docks, to which the great convoys came sweeping in from India and the Arabian Gulf,[2] bringing their wares to be exported in turn to Rome and the far West. The lighthouse of Pharos, which Cleopatra built, towered up on the flat coast-line and guided the ships in through the shoals and quicksands to the safety of the Delta. The exports and imports brought much revenue to the greatest trading centre

---

[1] cf. Merivale, *History of the Romans under the Empire*, Vol VIII p.235

[2] [The Ptolemies completed a canal, roughly on the line of the modern Suez Canal, in about 250 B.C. – GPB]

in the world. Alexandria was a rich city and a fair city; a city of open spaces, of palaces, of beautiful suburbs, where the sun shone and the wind blew pleasantly.[1] One who described it says: "Breezes blew through and round about, and healthy, fresh air, so that a man who spent much time there might imagine he were tarrying beyond the confines of our world, as he heard so often the murmur of the winds blowing over him with sunny breath."[2]

Yet Alexandria, in spite of her newness and commercial turmoil, possessed also the background of an almost endless age, which came from the antiquity of Egypt.[3] The corn she sent to Rome was grown by the unceasing toil of Egyptian peasantry as it had been grown for generations. The Pyramids, the Nile and the desert looked as unchangingly on the city of the Ptolemies as, hundreds of years before, they had smiled at the youth of Solon's Greeks. It was the Nile more than anything else, which summed up the permanent element of life to the Egyptian: the growth of wheat depended on its flood-mark being high; in its regular rise and fall was centred all that was real. There is a hymn of one of the ancient kings of Egypt, who was a monotheist reformer, in which he thus addresses God: "Thou createst the Nile in the other world, thou bringest it at thy pleasure to give life to mankind: for thou has made them for thyself, O lord of them all who art ever with them, O lord of all the earth, who risest for them, O Sun of day... the mighty one in the remotest lands, thou givest them their life, thou sendest forth the Nile

---

[1] Cf. Ammianus Marcellinus XXII. 16 and Strabo Bk XVII pp.785-98 for descriptions of Alexandria and Egypt.

[2] Ammianus Marcellinus XXII. 16.

[3] cf. Westcott, *Essays in the History of Religious Thought in the West*, p.197

in heaven, that it may descend upon them; it raisest its waves mountain-high like the sea, it waters the fields of their cities. How glorious are thy counsels, O lord of eternity, thou art a Nile in heaven for foreign men and cattle throughout the earth! They walk on their feet and the Nile cometh to Egypt from the other world."[1] In this way the Egyptians loved and venerated their river. So by the very circumstances of its founding and the position in which it stood, Alexandria linked together the old and the new.

The races who lived and traded and studied and ruled in the city were as diverse as its surroundings[2] so that it well deserved the epithet Dio gave – πολυανθρωποτάτη τῶν πασῶν.[3] There were Egyptians, subject and sullen, Greeks of a peculiar Alexandrian type, owing more to the influence of Egypt than they would have acknowledged,[4] Jews with their own quarter in the city, their own officials and their own philosophy, Romans governing and not understanding; but governing well, because the Emperor would not allow so precious a province as Egypt to pass from under his direct control. There was work for the Roman legions in guarding the trade-routes to the East and keeping back the wild desert tribes to the South. There was work for the Governor of Alexandria in controlling the turbulent city-mob with its threefold character, Jew, Greek and Egyptian, mingled with

---

[1] Breasted *De Hymnis in Solem sub rege Amenophide IV conceptis*. p.47. Hymn to Aten.

[2] cf Merivale, *History of the Romans under the Empire*, Vol. VIII, p.234ff. Mommsen, *The Provinces of the Roman Empire* Vol. II. Chap .XII p.232 ff for account of Egypt and Alexandria.

[3] Dio Chrysostom, Or. XXXII 676 ["the most populous of all" – GPB]

[4] cf. Mahaffy, *The Greek World under Roman Sway*, pp.239-48 for character of the Alexandrian population.

Indians, Scythians, Bactrians, Arabians, Ethiopians,[1] and informed with a strange Bacchanalian spirit belonging more to the East than the West. It is possible to realise from reading Kingsley's "Hypatia" what the wild fury of such a mob could be. It was always impatient of authority and unsparing even of Emperors in the matter of ridicule and abuse.[2]

There is a vivid letter said to be written by the Emperor Hadrian, which gives the following description of Egypt and of Alexandria in particular:

> Hadrian Augustus to the consul Servianus greeting. I have come to know Egypt, which you praise so much, from end to end; and have found it fickle, unstable, and in a flutter at every breath of opinion. In Egypt the worshippers of Serapis are really Christians, and those who call themselves bishops of Christ are votaries of Serapis. There is not a chief of a Jewish synagogue, there is not a Samaritan nor a Christian priest, who is not an astrologer, a haruspex and an aliptes[3]. Why, when the patriarch himself, of whom you speak, comes to Egypt, one party forces him to worship Serapis, the other to adore Christ. They (the Alexandrians) are an excessively seditious, vain, and insulting people. Their city is wealthy and prosperous, and admits of no-one living idle in it. Some manufacture glass, others paper, others are linen-workers, all profess some trade or other. Even those whose feet are lamed by gout have something to do; the blind have an occupation; even those who suffer from gout in the hands do not live

[1] Dio Chrysostom, Or. XXXII 672

[2] Dio Cassius LXXVII, 22-4, Sen. Ad Helv. 19.6

[3] [i.e. "one who anoints" ; the manager of a wrestling-school – GPB]

> idle there. They have one god – money; he is worshipped alike by Christians, Jews and all nations. I wish the city had better manners and morals; its prosperity and its size really entitle it to be the first city of Egypt. I granted it all it asked for; I restored its old privileges and added new; and they could not avoid giving me a vote of thanks when I was there. Then as soon as I had gone, they said many things against my son Verus; what they said of Antinous I believe you have already heard.[1]

Even more piercing is the sarcasm of the orator, Dio Chrysostom, who rebukes the Alexandrians fiercely for their levity and readiness to listen to any false philosopher. "They (the philosophers) chatter in their lecture-rooms, so-called, having captured listeners and pledged them to be submissive:"[2] there are many Cynics in the city, yet they are "men, who know practically nothing and only need a livelihood. But in the cross-roads and the narrow streets and at the gates of temples they gather together and instruct falsely; children and sailors and all that type of mob, stringing together jokes and a great deal of gossip and those familiar retorts, which please the crowd. Therefore they do no good but rather the greatest possible harm, for they accustom the brainless to make a mock of philosophers."[3] He recalls the saying that the Alexandrian mob cared for nothing but abundance of bread and horse-racing,[4] and then goes on to describe the wealth and glory of the city, whose fame

---

[1] Vopiscus, Vita Saturnini (trans. by Bury *The Student's Roman Empire* p.520.

[2] Or. XXXII, 657

[3] ib.

[4] ib. 668

reached even to India and the ends of the earth, whence he is led to remark trenchantly: "That which brings the praise of men is obedience, gentleness, united wills, good order in government, attention to those who speak uprightly, no constant search after pleasures; but the coming and going of vessels and an abundant population are the praise and honour of the merchandise and the great gathering of ships and the harbour and the market-place, not of the city... but you, if anyone speak even in praise of the Nile, why you're just as proud and uplifted as if you were running all the way from Ethiopia yourselves."[1]

Even so the picture of the city is not complete, for there is no mention yet of the University, that great example of learning endowed by kings. Alexandria united in the bounds of one city a modern New York and a modern Oxford or Cambridge. There were scholars as well as merchants within her gates and no-one was considered a first-class doctor, who had not studied in the Alexandrian Medical School. The study of literature was chiefly analysis and assimilation of the work of the past: there was little original production, but in music and philosophy, astronomy and medicine, the professors of the Museum were pre-eminent even in the second century after Christ. The school of Medicine, in which Galen's name was all-powerful, the philosophy of the neo-Platonists, Ammonius Saccas and his successor Plotinus: these were the outstanding characteristics of the University in Origen's day. There was, in addition a Christian institution, at which lectures were given to heathen inquirers and Christians, anxious to find a philosophical expression of their faith. The history of this School is not

[1] ib. 669

very detailed or clear.[1] The converted Stoic, Pantaenus, gathered a few learners together informally in his house and taught them Christian philosophy, as he formulated it. There Clement found him and remained for many years till the pupil became more famous than the master, and it is Clement not Pantaenus who is regarded as the founder of the School. The study of philosophy was considered dangerous and subversive by a certain section of the Christian Church in Alexandria, whom Clement calls "ὀρθοδόξασται"[2], foreshadowing by the name the fact that such people are not peculiar to Alexandria.[3] But there were many students, who were anxious to do hard study of the doctrines of philosophy and the Christian faith; to these Clement, with his wide knowledge and deep love of Greek philosophy and literature, was a sympathetic teacher. The explanation of the Bible was the chief subject of the lectures, which were open to men and women alike and attended by both.

Such was the environment of Ambrosius and his friends - a city of merchants and sailors, students and professors, philosophers and votaries of every religion under the sun. Outwardly at least, as far as people and surroundings were concerned, Alexandria could justly claim to be the "clasp of the world." If we turn to thought and philosophy, religion and superstition, the clash of faiths and opinions is none the less manifest. It seems as though every possible kind of god had a sanctuary in Alexandria. There was the native Egyptian worship with its strange material ideas of the divine, its lack of power to speak in abstract terms, its animal worship and those mysterious superstitions, which excited

---

[1] Eusebius H.E. V 10-11. VI. 19.

[2] [Roughly, "fundamentalists" – GPB]

[3] Strom. I. IX. 45.6, I. 182 – II. 19, IX. 43.1.

the ridicule of Greek and Roman alike.[1] There were Eastern cults from Syria, Persia and India – magicians and impostors of every kind for the Alexandrian mob was noted for reverencing "τὸ δαιμόνιον".[2] There were Stoic and Cynic philosophers, who preached stern ethics to a pleasure-loving society; there was Emperor-worship reminding the inhabitants of Alexandria that their freedom to talk and speculate depended on a power, which kept the peace of the world; there was the ecstatic mystery-worship of Isis and of Mithras, with purifications and secret rites; there was the distinctive school of Jewish thought, inspired by Philo, when he strove to express Hebrew religion in the terms of Greek philosophy; there was the neo-Platonic school, which revived all that was spiritual in paganism; and, lastly, there was Christianity with all the heresies which grew up when the Christian faith was first being philosophically formulated and many free lances were striking out in all directions into the realm of pagan thought. Alexandria was, in a sense, a mirror of the spiritual life of the age. The pagan world was sick at heart from end to end: everywhere there was spiritual awakening and spiritual aspiration, everywhere a sense of dissatisfaction with ethics and philosophy, a longing for communion with the divine.

In this atmosphere of uncertainty and myriad-minded speculation we must imagine Ambrosius living. Practically no facts are forthcoming as to his life before his meeting with Origen about 218 A.D. From the short notices, which various writers allot to him, we gather that he was rich and held high office in the city. He had embraced some form of

---

[1] cf. Sayce, *The Religion of Ancient Egypt*

[2] Dio Chrysostom Or. XXXII 659. ["The Divine Essence" – GPB]

Gnostic heresy; Epiphanius says he was Marcionite or a Sabellian,[1] Eusebius a Valentinian,[2] but it is not necessary to pursue here the fantastic varieties into which these Gnostic systems spread; our purpose is rather to gain some insight, albeit tentative and imaginative, into the mind and character of Ambrosius.

There were probably two determining factors, which played the chief part in leading thoughtful students of religion into Gnostic beliefs – factors, which in every age are especially powerful with the young. Briefly stated, they are, first the revolt, conscious or unconscious, against the existence of evil and the consequent feeling of inability to reconcile it with the nature of God; and, second, the recognition of the value of the life and death of Jesus by those, who have any knowledge of the Gospel, however much they may alter and interpret it to suit their own ways of thinking. Heresy is often a conscientious effort to express intelligibly the state of mind, which is produced by the apparently glaring contrast between facts and ideals; it is an effort to be consistent, though the consistency so gained often weakens facts, and therefore ultimately the artificial system loses touch with life. So in the second and third centuries men fashioned what a modern writer has called "bizarre and fantastic cosmologies... which it seems so incredible that any reasonable being could have believed as a rational explanation of the great and awful problems of human life and destiny"[3] fashioned them to save God from

[1] Adv. Haer. 64

[2] H.E. VI. 18.

[3] Cairns, *Christianity in the Modern World* p.338. cf. "Gnosticism, to use Harnack's phrase, was 'an acute secularizing of Christianity', that is to say, it was a thoroughgoing attempt on the part of those early thinkers to

direct contact with matter, and at the same time they tampered with the facts of the historic Jesus, which gave the whole reality to His work of redemption, so that the Son of God might only in semblance have inhabited a human body. They were confronting what Origen himself called a very difficult question,[1] and it was more or less the same question for all though it came to them in different ways. Marcion rejected the Old Testament and the God of the Hebrews, as being utterly unworthy of the revelation of God in Jesus Christ, so unworthy, indeed, that in his system the God of the Old Testament was placed in an inferior position. Marcion had to make his own Gospel too, in order to exclude all the wrong ideas of the Evangelists, who identified Jesus with the Jewish Messiah. Was Ambrosius a Marcionite? He may well have been, for the influence of the master spread widely even after his death, and to one, whom Origen afterwards frequently characterizes as "θεοσεβέστατε"[2] there was much that was satisfying in Marcion's system, apart altogether from its attempt to reconstruct Christian thought. For, though the Christian Church might call him a heretic, Marcion and his followers also lived strictly by Christian ideals with that strange inconsistency which marks so many, who profess unbelief.[3]

---

graft the faith in Christ which they possessed upon a Pagan stem, to equate the Gospel with Weltenschauungen largely alien to it." ib.

[1] IV. 65. δυσθήρατος τῇ φύσει ἡμῶν ["hard for our nature to grasp" – GPB]

[2] ["devoted to God" – GPB]

[3] cf. Foakes-Jackson, *Christian Difficulties in the Second and Twentieth centuries* p 42 "Often, when men profess to know only the fantastic Christ of the last critic, they really believe in the Jesus of whom they were taught at their mother's knee."

So we may picture Ambrosius - a young man, endowed with the highest gifts and not shaming his gifts by his character (Origen calls him "γενναιότατε"[1]), one, who had met the best Alexandria could give in thought and life, who sought reverently for God and honoured Jesus Christ, but whose mind was confused by that struggle of thought to express spiritual facts, which reached its central whirlpool in his own city. This was the Ambrosius whom Origen converted from heresy to the Christian Church. Eusebius puts it vividly: he says, "a bright light shone into his soul and lighted it up,"[2] and so the half-light of Gnostic half-fact vanished in the new brilliance; henceforth, Ambrosius was Origen's faithful friend, a strong member of the Church, and one of that glorious list of devoted pupils,[3] who made their master's name famous – even to winning hatred for him from the rulers – by their persistent courage in martyrdom and persecution.

There must have been few thoughtful students of literature and philosophy, who were not brought into touch with Origen: we can gather from the account of Eusebius what a strong force his personality exercised, whether he lectured on the ancient Classics or the Hebrew Scriptures. "By giving proof of a philosophic life to those who saw him, he naturally aroused many of his pupils to similar zeal; so that prominent men, even of the unbelieving heathen, and them that followed learning and philosophy were led to his teaching."[4] "Coming one after another, from morning till evening, to his school, they scarcely gave him time to

---

[1] ["of noble character" – GPB]

[2] H.E.VI. 18.

[3] ib. 3 and 4.

[4] H.E. VI. 3.

breathe."[1] "Many others also, drawn by the fame of Origen's learning, which resounded everywhere, came to him to make trial of his capacity in sacred literature. And a great many heretics and not a few of the most distinguished philosophers studied under him diligently, receiving instruction from him not only in divine wisdom but also in secular philosophy."[2] His lectures on pagan literature were a true *praeparatio evangelica*, for those who attended them frequently went on to the definite Christian teaching given in the Catechetical School. From Origen's exposition of the Scriptures Ambrosius would gain a truer understanding of the character of God, while the fire of his personal Christianity would burn up all vague Gnostic theories about the life of Christ.

That Ambrosius loved and venerated such a master is not surprising. Origen's later pupil, Gregory Thaumaturgus, has left a sincere, if somewhat rhetorical, description of his own studies under Origen at Caesarea and from this it is possible to see how Origen's teaching captured his pupils in mind and heart. "He used to declare... that true religion was utterly impossible to one who did not philosophise. Heaping such sayings one upon another in great number, he would carry us away like enchanted creatures... and settle us I know not where by his arguments, with a power which was divine."[3] "When he had toiled much and seemed to have come to a standstill, then he treated us as a skilled farmer would some field, wild and... no-wise good soil... he... with his husbandman's skill surveyed us, and not only observed the faults beheld of all and openly to be seen, but dug down and

---

[1] ib. VI. 15.

[2] ib. VI. 18.

[3] Gregory Thaumaturgus, Farewell Address to Origen, Sec. VI (trans. Metcalfe)

searched to the inmost recesses, asking and propounding and hearing us answer. When he perceived anything which was not useless and unprofitable and ineffectual in us, he broke the ground, turned it over, watered it, used every device, applied all his skill and care, and wrought us into shape. The 'thorns and thistles' and all the tribe of wild grasses and herbs which our mad and startled soul had sent forth... he cut out and pulled up with his inquiries and restraint, grappling with us in argument, and sometimes overthrowing us in true Socratic fashion, if he espied us rushing off in all directions like wild horses, plunging out of the track and running aimlessly about, until by persuasion and compulsion, as if by the bit of reason in our mouth, he rendered us quiet to his hand. It was difficult and not without discomfort to us at first, as he produced his reasons to us unaccustomed and not as yet practised in following the argument as he produced it; yet he reformed us."[1] "He did not introduce but one philosophical argument, nor did he allow us to seek after them unaccompanied; but he introduced us to all, for he wished us to be unacquainted with no one of the dogmas of the Greeks, and he himself went in along with us... and led us by the hand as in an exploration, in case anything crooked, or hollow or adulterate should crop up by the way. In that case, as one well practised, from his long acquaintance with arguments neither unaccustomed nor inexperienced, he himself would remain above in safety, and, stretching forth a hand to us others, would draw us up like baptised ones. Everything in each of the philosophers that was useful and true he used to pick out and set before us, and sift out what was false, especially whatever concerned

[1] ib. Sec. VII

human piety."[1] "He himself would interpret and make clear whatever was dark and enigmatical... for he was a wondrous hearkener to God, and of most excellent understanding... This gift was his alone of all men whom I have known personally.... to keep (the precepts) in his own soul and teach them to others."[2]

This was the teacher, who held his pupils entranced not only for lecture-hours but for life. Ambrosius availed himself amply of the riches, which Origen's brain and spirit could afford. "To him Origen addressed many treatises."[3] "He was intellectual and enthusiastic about the sacred readings of God's Scripture, because of the deep thought in the divine books."[4] So enthusiastic, indeed, was Ambrosius about the interpretation of the Bible that he provided Origen with everything he could want for the quick production of books, paper, shorthand-writers and money, so that he was enabled to write the commentaries, which often reduced him to great weariness.[5] Sometimes the admiration of Ambrosius must have hastened beyond the bounds of discretion, for Origen speaks of his "rashness"[6] in publishing books, which were not yet revised. He had literary qualities himself; "he was of good birth and not without skill in graceful literary expression, as his letters to Origen show."[7] There is a fragment of one of Origen's letters, which shows the relationship between the two men and the love of Ambrosius

[1] ib. Sec. XIV.
[2] ib. Sec. XV (XIV Lommatsch).
[3] Jerome, de vir. ill. 56.
[4] Epiphanius, adv. Haer. 64.
[5] ib. cf. Eus. H.E. VI. 23.
[6] Ap. Jerome, Ep. 84, 10.
[7] Jerome, de vir. Ill. 56.

for deep discussions. "We scarcely have time for meals amid our discussions, nor when we have supped, for a walk or rest to our bodies. Even then we have to discuss points of grammar and check MSS. We cannot even give our frames the benefit of a full night's sleep, for we pursue our grammatical discussions until far into the evening. I say nothing about the time from the dawn till the ninth or tenth hour: for all serious students devote those hours to the study and reading of the divine oracles."[1] Such was the man whom Origen called his "taskmaster",[2] the faithful friend and the faithful pupil. All the years Origen continued in Alexandria we can imagine Ambrosius frequenting his lectures, urging others to attend them, beseeching him to write commentaries and never ceasing to learn from him Christianity as much in practical life as in theory. For, in the days when Origen had left the city and was settled in Caesarea, Ambrosius was serving the Church as deacon, witnessing in persecutions and, together with Protoctetus, receiving from their master the inspiring "Exhortation to Martyrdom". Distance evidently did not sever master and pupil, so that when Ambrosius, possibly during a visit to Rome,[3] was brought into contact with the arguments of Celsus, he naturally turned to the man to whom he had been wont to take difficulties for so long, and whom he knew could not be better fitted for the task of apologetic. Why, when Ambrosius sent him the book, was Origen so unwilling to refute it? He gives his own reasons in his preface, but it is possible also that he, like all great teachers, possessed a tendency against authorship. Socrates left no writings and

[1] Lommatsch. XVII. 5.
[2] Comm. In Johann. I. ἐργοδιώκτης
[3] Pélagaud, *Etude sur Celse*. Livre II[d]

Vittorino da Feltre, the great Humanist educator of the Middle Ages wrote no treatise, but continued only to practise his methods in his school. The same tendency doubtless belonged to Origen, but it was overruled by the persistence of his pupils, who insisted in the end on taking down his class lectures. So, at the age of 60, Ambrosius prevailed on him to write his apology for those "weak in the faith", whom it is so difficult to trace out. There had evidently been no demand within the Church itself for an answer to Celsus, but a man like Ambrosius, who had experienced the doubt and desire for sure knowledge of those who stood just outside its doors, was quick to see the force of Celsus' attack and to gauge the effect it would have on others. Probably the book would be read not only by Ambrosius but by many students of the Museum. They were a varied throng and might well be pardoned for uncertainty of mind in that flood of changing opinion.

There were students of pagan philosophy who had sat at the feet of Ammonius Saccas and associated with Porphyry, enemies of Christianity yet anxious to include its better points in neo-Platonism: there were also representatives of the medical school, where one doctor had set up such a high standard and handed on such a fine tradition. Galen was dead, but his love of scientific research for its own sake, and his deep belief in the good purpose, that ruled the Universe, had won for him such devotion from his pupils that his name remained magic in the school to which his life was given. No young doctor could read the treatise, "The best doctor is also a philosopher", without realising the greatness of his calling, and feeling shame if the motives, which led him to it, were only those of money-making.[1] "Galen perhaps by some is even worshipped",[2] says Eusebius, speaking of certain heretics, and there is no doubt that a strong character has a tremendous influence on University pupils, whatever the subject taught. Ambrosius might have known among them, as well as among those definitely within the Church, some who would welcome Origen's book. Philosophers, scientists, heretics and Christians could all, if they were thinking men, realise the value of Celsus' arguments and it was not always easy to find answers in that atmosphere of eclecticism, when experience of life was often lacking and theory tended to become academic and blurred. The man, to whom Ambrosius naturally turned, as being capable of meeting varied types of mind and understanding them, as capable of dealing with Celsus on his own ground, was Origen. It was an obvious choice for him to make: let us see how far Origen was fitted for the task.

---

[1] e.g. Galen ὅτι ὁ ἄριστος ἰατρος φιλόσοφος "It is not possible to attain the highest end of your calling if you set wealth above honour and study your profession to make money and not to help mankind... No, it is absolutely impossible to go in for money-making and at the same time practise so noble a profession."

[2] H.E. V. 28.

CHAPTER II
ORIGEN AND THE NEED OF APOLOGY

"Heresies, with their differences of opinion, have never sprung from any matter, whose first principle was not both worthy of enthusiastic pursuit and also of great value to the life of men. Take for example the science of medicine – men value it and cannot do without it, and there is much discussion and research among doctors about the treatment of bodily disease: so for this reason many 'heresies' abound in the medical world, and everyone knows it... Again, take philosophy: philosophy, by holding out the promise of truth and knowledge of real existence, lays down for us a method of life and strives to teach what is really best for us human beings; but the investigation of these questions always drags men in different directions, so that just as many heresies have been framed among philosophers... in the same way, when something wondrous and holy was shown to the human race in Christianity – not to the slave class alone, as Celsus thinks, but to many men of letters among the Greeks – it was inevitable that heresies should come into being, not in any way through faction and quarrelling, but because many, even among the student classes were eager to understand Christianity... But no one with any sense would avoid the advantages of medicine, because there are 'heresies' among doctors, nor would anyone with a fitting sense of proportion hate philosophy and offer, as the pretext for his hatred, its numerous heresies... But if these arguments are coherent, why may we not defend in the same way the existence of heresies among Christians? I always think Paul's remark on this subject very wonderful: 'There must be heresies among you, that those who are approved may he recognised.' For as that man is 'approved' in the medical profession, who, on account of his experimental training in varied 'heresies' and his honest examination of most of them, has chosen the best, and, as the leader in philosophical thought is he, who after studying the majority of views and testing them, has given his adherence to the strongest cause, so I would say that he who had carefully studied the heresies of Judaism and Christianity was the wisest type of Christian. But the man, who finds fault with Christianity because of its heresies, would find fault else with the teaching of Socrates from whose school many others have come with dissentient views. Why, one might even find fault with the opinions of Plato himself, because Aristotle left his school and founded a new one."[1]

So Origen answers the charges against Christianity, which Celsus bases on the existence of heresy, but, apart altogether from its context, this passage seems to sum up the Alexandrian world of thought, as Origen saw it, and his own special relation to it. The word "heresy" has lost its original meaning of "choice" and at the same time has been narrowed down, in application, to the paths of theological unorthodoxy. In third century Alexandria, however, "αἵρεσις" was predominant in that sea of opinion, ever blending and changing its hues, often confused and blurred, which well deserved the names we give to it – eclecticism and syncretism. A man, who was to speak with definite authority in that University, had indeed to be "approved", before he could lay claim to public notice, and authority of this kind could only be gained by one who possessed a

[1] III. 12 and 13.

comprehensive knowledge of the varied branches of thought, wherein men were occupied, one who could rise above his knowledge to the heights of selection and interpretation, and – most necessary of all – one who could express himself in the ordinary student language, in terms which his audience understood. Origen was gifted with all these qualities and, at the same time, possessed a personality, which ensured him a hearing. It is here that the contrast between himself and Clement is most obvious. Alexandria has given its name to Clement, and it is he who most truly reflects the infinite diversity of her life and thought. Origen is much stronger and more definite, his intellect is greater and his vision more piercing; therefore, he is not so much the plastic creation of his surroundings as the master hand, who lifts up the tendencies of his time and by his touch moulds them until they reflect himself. What the surroundings of a third-century Alexandrian were we have already tried to imagine. We have next to show how Origen was in touch with thought and life in his city and specially fitted to speak to those for whom Ambrosius demanded teaching. Ptolemy's "bird-cage of the Muses" had been the centre for the last outburst of Greek literary production, but, after the days of Theocritus and Callimachus, literature was choked by learning and Hellenistic erudition, isolating itself from life, remained untouched by the new stream of inspiration which flowed from Augustan Rome: for the Greeks did not generally condescend to read Latin literature. The Museum, however, was still famous for the study of science, though the word conveys rather an ambiguous meaning to the modern ear: so different were ancient categories and canons, conceptions and methods, to say nothing of existing and ascertained facts, that practically all which modern science supplies to the intellectual atmosphere of the twentieth century was literally non-existent in the ancient world. Nevertheless, both astronomy and medicine had large schools in the "new" University of Alexandria.

The researches of Eratosthenes had been continued by numerous disciples, and Origen seems to have been familiar with the pursuits of astronomers in his own day. The dark blue of an Eastern sky, studded with points of burning light, is in itself sufficient reason for the fact that the home of astronomy and augury lies in the East. When, as in Egypt, this sky is spread over the silence of the desert, men are irresistibly summoned to contemplate the heavens, whence it is but a short step to worshipping sun, moon and stars, and attributing to them rational, living souls. In spite of his condemnation of sun-worship,[1] Origen speaks with awe and wonder of "the heavenly bodies, whose being and splendour we perceive, when we gaze upon them."[2] And again – "it is with no intention of dishonouring such wondrous works of God, the Creator, or calling them like Anaxagoras 'fiery masses' that we speak as we do about sun, moon and stars, but because we perceive the surpassing divinity of God, which is far beyond all words."[3] These are the words of one, who has gazed himself upon the heavens and found them "very good". He leaned also to the current belief that stars were living and had living souls: "We are certain that the sun itself and moon and stars pray to God, who is over all, through His only-begotten Son and so we think we ought not to pray to these, who pray themselves."[4] The connection

[1] V. 10-13.

[2] VI. 73.

[3] V. 11.

[4] V. 11. cf. Milton, Ode on the Morning of Christ's Nativity

between philosophy and science was closer in ancient thought and it was natural that one who contemplated the Creator should be in touch with those who contemplated the celestial creation. On the more technical side of astronomy we find that Origen has information. He has read the "Treatise on Comets" by Chaeremon, the Stoic,[1] and quotes it to confirm and justify the appearance of the Star of Bethlehem. Indeed he speaks of stars as one who had studied the subject personally. "The star, which was seen in the East, we think to be a new star and like none of those to which we are accustomed either in the firmament or in the lower orbs, but in nature like those which appear from time to time, comets, or meteors like beams of wood, or beards, or wine-jars or any other of the names by which the Greeks are wont to call their different shapes."[2]

It is evident that Origen was at home in the company of astronomers. He seems also to have a great interest in medicine and to sympathize with the actual work of doctors. His master, Clement, may have known Galen, and no one who attained eminence in the University could fail to come into touch with the medical School. Origen frequently takes metaphors and analogies from medicine,[3] as one to whom

---

The stars with deep amaze,
Stand fixed in steadfast gaze,
Bending one way their precious influence;
And will not take their flight
For all the morning light,
Or Lucifer that often warned them thence;
But in their glimmering orbs did glow
Until their Lord Himself bespake and bid them go.

[1] I. 59.

[2] I. 58.

[3] III. 12-13, 62.

the operations of doctors were familiar. He speaks of "the people who are operated on or cauterized by surgeons,"[1] and of "the doctor, who looks at dreadful sights and handles unpleasant things, that he may cure suffering."[2] And, in speaking of the great change, which Jesus brought into the lives of so many men, he sums up the beginning and end of all medical research in a manner after Galen's own heart. "Even those, who heal many sick bodies, do not attain their object, which is the health of those bodies, without God."[3]

It was, however, in the sphere of literature and philosophy that Origen was supreme, being as Porphyry said, "a Greek educated in the wisdom of the Greeks;"[4] we have already noted the attraction of his purely Classical lectures to pagan and Christian alike. Evidences of his own study of Greek poetry and his familiarity with "the Greek who loves learning and is soaked in Grecian lore"[5] escape from him constantly in his defence of Christianity. He quotes Euripides[6] in the same breath as the Psalmist on the subject of the fulfilment of prophecy and oracular responses. He cites "the whole of Greek and barbarian history"[7] to prove how often men break covenant with their hosts, giving as an example a quotation from Archilochus. Homer, on whom he has read commentaries, he calls "the best of the poets",[8] and though he seems to adopt a Platonic attitude of contempt

---

[1] VI. 56.
[2] IV. 15.
[3] I. 26. cf. Harnack, *Expansion of Christianity*, Vol. I, Bk. II, Chap. II for Jesus regarded as physician in the early Church.
[4] Ap. Eus. H.E. VI. 20.
[5] I. 67.
[6] II. 20 (Ps. 109 vv 1-2 and Eur. Phoen. 18-20) cf. II. 34.
[7] II. 21 cf. II. 20.
[8] VII. 6.

towards the representations of tragedy,[1] he shows knowledge of the tragedies and. in a discussion of the suitable portrayal of character, turns naturally to Greek poetry for his illustrations, and not only to the universally admired characters of Homer – Nestor, Odysseus, Penelope, but also to the philosophising slave of Euripides.[2] He refers to the plots of the Old Comedy[3] and gives a long quotation from Hesiod's "Works and Days".[4] Plato's style he calls "beautiful and polished",[5] and quotes elsewhere the myth of Eros from the Symposium.[6] It is only by such sidelights as these that insight can be gained into Origen's literary taste. Of the philosophers he speaks more frequently, and indeed their writings were closer to his own work of explaining the Bible and setting forth Christianity to his pagan pupils.

Origen's method of approach to the Greek philosophers was that of a man, who was conscious of a higher revelation than they had received, but who, at the same time, honoured them for their enthusiastic pursuit after truth.[7] "Out of love for truth", he says, "we bear witness of certain Greek philosophers that they knew God, since 'God made the knowledge of Himself plain to them', although 'they have

---

[1] VII. 6.
[2] VII. 36.
[3] VI. 49.
[4] IV. 38.
[5] VI. 2.
[6] IV. 39
[7] cf. Eus. H.E. VI. 19. προσῄεσαν ὅτε μὲν αἱρετίκοι, ὅτε δε οἱ ἀπὸ τῶν Ἑλληνικῶν μαθημάτων, καὶ μάλιστα τῶν ἐν φιλοσοφίᾳ ["I was sometimes visited by heretics, sometimes by those who were conversant with the studies of the Greeks, especially those that were pursuing philosophy" (a letter of Origen, quoted by Eusebius) – GPB]

not glorified Him as God nor given thanks to Him; they have turned to futile speculations till their ignorant minds grew dark. They claimed to be wise, but they have become fools; they have exchanged the glory of the immortal God for the semblance of the likeness of mortal man, of birds, of quadrupeds, and of reptiles'."[1] These words of Paul are Origen's favourite indictment of philosophers[2] – they have misused the gifts of God. He is also careful to point out that in spite of the great value of wisdom, the words of the wise are not always of use to the plain man. "Let the ancients then and their wise men set forth their words to those who can understand them."[3] This plea on behalf of the unlearned does not make void his appreciation of educated religion. "To be really wise is excellent, not only to seem wise... and far from being a hindrance to the knowledge of God, education and study of the best thought and wisdom all help towards it."[4] Origen himself was renowned as a Christian Platonist,[5] but it is evident that he had a deep acquaintance with the history of philosophy and the tenets of different schools, Platonists, Aristotelians, Epicureans and Stoics,[6] even though he distorts words of Celsus, which show him plainly to be a Platonist, in an effort to prove them the malicious utterance

[1] Rom. l. 19, and 21-3 (trans. Moffatt): Ap. IV. 30.
[2] cf VI. 3.
[3] VI. 3 (ad init.)
[4] III. 49.
[5] I. 3, II. 12, and 41. cf. Eus. H.E. VI. 18. "He was celebrated as a great philosopher even among the Greeks."
[6] III. 75, V. 20-21, VI. 48, 71. cf Porphyry Ap. Eus. H.E. VI. 19. "He was always in company with Plato, and had the works also of Numonius and Cranius, of Apollophanes and Longinus, of Moderatus and Nicomachus, and others, whose writings are valued in his hands. He also read the works of Chaeremon the Stoic and those of Corrutus."

of an Epicurean;[1] there are also passing references to contemporary ideas about matter and spirit, which point to the founders of neo-Platonism,[2] and Origen had studied that strange mixture of quackery and philosophy, found in the story of Apollonius of Tyana.[3] His own reasons for studying the Classics are preserved by Eusebius. "While I gave myself to the teaching of the Word, the report of my occupation spread abroad and there came to me at different times heretics and Hellenic scholars, especially philosophers, so that I decided to examine the opinions of heretics and the tenets of the philosophers who profess to discuss truth. This I did, copying both Pantaenus, who before my day was so great a help to many, in that he gave much attention to those studies, and also Heraclas, who at this very time is a member of the Alexandrian presbytery: I found the latter in the lecture-room of a philosopher, wherein he had persevered for five years before I began to attend that kind of lecture... Therefore.... up to this day... he continues his literary researches among the writings of the Greeks, as far as he is able."[4]

In all schools of thought in different ages there are certain characteristic modes of expression, certain pre-conceptions taken for granted, which influence men's minds in every branch of learning and give them, to a certain extent, a uniform point of view. It is these characteristic ways of thought and expression, which, as a rule, become most quickly obsolete; so much so, that they are almost a stumbling-block to later generations, who think and speak

[1] I. 7, 10, 32. III. 80. Iv. 4, 54, 76, V. 3.
[2] III. 41-2. IV. 56.
[3] VI. 41.
[4] Ap. Eus. H.E. VI.19.

from a different standpoint, and therefore frequently find the discoveries of the past vitiated by the perspective, which makes them most characteristic of their own age. It is a common-place that the whole intellectual atmosphere of today is coloured by the methods and ideas of the theory of evolution. In every art or science and most of all in religion is found what Samuel Butler calls a "pestering of the unborn" – that seeking for origins and tracing of development, which makes for a strong historical sense and a definite idea of gradual progress. This characteristic finds its exact opposite in the mental outlook of ancient Alexandria. Modern conceptions of progress were almost entirely absent, and the study of history and literature took more and more the trend of allegorical interpretation. The old idea of the magic nature of words had not vanished[1] and Origen shows that theories on this subject were a common matter of debate. "Here is involved a deep and mysterious subject – that of the nature of names,"[2] he says, and goes on to quote both Greek and Eastern philosophers and to apply the "philosophy of names" to Jewish and Christian beliefs. When such mystery is attached to words, it is a short step to the figurative interpretation of documents, be they historical or literary. It is a kind of poetic imagination running riot. As alchemy among the sciences, so is allegorical interpretation in the realm of literature and philosophy. "I remember reading" says Origen, "in the book of a certain Pythagorean on the hidden meanings in the poet (Homer)".[3] Hellenes, as well as Christians, used this method to explain their sacred

---

[1] cf. Hatch. *The Influence of Greek Ideas and Usages upon the Christian Church* (Hibbert Lectures 1888), Lecture III.

[2] I. 24-5.

[3] VII. 6.

writings – a fact which Origen does not fail to note. "Are the Greeks allowed to refer such stories to the doctrine of the soul or to interpret them figuratively, while for us the door of a consistent explanation is closed?"[1] Origen's own allegorical exegesis of the Scriptures will be treated more fully later. Here it is sufficient to say that he found even in the Gospels symbolism,[2] and in the Jewish law "the pattern and shadow of heavenly things."[3] Herein he was in line with the practice of his day: allegory was used even by the neo-Platonist, Porphyry. It is a method which is peculiarly unsatisfying to this generation, but it is necessary to remember, when estimating Origen's work, that here he was on common ground with his opponents, and that, though they might differ as to details of interpretation, the principle was granted unquestioned.[4] It was a characteristic of the age. "The Alexandrians," says Bigg "... found symbols where there was no symbol... they neglected the difference between before and after... but they are always intelligent and reasonable and their extravagance is that of the poet philosopher, not that of the dogmatist. And they did not invert their allegorism... They evaporated the letter; they did not stereotype the Spirit."[5]

Up to this point we have been considering Origen's relation to the intellectual outlook of his day and discovering his familiarity with all sides of the University. It is, however, in his personal character that the power of his work is ultimately found, and in a discussion of his apologetic

---

[1] IV. 17.
[2] II. 69.
[3] II. 2.
[4] Elsee – *Neo-Platonism in relation to Christianity*, p.94.
[5] *The Christian Platonists of Alexandria*, pp.188-9.

Origen, the man, is of greater importance even than Origen, the scholar. The circumstances of his own life had brought him into close touch with hard fact and the unacademic world; his youth was clouded and stormy, his manhood strenuous and beset by many dangers, his old age troubled by exile from his native city and the disapproval of the Alexandrian Church. He was no more than seventeen, when he learnt the sternness of reality by his father's martyrdom. It does not need much imagination to read between the lines of the plain account in the history of Eusebius. "When Severus stirred up persecution against the churches, a brilliant witness was given by the champions of religion everywhere, but especially did it abound in Alexandria; for thither from Egypt and all Thebais they were escorted like athletes to a great stadium of God, and through their unconquerable endurance of varied tortures and ways of death they put on the victor's fillets, given them by God. Among these also was Leonidas, said to be the father of Origen; he was beheaded, leaving his son behind very young."[1] It is all told in a few lines but it was a hard experience for a sixteen-year-old boy. Eusebius, who had access to first-hand evidence about Origen,[2] gives a picture of his early home-life. He was evidently gifted far beyond the average with a love of study and literature, and his father seems to have taught him personally with a loving pride which recalls Quintilian's

[1] H.E. VI. 1.

[2] ib. VI. 2. "ἐκ τινων ἐπιστολῶν καὶ ἱστορίας τῶν καὶ εἰς ἡμᾶς τῷ βίῳ πεφιλαγμένων αὐτοῦ γνωρίμων τὰ δηλούμενα φέροντες" ["(we adduce the facts) from certain epistles and histories which have come down to our own day, by those of his familiar friends who are yet living." – GPB]

delight in his scholarly sons.[1] The words of Eusebius are very vivid here: "he gave his father trouble by asking what was the intent and meaning of the God-inspired Scriptures. His father, outwardly indeed, rebuked him and told him not to enquire into things beyond his age nor to search beyond the obvious meaning of Scriptures. But in his own heart he was greatly delighted and gave sincere thanks to God, the Author of all good, that He had given him the honour of being the father of such a child. And they say that frequently, when standing over his sleeping boy, he would uncover his breast and kiss it, as a shrine made holy by the Spirit of God, and congratulate himself on a son of such promise."[2] It was into the peace of this Christian home that the storm of persecution broke. In the year 202 A.D. it was not yet so safe to be a Christian that men could connect it with dulness and respectability. The unique value of Christ was not confused or obscured by less fundamental issues, and men died for this possession of supreme worth with thanksgiving to God on their lips: and these "martyrs" or witnesses of Christ were honoured as athletes were honoured, who had won a glorious victory in the games. It was no wonder then that in this atmosphere, "the love of martyrdom took such a hold on the soul of Origen, though as yet only a boy, that he longed to leap forward and rush upon the conflict."[3] He was at the age, when the demand of a great cause makes a strong appeal, and it was only the action of his mother which prevented him from precipitating himself into youthful martyrdom. Held at home himself, he could not keep quiet, but wrote his father a letter full of encouragement, saying, "Stand fast and do not

[1] Quint. Inst. Or. VI. Pref.
[2] H.E. VI. 2.
[3] Eus. H.E. VI. 2.

change your mind for our sakes."[1] Thus the gifted boy was bereft of his father and teacher, and his "burning enthusiasm" was put to a searching test. The property of Leonidas was forfeited to the imperial treasury; and his family of six, of whom Origen was the eldest, were left almost penniless;[2] to have faced death and imminent danger of starvation at the age of seventeen is an education in reality, which cannot be easily lost. It left its mark upon Origen, and throughout his years of academic work he never lost touch with life.

A wealthy and distinguished lady of Alexandria received him into her house and he maintained himself by teaching Greek literature: a leader of certain heretics, one Paul, was also sheltered by the same patroness, but Origen, though so young, showed already a hatred of heretical doctrine and took the firm line of refusing to join in Paul's services.[3] "But" says Eusebius, "while he was thus busy with his school.., and there was no one in Alexandria, who gave up his time to instructing people in the principles of the faith, but all were driven away by.... persecution, some of the pagans came to him with a mind to hear the word of God:"[4] and again, "he was in his eighteenth year when he conducted the school for preliminary instruction in the faith... at the time of the persecutions of Aquila, governor of Alexandria; and then he obtained a celebrated name among all the believers on account of that enthusiastic kindness, which he showed to all the holy martyrs, whether known to him or not. For not only was he with them, when in bonds, nor only until

[1] ib.
[2] ib.
[3] H.E. VI. 2 (ad. fin).
[4] ib. VI. 3. (ad. init.)

the last of their trial at the tribunal; but even after this, when they were led away to die, he conversed freely with these holy martyrs and advanced in the face of danger. So that as he... with great boldness saluted the martyrs with a kiss, the multitude who stood around, mad with rage, had more than once almost stoned him to death, had he not experienced the helping hand of God and by a marvel escaped... so great, indeed, was the hostility of the unbelievers to him that they formed themselves into companies, to station soldiers about the house where he dwelt, on account of the numbers that were taught by him the principles of the faith. The persecution daily blazed forth against him with such violence that the whole city of Alexandria could no longer contain him, as he moved from house to house, driven about in every direction, because of the great number of those, who had been brought by him to learn about God."[1] So stormily was Origen's headship of the Catechetical School inaugurated: for, in spite of the youth of the teacher, the bishop, Demetrius, gave church authority to the work Origen was doing informally and for nearly thirty years he continued to hold the post – thirty memorable years both for the University of Alexandria and the Christian Church. "His daily life gave wonderful examples of the conduct which comes from true philosophy. For, 'as his teaching' they say, 'so was his life; and as his life, so also was his teaching'. Therefore, with the help of God's power, he induced many to emulate him."[2]

It is evident that Origen not only taught but also lived the Gospel, and that the key-note of his philosophy was the

[1] H.E. VI. 3.
[2] ib.

application of stern principles of self-denial to every-day life. Long before the age of friars and monks had carried asceticism to its extreme, he disciplined himself by fasting, slept always on the bare ground, and followed the precepts of Christ not to possess two coats or wear shoes or pass time in cares for the future. "Showing an ardour beyond his years, he persevered in cold and nakedness, advancing to the greatest extremes of poverty... many, indeed, who wished to share with him some of their money, were grieved because of the heavy toil he endured for the sake of teaching God's truth. He did not, however, relax in his perseverance."[1] In order to be financially independent, he sold his classical library and received an allowance of four obols a day – a great sacrifice for a scholar.[2] "For many years he continued to lead this life... during the whole day undergoing no trifling amount of laborious exercise and at night devoting himself most of the time to the study of the Holy Scriptures."[3] Origen had early mastered the lesson of self-control and learnt in practice what he taught in theory. The charm and power of his teaching have been already mentioned; his pupils increased so greatly that he appointed Heraclas, a friend and former pupil to lecture to the more elementary scholars.[4] His curriculum was varied to suit the needs of different types of people at different stages of learning. "All whom he saw to be endowed with ability he introduced to the study of philosophy, through geometry, arithmetic and other preparatory work; then advancing them to the opinions current among philosophers, and explaining their writings,

---

[1] ib. VI. 3.

[2] ib.

[3] ib. cf. H.E. VI. 8.

[4] ib. VI. 18.

he commented and speculated upon each, so that he was renowned as a great philosopher even among the Greeks. He also gave many of the more common people a liberal education, often declaring that they would get no small help from this for understanding the Holy Scriptures; whence also he considered the study of secular philosophy particularly necessary for himself."[1] It was not surprising that many "led by the fame of Origen's learning" came to make trial of his teaching. It was during these years too that Ambrosius was converted and that Origen's attention was first turned to literary work; he now spent many hours on his great critical text of the Bible and on various Biblical commentaries, notably that on the Gospel of St. John.[2] In Alexandria also was written the famous "περὶ ἀρχῶν",[3] which laid the foundation of dogmatic theology. "He had more than seven secretaries, when he dictated, who relieved one another at appointed times. He had no fewer copyists as well as girls, who were skilled in elegant writing."[4] All these were supplied by the zeal of Ambrosius.

Occasionally, Origen left his pupils and his books to undertake journeys, journeys too of very varied purpose. About 215 A.D. he visited the "very ancient church of the Romans", but "after no long stay" returned to his work in Alexandria.[5] On another occasion, "a soldier arriving handed letters both to Demetrius, the bishop of the district, and to the prefect of Egypt from the governor of Arabia; the purport was that he should send Origen to him in all haste, that he

[1] ib. VI. 18. cf. Plato, Republic Bk. VII.
[2] ib. VI. 18, 23, 24.
[3] ["First Principles" – GPB]
[4] ib. VI. 23.
[5] ib. VI. 14.

might communicate his teaching. So he was sent. Soon, having accomplished the object of his visit, he returned again to Alexandria."[1] It was not only among Christians and the academic circles of the Museum that Origen was renowned; it seems that his fame spread even to the court of the Emperor. "Mamaea, the Emperor's mother, a woman distinguished for her piety and religion, when the fame of Origen had been spread abroad so that it reached her ears too, was very eager to be honoured by seeing him and to make trial of his wisdom in the things of God, at which all men wondered. Therefore while staying at Antioch, she sent for him by a military escort. With her he stayed some time, giving much teaching to the glory of the Lord and to show the excellence of divine learning; then he hastened back again to his usual occupations."[2]

About 215 A.D. it chanced that there was war and insurrection in Alexandria, so that Origen for safety visited Palestine. He stayed in Caesarea and "was requested by the bishops to explain the Holy Scriptures publicly in the church, although he had not yet received the priesthood by the laying-on of hands."[3] This was the beginning of trouble and dissension between Origen and his home-church in Alexandria. It is evident that Demetrius, bishop of Alexandria, and his clergy "were not altogether sympathetic with Origen: his intellect was far beyond them and they were very jealous for Church discipline. Demetrius, who was a man of humble birth and little education,[4] wrote on this occasion to the bishops of Jerusalem and Caesarea,

[1] ib. VI. 19.

[2] ib. VI. 21.

[3] VI. 19.

[4] Chronicon Orientale – cf. Farrar *Lives of the Fathers* Vol. I, pp.411-16.

emphatically condemning the action of Origen: "This has never before been heard, nor has it occurred in our time – that laymen should give discourses in the presence of the bishops."[1] The two bishops wrote a defence of Origen to the agitated Demetrius but, in spite of their statements confirmed by the quotation of precedent, Origen was recalled to his duties in Alexandria, first by letter and then by members and deacons of the Church sent for that purpose, nor did Demetrius ever ordain him priest – a strange fact considering his important position as head of the Catechetical School. It is impossible because of the lack of definite evidence to discover the ins and outs of the relations of Origen with his ecclesiastical superior, but evidently all was not well, and about 230 A.D., when Origen was ordained priest on a visit to Caesarea, the storm broke.[2] Demetrius gathered a council of his bishops and formally excommunicated Origen, who was ultimately compelled to give up his work and leave Alexandria.[3] "All the disturbance about him in this matter," says Eusebius "and the decisions of the bishops of the churches thereupon... as it demands a separate treatise, we have made a sufficient statement in the second book of the treatise we have written in his defence."[4] The "separate treatise" has not survived and it is only by conjecture that we can discover the actual rights and wrongs of the cause. It is significant that, though apparently the sentence of excommunication was accepted at Rome, yet Origen was treated as an honoured friend and teacher by the Eastern bishops of Palestine. Yet, when Demetrius died a few years

[1] Eus. H.E. VI. 19.
[2] ib. VI. 23.
[3] ib. VI. 26.
[4] ib. VI. 23.

later and Heraclas, Origen's old pupil and successor in the headship of the Catechetical School, was appointed bishop of Alexandria, he did not recall Origen.[1] It may be that public opinion in Alexandria was too strong even for the friendship of Heraclas, but it is even more likely that Origen himself could not bear to return to the city, where he had worked so strenuously, been so prominent a figure and tasted the bitterness of such grievous enmity and opposition. No-one can read for long the writings, which Origen has left, without discovering him to be a man of fierce passions and intense feeling; to one so sensitive the apparent wreck of his work, coupled with disgrace and exile from the city, must have brought unfathomed torture and pain. He has left in the introduction to part of his commentary on St. John (which he was writing at the time), a few words from which we can judge how fierce had been the conflict within himself and how complete his ultimate victory. "Afterwards when my enemy waged most bitter war against me by his fresh letters, which were truly at enmity with the gospel, rousing all the winds, reason exhorted me to stand to the contest and to save the ruling principle within me lest troublous disputes should avail to bring the storm even upon my own soul, rather than to compose the rest of my commentary before my understanding received calm... But now, since God has quenched the many fiery darts which have been hurled against me so that their force is spent, and my soul… is constrained to endure more easily the assaults that have been made upon me, having, as it were, obtained some fair

[1] ib. VI. 26.

weather, I wish to defer no longer the dictation of what remains."[1]

So ended Origen's long and brilliant ministry in Alexandria, and so he left the city, which he seemed so peculiarly fitted to serve, the city whose ways and manners, whose people and pastimes, whose sins and beauties flash out even in the midst of theological argument and show that they had their own place in the sympathy and knowledge of one who spoke, not as a lecture-room theorist, but from experience of life.

It was not often that political questions of the day received much attention from the professors of the Museum, but Origen acknowledges the advantages of the world-peace, which the Roman Empire at its beginning had established;[2] a debt which isolated Alexandria was apt to pass over. We cannot discover whether he took any part personally in civic affairs but he certainly speaks of "the popular ecclesia at Alexandria"[3] in the tone of one who knew it from experience, contrasting it, coupled with the assemblies of Athens and Corinth with "the ecclesia of God" in those cities; he found the Church councils far superior to the political administration, calling the former gentle, courteous and steadfast, and the latter full of sedition and quarrelling. He knew well the streets and market-places of the city,[4] where the crowds would gather round any strange juggler or the Cynic philosopher would endeavour to deliver discourses on virtue – streets, jostling with the men of many nations, and enlivened by the abuse of women slandering one

[1] Comm. ad Joann. T. VI (trans. Farrar – op. cit. Vol. I p.412)
[2] II. 30.
[3] III. 30.
[4] III. 50. cf. Dio Chrysostom Or. XXXII.

another.[1] The inner side of the social life of Alexandria did not escape the piercing eye of this student of humanity; he knew all the attractions of dancing, theatres, games, rope-walking[2] and the other trifles, which formed the centre of life for the rich. "We turn away women" he says "from self-indulgence, home-quarrels and all their theatre-manias, dancing-manias and superstition."[3] In spite of his learning and reverence for wisdom, Origen was supremely alive to the value of all human personality[4] and we may be sure that he had links among the poor and unlettered of the city as well as among his own students and colleagues. So Alexandria lost what the leaders of her church were unable to appreciate.

The remainder of Origen's life was spent in Asia, chiefly at Caesarea, and the story of it is best told by Eusebius. "The bishop (of Caesarea in Cappadocia) was so enthusiastic about Origen that he summoned him to his own diocese to help the churches; another time he went to see him in Judaea and stayed with him there some time, to increase his knowledge of God. Moreover, Alexander, the bishop of Jerusalem, and Theoctistus, bishop of Caesarea, attended him nearly always, like pupils their master, and allowed no one else to explain the Holy Scriptures and other questions of Church doctrine."[5] "While Origen was performing his usual duties at Caesarea, many frequented his school, not only of the inhabitants but also innumerable others from abroad, who left their country in order to attend his lectures.

---

[1] III. 52

[2] III. 69.

[3] III. 56.

[4] III. 54.

[5] H.E.VI. 27.

Of these the most noted, whom we know, is Theodorus, known also known by the name of Gregory, and so celebrated among the bishops of our day; also his brother Athenodorus. Origen, seeing them wrapt up in Greek and human learning, instilled into them the love of philosophy and induced them to exchange the zeal they showed in their former studies for training in the wisdom of God. After being with him five years, they made such advance in sacred studies that both, though very young, were honoured with the episcopate in the churches of Pontus."[1]

Reference has already been made to the farewell address of this Gregory to Origen; he describes in it how he and his brother were diverted from studying at Berytus by Origen,[2] who "began by using every device to bind us firmly, us who were like some wild beasts, or fishes, or birds, fallen into snares or nets, trying to struggle out and escape away, and wishful to depart from him to Berytus or our fatherland... He laid special stress on the things which were exciting us, while – said he – we were neglecting the chief of our endowments, namely reason. I cannot now tell how many sayings of this sort he was wont to utter, urging us to philosophise, and not on one day only, but all those early days when we first resorted to him transfixed by his word as by a dart, and in our new youth (for he was compounded of a certain sweet grace and persuasiveness and a certain cogency), while we were still casting about and considering and essaying to philosophise but not yet fully decided, yet withal somehow unable to draw back, and attracted to him by some constraining power greater than his words... Like

[1] ib. IV. 30.

[2] Gregory. op. cit. Sec. V

some spark kindled within my soul there was kindled and blazed forth both my love toward Him, most desirable of all for His beauty unspeakable, the Word holy and altogether lovely, and toward this man his friend and his prophet... and the soul of Jonathan was knit with David."[1] The last words of the address show that Gregory's youthful affection was strengthened into a life-long friendship. "But do thou, beloved one, rise and bless us as thou sendest us forth. Thou hast been our salvation while we frequented thy holy instruction. Save us with thy prayers also when we are gone. Hand us over and commit us, yea hand us over to the God who led us to thee... For when we are gone, we shall not hearken to Him in that same freedom which we enjoyed with thee. Entreat some consolation to come to us for our parting from thee; send some good escort, some companion angel. Ask too that He may turn us again and lead us unto thee. That above all things will be our consolation."[2] Age and exile had not weakened Origen's teaching powers.

Eusebius gives also an account of the commentaries and discourses, which he wrote in Palestine, including the "Reply to Celsus" and various letters, for "he also wrote to Fabianus, bishop of Rome, and to many other bishops of churches on the subject of his orthodoxy."[3] Another side of Origen's activities is illustrated by the incident of Beryllus bishop of Bostra in Arabia, who "perverting the definite teaching of the church, attempted to introduce certain opinions that are foreign to Christian faith, daring to assert that our Lord and Saviour did not exist in the personal sense of existence before his dwelling among men; neither had he a divinity of

---

[1] Gregory, op. cit. Sec. VI.
[2] ib. Sec. XIX (XVIII Lommatzsch)
[3] H.E. VI. 32, 36.

his own, but only that divinity which dwelt in him from the Father. When the bishops had had many examinations and discussions with him, Origen, who had been invited with the rest, entered into conversation with him, in order to find out what opinion he held. But when he understood what he meant, after correcting his error, by reasoning and proof he convinced him, and thus recovered him to the truth of doctrine and brought his back again to the former sound opinion."[1]

So Origen lived, writing, teaching, exhorting and travelling, a bulwark of the Church and a champion against false opinions, till about the year 250 A.D. when the Emperor Decius stirred up a persecution against the Church and once again we read in Eusebius: "the number and greatness of Origen's sufferings during the persecution, and the nature of his death, when the spirit of darkness drew up his forces for the contest, and waged war with all his arts and powers against him... the nature and number of bonds, which he endured for the word of Christ, and all his torments of body, the sufferings too, which he endured under an iron collar and in the deepest recesses of the prison, when for many days he was extended and stretched to the distance of four holes on the rack; the threats of fire too, and whatsoever other sufferings inflicted by his enemies he nobly bore, and finally the issue of these sufferings, when the judge eagerly tried with all his might to protract his life... his letters tell."[2] Soon after this Origen died – the result of his tortures. He died a martyr as he had lived a saint.

---

[1] ib. VI. 33.
[2] ib. VI. 39.

It is never easy to describe human personality by means of words and the greater the personality, the more inadequate do the words seem. Gregory, who had known Origen intimately and studied under him for years, was acutely conscious of this inadequacy. "I am about to recall" he says "whatever is most God-like in him, whatever in him is akin to God, whatever, though imprisoned in this appearance and mortality, is forcing its way with all welcome toil unto likeness with God. I am about to touch... on things too great for me... and... I who am so little and utterly devoid of wisdom, shrink and hesitate and fain would be silent... Yet, beloved one, no detraction or insult can touch thy qualities, still less the divine, abiding in their place as they do, unshaken, unaffected by our little unworthy words."[1] It is a fitting preface to any attempt to sum up the character of Origen.

Even from the short account given so far of Origen, it is possible to realise that he was a man exceptionally gifted by nature with powers of mind and spirit, and formed by the circumstances of life into a peculiarly strong and effective personality. Perhaps the most striking point both of his own writings and of all the accounts, which those who knew him have left, is the note of perfect reality and sincerity. "As he lived, so was his teaching; and as he taught, so was his life."[2] "It was not by words only, but in a manner by deeds, that he directed the impulses within us."[3] "Our teacher did not discuss the theory of the virtues with us; rather he exhorted us to their practice, and that more by his example than by his

[1] Gregory, op. cit. sec. II.
[2] Eus. H.E. VI. 3.
[3] Gregory, op. cit. sec. IX.

precept."[1] "I had met... with some few professed teachers; but they all made philosophy consist in mere phrases. But he was the first to incline me to philosophise, by his words, it is true, but anticipating their impulse by his deeds. He did not merely pronounce studied phrases; he never thought of speaking unless he did so with a mind sincere and striving to give effect to his utterances."[2] Origen's own words agree with Gregory's: "Nothing unreal must dwell in the soul which is truly given to God."[3] There is no doubt that to Origen Christianity was not a system of rules but a life to be lived, as much in daily practice as in speculation. He quotes with approval Thucydides' phrase, "To keep a feast is nothing else but to do one's duty"[4] and adds, "that man truly keeps a feast, who does his duty and is ever praying... and the perfect Christian, who is ever in his words and deeds and thoughts abiding in his natural Lord, God the Word... is also ever keeping the Lord's day."[5] The driving force which absolute sincerity gives to a man of Origen's calibre and powers cannot easily be estimated: it is hard to set a limit.

He was naturally endowed with characteristics, which attract men and exert influence. In addition to his powerful intellect and vast learning, he possessed wide sympathy with varied types of people and a faculty for understanding them, which was increased by his vivid imagination and supported by his broad-minded outlook on all who were searching for truth. Much as he appreciated speculative wisdom himself, he rejoiced in the value of the Gospel for all men, rich or

---

[1] Gregory, op. cit. sec. XI.
[2] ib.
[3] VII. 66.
[4] VIII. 21.
[5] VIII. 22.

poor, wise or foolish, and the debt which all Christians owed to them.[1] "We wish to educate all men in the Word of God... and to show to slaves how they may win back freedom of mind and become the children of highest nobility through the Word."[2] Perhaps the imagination of Origen strikes a modern reader most forcibly in his allegorical interpretation of the Bible, when his mind seems to run riot among strange, remote symbols and figures: but it shows itself in a way more natural to present-day thought, when he summons up vivid ideas of the sun and moon at prayer[3] or exhorts his readers "to go back in thought to Jesus"[4] and imagine the historic circumstances of his words and works. It is strange that so much sympathy and imagination could exist in a man, who seems from the ordinary standpoint to have been lacking in sense of humour. Perhaps his theological writings are not the best place in which to find it, but it is certain that if he had not labelled his one joke about the tears of the angels[5] as a jest, modern readers would pass it by unnoticed, or at least judge it laboured and heavy. But, in this respect, a genius is unhampered where lesser men would fail, and Origen's lectures must have been alive or his pupils would not have loved them as they did. Gregory speaks of his "wise and gentle"[6] manner, and says "the goad of friendship" was struck into them by "the keenness and great urgency of his ability and good disposition, which shone so benevolently upon us in his very tones as he discoursed or talked, trying

[1] III. 49.
[2] III. 54.
[3] V. 11.
[4] II. 13. "ἀνάβα μοὶ τῷ λόγῳ ἐπὶ τὸυ᾿ Ἰησοῦν λέγοντα ταῦτα"
[5] V. 55.
[6] Gregory, op. cit. sec. IX.

not to get an easy victory over us in argument, but by his able and kindly and genuine ability to save us."[1]

The same Gregory gives proof of Origen's broadmindedness in urging himself and his brother to read all the ancient writings of poets and philosophers and to give a hearing to all.[2] We know that he was "renowned as a great philosopher even among the Greeks",[3] and that in Alexandria he used to attend the lectures of his rivals, the neo-Platonists, while his own knowledge of the varied types of religion, philosophy and superstition, which abounded in the city, was exceptionally deep.

All these sides of Origen's nature were tested, developed and strengthened by the schooling of life, and he emerged triumphant and approved, like the athletes, who were so often on his lips, in his metaphors about Christians and their struggles for character and righteousness.[4] The ground was made firm under his feet by the solid fact of personal experience. Added to this, he possessed united two qualities which are often divided, enthusiasm and the love of hard persistent work.[5] Therefore the blaze, which his own fervent spirit kindled, was never allowed to die down from lack of care. There was nothing specious or unreal about the character of Origen. He possessed too that spirit of wonder

[1] ib. Sec. VI.
[2] ib. Sec. XIII.
[3] Eus. H.E. VI. 18.
[4] e.g. I. 69. (Jesus called "μεγαν ἀγονιότην"). III. 60, VIII. 55, II. 42 "τὸ δ᾽ ἐν τῷ ἐνεστῶτι αἰῶνι λεγομένῳ ζῆν συμφορὰν εἰναι ἠ ἀγῶνα τὸν πρῶτον καὶ μέγιστον τῆς ψυχῆς ." ["a great wrestler"; "in what is called the 'present world' life is a calamity, or at least the first and greatest struggle of the soul." – GPB]
[5] Gregory, op. cit. Sec. XIII. φιλοπονία καὶ σπούδη

and awe, mingled with the desire to know, which has characterised all the great and wise from the beginning of time. It is a "humility of soul"[1] (to quote Gregory once again), which is lost in wonder before the works of the world which are too great for it, whether their Author be named Nature or God. This in Origen had become a reasonable and reasoning wonder, at the management of the Universe by the Creator. He never lost the freshness of his joy at the exceeding goodness of God or his wonder at the unique Person of Jesus.[2]

He was qualified far above the ordinary to deal with men, for he understood their fundamental inconsistencies and weaknesses,[3] while recognising their diversities and possibilities and the way their minds worked on the ideas and beliefs which filled them.[4] To the Greeks he was the University professor, deeply versed in their literature and philosophy, himself also no mean philosopher and scholar, one who entered into their thought and worship, who tried to understand their wise men and their mystery religion, who sympathised with their art and athletics, and their expression of social and political life.[5]

To the Jews, though a representative both of that Greek literature, which in spite of Philo they did not read,[6] and of those apostate followers of Jesus Christ, Whom they hated

[1] Gregory op. cit. Sec. IX.
[2] II. 42. τεθήπαμεν αὐτὸν καὶ ὁσημέραι βεβαιοῦμεν τὴν εἰς αὐτὸν πίστιν ["we are lost in wonder at Him, and have our faith in Him daily confirmed." – GPB]
[3] II. 8, III. 64. (ad fin.).
[4] VI. 45.
[5] II. 27, III. 30, 60, 67, VIII. 17.
[6] II.34, 55. cf. VI. 21 (ad fin.).

and calumniated,[1] yet Origen was evidently an honoured opponent and well-known for his fairness and appreciation of Jewish ideals. He seems to have frequently attended the discussions of their learned men[2] where the meaning of a messianic prophecy and its reference to Jesus were hotly debated, – Origen, on one occasion, pressing a rabbi hard with a passage and the rabbi becoming perplexed;[3] but his admiration of the Jewish "polity" and the Hebrew consciousness of the one, supreme God find frequent expression in his "Reply to Celsus", notably in one passage where he gives almost the highest praise he knew, calling them "a whole nation of philosophers",[4] and in another, where he says; "Would that they had not sinned by transgressing the law, first slaying the prophets and later plotting against Jesus, so that we might possess a pattern of the heavenly city, which Plato also sought to describe; though I doubt whether he could have accomplished as much as the strength of Moses and his followers wrought, for they nurtured a 'chosen race' and a 'holy nation', dedicated to God with words free from all fear of demons."[5]

There is a tradition, supported by Epiphanius[6] though Eusebius does not mention it, that Origen was by birth an Egyptian, and attempts have been made to connect his name by derivation with that of the Egyptian god, Horus. However that may be, he certainly was familiar with the various cults and worships, which filled Alexandria in his day, whether

[1] II. 29.
[2] I. 45, 55-6, II. 31.
[3] I. 56 (ad fin.).
[4] IV. 31, cf. VIII 47.
[5] V. 43.
[6] Adv. Haer. Lib. II. Tom. I. Haer. 64.

they were of specific Egyptian origin or whether they came from Babylon and the East, whether they were concerned with material worship of animals or with the allegorical explanation of such worship. How far his mark touched real Egyptians it is hard to say. The evidence of papyri goes to prove that "up to the end of the third century the vehicle of the new religion was Greek, and that although there may have been many non-Greek speaking native converts, Greek ideas and Greek education, tinged perhaps with native Egyptian elements, were the guiding influence of the early Church."[1] It is also evident from papyri that there was a wide gulf at the end of the second century A.D. between the Alexandrian Egyptian, who had studied Greek philosophy, and who devoted himself to a cult of Serapis and Isis, full of asceticism and mysticism, and the ordinary peasantry, who tilled the banks of the Nile and clung, as their fathers had clung for generations, to material ideas of the Gods[2] and belief in the great judgment of Osiris, where the future of the dead was decided. Dionysius of Alexandria[3] uses the word Αἰγύπτιοι to distinguish the natives of Egypt from the Alexandrians, who were largely half-Greek by birth, and this marks the difference in religion also. There are signs that Origen was temperamentally akin to the native Alexandrian in his passionate nature and in his tendency towards asceticism.[4] There are many references in the Reply to Celsus to the Egyptian worship of animals and the superstitions connected with it, to the myths of interpretation made by wise men, and especially to the widespread belief in

[1] Scott-Moncrieff – *Paganism and Christianity in Egypt*, chap. IV, p.96.
[2] I. 12, 52. cf. Sayce, op. cit.
[3] cf. Feltoe – *The Letters of Dionysius of Alexandria*, p.13, note 9.
[4] cf. V. 49.

magic, which ranged from divination and study of the magic properties of names to all kinds of jugglery, for which the Egyptians were famous.[1]

Along with the philosophy of the Greek and the religion of the Jew Origen had also to face the superstition based on the fear of demons, which held thousands of pagans bound as with chains at the beginning of the Christian era: and here also he could confront its terrors unafraid. For, in the end, it was not Origen's learning or experience, not his brain or his personality, not even his human sympathy and insight, which marked him out as the man to meet the varied need of Alexandria in the third century. The secret lay in the fact that Origen possessed ardent, definite and sincere, a conviction of the supreme value of Jesus Christ for men; which could conquer all opposition and fulfil all want.

This was the central power of his life, which lifted up and transformed his varied gifts and energies, so that he stands for all time as an example of one, in whom the life of faith and the potency of intellect were united to a degree which made him as much a leader of those who worship as a master of those who know.

It was personal experience of the power of Christ and personal experience of the power of sin, which lay at the root of the eagerness of Origen's personal Christianity. Again and again he speaks of the helplessness of men without God; they are diseased and need a physician; nothing can change their lives and control their actions for good but the power of God made manifest in Jesus Christ. "Jesus did not only do

---

[1] Animal-worship I. 20, III. 17-21, IV. 90, V. 51, VI. 4.
Magic I. 23-4, 28, 68 II. 50, 52, III. 36-8, 46, IV. 93.
Allegory IV. 38~9, V. 35.

good to men during the days of His life in the flesh, but even up to this present time the power of Jesus works in those, who believe in God through Him, bringing about a turning-point in their lives and a change for the better."[1] It is the same "evident power" of which Origen speaks in the preface, saying that no one, who has made it his own, can be seriously shaken by the arguments of Celsus.[2] He lays great stress on the humanity of Jesus – the fact which made neo-Platonists, Gnostics and all manner of heretics to stumble.[3] "For Jesus Himself wished and His disciples too that these, should not only put their faith and trust in His divine nature and miracles – as though He had no share in the nature of man and had not taken upon him that human flesh, which 'lusteth against the Spirit;' for in point of fact, they saw that the power also, which came down into man's nature and man's sorrows and assumed man's body and soul, by means of faith, joined with man's leanings towards God for the saving of those who have the faith – when they see that from Him the nature of God and the nature of man began to be knit together, so that man's nature, by communion with that which is nearer God, may become like God, not in Jesus alone, but in all those, who with faith enter on the life, which Jesus taught and which leads to friendship with God and communion with Him everyone who lives as Jesus ordained."[4]

Origen finds in Jesus the revelation of the character of God no less than the salvation of men from evil. There is a long passage in the sixth book against Celsus, where

---

[1] I. 43.
[2] Introd. 2.
[3] VII. 16.
[4] III. 45.

Origen's personal conviction about God and Christ is declared with passionate force. "He (Celsus) introduces a character who says 'How then am I to know God? And how am I to learn the way to Him? And how do you show Him to me? For at present you do but cast darkness over my eyes and I see nothing clearly'.... we shall say... 'The people sitting in darkness... have seen a great light and for those sitting in the land and shadow of death has a light uprisen' – even the God, Jesus. Therefore, no Christian answers Celsus... 'How am I to know God?' For each of them learns to know God, as far as it is possible for him. And no one says, 'How am I to learn the way to Him?' For he has heard the words, 'I am the Way, the Truth, and the Life,' and has tasted, as he journeys along the Way, the good gifts that it brings.[1] Therefore, if Celsus were to ask us how we think we know God and how we think we shall win safety in His sight, our answer is this:– The Logos of God, won by those who seek Him or those who accept Him when He appears, is able to make known and reveal the Father, unseen before the coming of the Logos. Who else has the power to save and lead up the soul of man to God, who is over all, if it be not the Logos of God? For, being 'in the beginning with God,' He became flesh for the sake of those, who clave to the flesh and became as flesh, in order that he might be received, by those who could not look upon Him, inasmuch as He was 'the Logos' and was 'with God', and was God. So, in human form He speaks and announcing Himself as flesh, He calls to Himself those who are flesh, that first He may make them to be changed according to the Logos, who had became flesh; and that after this He may lead them up to behold Himself as

[1] VI. 66.

He was before He became 'flesh'; so that in the end they, being made better and having gone up from their first initiation, which was according to the flesh, say 'Even if we once knew Christ according to the flesh, we know Him so no longer.' Flesh therefore, He became, and having became flesh, He tabernacled among us, not being outside us, but after He had tabernacled and dwelt in us, He did not abide in the same form but led us up to the lofty mountain of the Logos and showed us His glorious form and the brightness of His garments, and not of Himself only, but also of the spiritual law, which is seen 'in glory;' with Jesus – Moses: and He showed us also the whole of prophecy, for it did not die after He dwelt among men, but was taken up into heaven and its symbol was Elijah. The man who looked upon this might well say those words: 'we beheld His glory, a glory as of the only begotten of the Father, full of grace and truth'."[1]

Such was Origen's personal faith, expressed as a scholar and philosopher would express it, but in its essence the Gospel of the early Church. The term "Logos" has not the personal significance to a modern spirit, which can alone attempt to express the meaning of Jesus Christ for the individual. But it was full of meaning for Origen and we find also again and again that he speaks of 'Our Jesus' and 'my Jesus' in tones which are the height of personal love and possession.[2] Christianity is for him "a holy and wondrous thing;"[3] "something fresh and unique (καίνον) happened after Jesus suffered";[4] and the sum of the whole experience

[1] VI. 68.
[2] I. 25, 29,, II. 55, III. 23, 31, 32, V. 51, 63.
[3] III. 13, σεμνόν τι
[4] VIII. 43.

for Origen did not end with himself, for "Christ is the Saviour of all men."[1]

This was the ultimate and moving cause of Origen's greatness in teaching, in theology, in apologetic; it was not only that he knew his opponents and their learning, not only that he knew those to whom he was speaking and therefore could strike home and be understood; it was not only that he was conversant with heretics, Marcionites, Gnostics, docetists and the rest;[2] it was the fact that he possessed a Gospel, a Gospel which he knew to be "for all men" and by his very personality and life set forth that Gospel. "By force of his virtue," says Gregory, "he implanted in us the love of the beauty of righteousness, whose golden face he showed to us."[3]

This man of all others was fitted to take up the task which Ambrosius laid upon him. Westcott has spoken of the age and the man in a few striking phrases: "Origen, standing in the meeting-place of struggling thoughts, knew that he had that to speak which could harmonize and satisfy every spiritual aspiration of man: an answer to the despair of the West which saw in man's good an unattainable ideal; an answer to the despair of the East, which saw in man's way a vain delusion... the interpreter of a universal hope."[4]

---

[1] III. 49.

[2] Marcionites II. 27, V. 54, VI. 53, 74.
Gnostics I. 69, II. 16, IV. 15, VI 31-2, 35,
Various IV. 19, V. 61-2.

[3] Gregory Op. cit. sec. XIV.

[4] Op. cit. p.249.

CHAPTER III
CELSUS AND THE *TRUE WORD*

It is never an easy task to recover the attitude of an antagonist, against whom the centuries have given their decision, more especially if, as in the case of Celsus, it is only through the writings of his enemies that any direct knowledge of his ideas can be gained. Knowledge of the age, of life and thought as it affected Celsus, may help towards a greater understanding of his aim and motive, but the only firm evidence for the nature of his character and ability must be sought in the fragments of his own book, preserved in the refutation of Origen. The question as to how far Origen was honest in his quotations and whether he is to be suspected of seriously mutilating the text of the True Word has been carefully examined by a considerable number of authorities, and in spite of the contention of Pélagaud,[1] who is supported by Aube, that the book is "singulièrement tronquée", the good faith of Origen in this respect is definitely established. It is only natural that the mere fact of quoting a treatise, even in large sections, should remove to a great extent, its coherence and effective power, but the extracts are obviously treated in order and not arranged haphazard. There are passages where the connecting link is difficult or impossible to find; there are passages where Origen quotes not the actual words but their substance for refutation; there are other places where he notes the fact that he is taking a sentence or two out of proper order, but in spite of all this it is possible to reconstruct the main outline and argument and

[1] Pélagaud, *Étude sur Celse* Liv. III. p.203

to gain an impression of the original.[1] Various[2] attempts have been made to discover in detail the scheme of the book, and of these the one most generally used and accepted is that of Keim, but like all the others it can never be more than tentative and its chief claim is not that it ever existed in the True Word, but that it follows very closely the line of argument and is therefore valuable as an aid to its analysis. Other modern writers,[3] in giving summaries of the treatise, generally follow one or other of these tentative schemes with alterations and additions of their own, sometimes combining comment and explanation with the summary. The plan of this chapter falls into two divisions: first, an outline sketch of Celsus' own position and the main lines of his attack on Christianity; second, a translation of his own words as far as it is possible to extract them from Origen's answer. This is sometimes done at the expense of clear connection, but additional vividness can frequently be gained by the preservation of the trenchancy of Celsus' personal address.

The date of the True Word and the identity of the author have offered a wide battlefield for many critics, but the date now generally accepted is the end of the reign of Marcus Aurelius, probably between the years 176 and 178 A.D.[4] Egypt, Phoenicia, Palestine and Persia have all been considered as possible places for the composition of the

[1] cf. I. 8, 12, 32, 34, II. 5, 34, V. 33.

[2] Keim, Aube, Pélagaud

[3] Glover, *The Conflict of Religions in the Early Roman Empire*, Ch. VIII.
Patrick, *The Apology of Origen*, Part I, chap. II.
Froude, *Short Studies in Great Subjects*.
Pressensé, *The Early Years of Christianity*, Vol. II

[4] For evidence and discussion of other views see Keim, *Celsus Wahres Wort*, pp.261~73.

book; but the knowledge of these countries, which Celsus displays, could well have been gained by travelling, while the general tone and spirit of his writing is so distinctively Roman that, apart altogether from reference to definitely Roman heresies and practices, Rome seems to be the most likely place of writing. Even when these hypothetical questions of time and place have been settled it is hard to trace the identity of one who held the common name of Celsus. In addition to the two mentioned by Origen,[1] some two dozen can be counted in the first three centuries. Discussion mainly centres round the identification of Origen's Celsus with the Celsus to whom Lucian addressed his "Alexander". Lucian's description of his friend, whom he loved and honoured "above all men for his wisdom, love of truth, gentle manners, moderation, his peaceful life and his tactful treatment of those he met",[2] fits, in the opinion of many, the author of the True Word so exactly that the two men must be one and the same.[3] Nearly all older Church historians accept this identification, and Keim has stated fully all the evidence in its favour, but, as Pélagaud[4] and others have recognised, there is no reason why two persons of the same name and certain similar characteristics should not have lived at the same time with widely differing opinions. For the opinions of Celsus on magic cannot easily be reconciled with those of a man, who has written a special book on the subject, and the attitude of Lucian towards the Christians differs from that of Celsus, as widely as a cynical Epicurean can differ from an enthusiastic, if eclectic,

---

[1] I. 8.

[2] Lucian Alexander 61

[3] Keim, Op. cit. pp.276-92.

[4] Pélagaud, op. cit. Liv. IV. pp.230-48.

Platonist. The charges of Epicureanism which Origen brought against Celsus have not clear enough proof to allow them to stand against his undeniably Platonic views, and although in many respects the friend of Lucian seems akin to this Celsus there is no doubt that Lucian himself was in his attitude towards religion and philosophy, in his aims and motives, far removed from the author of the True Word. Lucian is essentially the brilliant looker-on, who will only criticise, and who refuses to compromise his intellectual superiority by any enthusiastic partisanship; Celsus, on the other hand, does not hold himself aloof from life: he is a keen partisan of ideas and institutions, which seem to him essential, and is sarcastic and critical only when the sacredness of those ideas is violated. To understand the motives of Celsus and to recover the point of view which drove him to apply all his energies of intellect and personality to his attack on Christianity, it is necessary to realise how far Greek ideas, Greek education and Greek associations had modified the Roman world by the middle of the second century. It is a commonplace to say that it was an age of eclecticism, but to a Roman citizen, it was more – it was the effort to reconcile Roman practice with Hellenic theory, to govern a vast empire, involving thousands of practical problems, with a background of alien education, filled with ideas coming not only from Greece, but from Persia and the far East. A philosopher-Emperor, who wrote in Greek, is but a sign of the times, and Celsus himself is typical of his age. The general policy at Rome towards new ideas and speculative thought was that of large toleration; the introduction of strange gods and new worships was by now unhindered and even legalised, but with this reservation – anything which was in the least subversive of imperial control or which could turn men from their duty to the world-wide state was severely crushed. This is a sufficient reason for the persecution of the obscure sect, called Christians, and just because of this reservation the ultimate position of Roman governors and Roman citizens alike was a compromise. And perhaps the compromise is even more apparent in the character of an individual, such as Celsus than in the complicated working of the Roman Empire.

Among the qualities which Romans of old valued most highly, qualities which contributed to that sum of excellence described by the word "virtus", there were two greatly prized – "pietas" and "gravitas". They seem to contain within themselves the most characteristic traits of the race. Within the bounds of "pietas" lay practically the whole sphere of conduct towards God and man: and "gravitas" is symbolic of the dignity and firm purpose, which marked all truly Roman actions – nothing light, nothing puerile, nothing frivolous. Almost of necessity it implied conservatism and a very stern testing of new ideas. Anything which conflicted with solid traditions and "mos maiorum"[1] was liable to stir up severe criticism. These fundamental characteristics persisted on from the days of Pyrrhus and the Samnites, through the troubled end of the Republic, through the Augustan age, when Vergil could write of young Marcellus "heu pietas, heu prisca fides!",[2] right on to the second century of the Empire, when the cosmopolitan emperor, the scholar Marcus Aurelius still led forth his frontier legions against barbarian hordes. And these characteristics are the foundation of the character of Celsus. The very keynote of his accusation

[1] ["Ancestral custom" – GPB]

[2] Aen. VI. 878. ["Alas for piety! Alas for the ancient faith!" – GPB]

against the new religion is criticism of its irreverent ideas about God. "They blaspheme God" he says "and speak lies".[1] He possessed a deep sense of what was right and fitting in men's thoughts about God and God's actions towards men, blended with a spirit of reverence and devotion which the word "pietas" most adequately describes.[2] He is also possessed by a natural desire for dignity and authority not only in things religious but also in the sphere of the state. It is the aristocratic spirit of one, who despises small and unlearned peoples, who scorned the delusions of the vulgar, and who waged a relentless war against all that could overthrow the order of Roman government. He speaks with admiration of imperial rule and is tenacious of tradition, in essence, a Roman conservative. Yet upon this foundation had been laid a thorough classical education, which meant the study of Greek thought and literature, probably at the University of Athens. His Hellenic learning is apparent on every page of his book, whether it show itself in a reference to Herodotus or a quotation from Plato, whom he honoured alike for his thought and his style. His knowledge embraced the wider field of Eastern history and mythology and he shows acquaintance with certain Asiatic beliefs and cults, which may have been gained either by travelling in the countries themselves or from the motley crowd, who were to be found in the universities of the time, especially in Alexandria.

It is interesting to note the result of this mixture of different elements in the character of Celsus. It is evident that his Greek education had freed his mind, and made him,

[1] III. 64, cf. IV. 10.
[2] VIII. 66.

at least in thought, a citizen of the world. He had studied speculative thought at its highest level and had found in the philosophy of Plato a conception of the Ideal and an expression of the Supreme God, which satisfied all his spiritual aspirations. His ideas of Being and Beauty, of the Divine will in the Universe, who is Reason, are all clothed in Platonic language and show plainly on what theory Celsus based his scheme of life, and the value he set on things spiritual. "We must never in any way lose our hold on God, neither by day nor by night, in public or in private, in any word or deed, but apart from these actions or with them let the soul ever be fixed upon God."[1] There is an irresistible reminder of Epictetus – "what can I do, a lame old man, but sing hymns to God?" Yet Celsus, in spite of his Greek learning was not a Greek; he was a practical Roman and saw that the affairs of life demanded a compromise. What of the countless other powers spiritual and temporal whose working was visible every day on earth? "How is it wrong to gain the goodwill of the rulers on earth, whether they be human princes and kings or other beings. For it is through the strength of daemons that human men gain their power here."[2] And again, "If anyone command you to swear by a human king there is nothing wrong in it, for to him have been given the things upon earth, and whatever you receive in this life you receive from him."[3] This is a characteristically Roman statement of the compromise which Plutarch made, when he tried to reconcile the highest idea of God with pagan beliefs and pagan practices. The same effort is made by Celsus: "If anyone command you to sing praises

[1] VIII. 63.
[2] ib.
[3] VIII. 67.

to the sun or to glorify Athena devotedly with a beautiful hymn, you will, if you sing praise to them, seem to give still greater honour to the Great God, for the worship of God becomes more perfect if it extends through all things."[1] This was a plausible theory and Plutarch set it forth as plausibly as possible, but nevertheless, as even Celsus admits, daemon-worship remained cruel and degrading. Yet it was in the daemon environment that the lives of all ordinary men were passed and some compromise had to be made by those, whose philosophy could not abstract them entirely from the affairs of the world. With Celsus the motive was even more urgent than for Plutarch, for Plutarch aimed at the restoration of the worship of the Hellenic Gods, by men whose Hellenic speculation had made them cast it away, at the recovery of the free political life of a Hellas, who was lost for ever: it was a reaching-out to the past. But Celsus was concerned with the immediate pressing problems of a vast empire, with the duties of citizens and the necessity of firm government; his practical Roman nature knew instinctively what was needed and sought only secondarily its philosophical justification. He found it in the logical idea of a hierarchy of power and authority, but the compromise was plain, though almost inevitable.[2] It was the effort to combine religion with devotion to the State, which led Celsus to make concessions to Paganism, inconsistent with his philosophy, but patriotism and religion are so inseparably bound together in the history of Rome that it only proves him once more to be what he was – a typical Roman.

---

[1] ib.

[2] VII. 68, VIII.2, 24, 28, 33, 45, 48, 58.

Even so, a type is not a person and it is very difficult to gain much knowledge of personality from opinions. Apart altogether from theory and practical politics, there are characteristics emerging in his writing which individualise the man Celsus. Reference has already been made to his religious nature and there are two passages, where his personal experience seems to flash out in the midst of argument. "A more effective teacher... is Plato... in the Timaeus. The maker and Father of this universe it is hard to find, and even having found Him, it is impossible to speak of him to all."[1] And again when he is answering the imaginary question of the Christians, "How can we know God, if we do not comprehend Him by our senses?" Celsus says, "This is not the language of a man or the soul, but of the flesh... if, silencing the senses you look upward with the mind and turning away from the flesh, awaken the eyes of the soul, in this way only you will see God."[2] The search of the soul for God through a baffling and bewildering Universe and the final consummation of that search is for Celsus a real and living fact. There is a note in his words which re-echoes through the Platonic phrasing of St. Augustine's wonderful description of the ecstasy of himself and St. Monica: "And we began to say, 'If to any the tumult of the flesh were hushed; hushed the images of earth, of waters, and of air; hushed also the poles of heaven; yea, were the very soul to be hushed to herself, and by not thinking on self to surmount self; hushed all dreams and imaginary revelations, every tongue and every sigh; if all transitory things were hushed utterly, – for to him that heareth they do all speak, saying

[1] VII. 42.
[2] VII. 36.

"we made not ourselves, but He made us, who abideth for ever" – if, when their speech had gone out they should suddenly hold their peace, and to the ear which they had aroused to their Maker, He Himself should speak, alone, not by them, but by Himself, so that we should hear His word, not through any tongue of flesh, nor angel's voice, nor echo of thunder, nor in the dark riddle of a similitude, but might hear indeed Him, whom in those things we love, Himself without these, – as we but now with effort and in swift thought touched on that eternal wisdom, which abideth over all – ; could this be continued, and all disturbing visions of whatever else be withdrawn, and this one ravish and absorb, and wrap up its beholder amid those inward joys, so that life might ever be like that one moment of understanding, which but now we sighed after; were not this ENTER INTO THE JOY OF THY LORD?'"[1] Not that Celsus was a mystic or that he found his way to God by the path of the mystic; but he sought through reason and the flights of speculative thought the supreme Good of the philosopher. He was earnest and sincere; the very depth of his convictions made him merciless and intolerant. He was a strange mixture. In the disciple of Plato was found the fierceness of a Tertullian and the proud scorn of a Lucretius for error in ideas about the universe and God: and in the mixture lay his weakness. Lucretius in an age when men's hearts were indeed "blind",[2] preached with the zeal of a missionary a system which should bring them light, and free them from the bonds of superstition. Even if his gospel was a gospel of despair, it was at least a trumpet call from a high mountain to the men

[1] Aug. Conf. IX. 10. (trans. Bridges).

[2] Lucr. II. 14; O miseras hominum mentes, O pectora caeca ["O wretched minds of men! O blinded hearts!" – GPB]

of his day – an uncompromising call; for Lucretius made no truce with the practices of pagan religion. Tertullian, the follower of Christ, seems poles apart from this devoted disciple of Epicurus, yet their spirit and attitude is the same. Tertullian is fierce because he cannot help it, because of his passionate conviction of the truth in Christ; he is thorough going and uncompromising, and, like Lucretius, he stands for advance, for higher ideas and progress. But Celsus, while he is akin to both, has, in spite of all his intellect and brilliance the greatness of neither; he is looking not forward, but behind, striving to preserve the old rather than to create the new, "a man with his back to the East."

As a preliminary to sketching the main points of Celsus' attack on the Christians, it is necessary to estimate his knowledge of them, and his appreciation of their point of view. He seems to possess a curious mixture of accurate information, acute perception and complete lack of understanding. He had certainly studied Christianity carefully, both in its literature and the life of its adherents. "I know the whole thing"[1] he says, and he manifests knowledge of the Synoptic Gospels,[2] of Genesis and Exodus,[3] of certain uncanonical literature (The Heavenly Dialogue,[4] Jason and Papiscus,[5] the diagram of the Ophites[6],) and he is familiar with the teaching of Marcion[7] and with other phases of Gnosticism, also with the beliefs and practices of countless

[1] I. 8, παντὰ γὰρ οἰδα.
[2] e.g. II. 55, V. 52, VI. 6.
[3] e.g. V.59.
[4] VIII. 15.
[5] IV. 52.
[6] VI. 24-5, 27, 30, 33, 38.
[7] VI. 74.

heretics,[1] some of whom were even unknown to Origen. Further it is evident that he has read other books in the Old and the New Testament and other early Christian writings,[2] but since he does not mention their names, no definite assertion can be made about them. The question as to whether he used Apocryphal Gospels or was engaged in a controversy with the early Apologists, who cluster round Justin, has been debated by several modern scholars, with opposite conclusions;[3] the main fact which emerges is that Celsus, with few exceptions, bases his charges against Christianity on the writings which Christians themselves held to be authoritative and that he recognised the difference between the doctrine of "the Great Church"[4] and any chance heretic, even though he made heresy and quarrelling a charge against them. It shows both a fair mind and good controversial ability. It is a tribute to his keen perception that he selected for attack the elements in the new faith, which were really cardinal and essential. He did not, after the manner of earlier antagonists, bring baseless slanders upon the moral character of Christians, but attacked the centre and heart of their belief. It was an attack on what seemed a totally wrong and irreverent idea of God, which meant an attack on the Person of Christ,[5] and it was also a violent protest against the conduct of people, who guided their lives by their belief in God, made manifest in Christ. Celsus recognised, while despising it, the revolution which Christ made not only in the realm of philosophic dogma but in the

---

[1] V. 61-4.
[2] e.g. II. 44.
[3] Keim op. cit. pp.219-32. Patrick op. cit. pp.84-104. Reuss. Aube.
[4] V. 59, cf. III. 10, 12.
[5] e.g. II. 23-4, 26-39, 41-3.

world of daily life: and, with all his digressions on minor points, he generally hits squarely at the author of the revolution. Yet even allowing for Celsus' study of Christian literature and his grasp of the vital points in Christian teaching, we find a lack of sympathy in his attitude, which shows that his own pride of intellect and aristocratic feeling were too great to permit him even to attempt to see the point of view of the people he attacked. It is not only that he misrepresents definite words and actions of Christ as related in the Gospels,[1] but he treats the personality of Jesus and his relations with his followers in a manner as unsympathetic as it was wholly inadequate.[2] "A good general... has never been betrayed, nay more, not even a wicked brigand, a captain of the very scum of the earth, whom his comrades deemed valuable; but Jesus was betrayed by those under him, and neither ruled as a good general nor, when he had deceived his disciples, did he even produce a feeling of goodwill... such as a brigand chief would win."[3] This is either deliberate falsification or an entire failure to grasp the meaning Jesus had for those with whom he associated. The same attitude appears, when Celsus contemptuously contrasts the call of the Greek Mysteries with the summons of Christ: "Those who summon to the other mysteries make this proclamation 'whosoever is clean of hand and wise of tongue', and again others say, 'Whosoever is pure of all stain, and whose soul is conscious of no evil and whose life has been good and righteous.' So they proclaim, who promise cleansing from sins. Let us hear whom these Christians invite. 'Whosoever'

[1] II. 24.
[2] e.g. II.35, VIII. 39.
[3] II. 12, cf. II. 18.

they say 'is a sinner, whosoever hath an[1] understanding, whosoever is childish, and to put it in a word, any miserable wretch, him will the Kingdom of God receive.' Now do not call him a sinner, who is unjust and a thief and a burglar and a poisoner and a temple-robber and a tomb-breaker? What others could a robber call if he made a proclamation?"[2] The saving power of Christ for him meant nothing, as is apparent from his sarcastic caricature of the purpose of the Incarnation. "There are many even nameless people who assume this so-called inspired action... each is wont to cry glibly 'I am God, I am the Son of God, I am the Spirit of God. I am come, for already the Universe is perishing, and you, O mortal men, through your unrighteousness are as the dead. But I wish to save you, and you shall see me again coming with the power of heaven. Blessed is he who now gives me homage. On all the rest I will send down everlasting fire, both cities and lands, and men, who know not their punishment, shall repent in vain and weep bitterly; but those who believe me I will keep safe for evermore'."[3] As far as intellectual study, coupled with keen insight into the dangers of the new religion, could carry him, so far was Celsus an understanding and therefore an able critic of Christianity: he never understood its essence, even while he attacked it, for his character and prejudices took away for him all meaning from its inward vitalizing force, so that the most he could do was to wonder and scorn.[4]

The points of Celsus' thesis against Christianity are brought forward in a manner that is consonant with the most

---

[1] [*sic.* Should be "no understanding" – GPB]

[2] III. 59.

[3] VII. 9.

[4] cf. VI. 12.

notable traits of his character. It is the proud, religious aristocrat who speaks, contemptuous of the poor and unlearned, jealous for his God and for the service of his country; so on religious, intellectual, social and political grounds he opposed with all his force this unspeakable new doctrine. Celsus possessed a certain idea about God and attributed to Him a definite character which the Christian teaching of the divinity of Jesus seemed to violate with hopeless irreverence. "The question is" says Celsus "not whether a thing has or has not been predicted but whether or not the action is worthy of God and honourable... How then can the story of this man's life be reverent or right as applied to God?"[1] Therefore a large portion of the argument is given up to showing with sarcastic fervour how absurd and impious it is to imagine for one moment that God could have lived a human life, subject to human passions like Jesus, and incidents are quoted with all the loathing expressed in the following extract:[2] "That God should eat the flesh of sheep and drink vinegar or gall was nothing else but sheer feeding on filth."[3] Every effort is made to disparage the character of Jesus and show that he is utterly unworthy of any connection with God. And here Celsus' idea of God becomes involved with his idea of man for it is on the subject of the relations of God and man that he is most at variance with Christianity; God is to him perfect and immortal, sought after by man, but not seeking man out.[4] "There is something in man better than the element of earth, akin to God... they in whom this

[1] VII. 14, cf. I. 39.
[2] I. 66-7, 69, 70-1, II.9,16, 17, 20, 24, 30-1, 36-8, III. 41-2, VI. 10, VII. 27.
[3] VII. 13.
[4] IV. 72, 99, VI. 15, 18.

element is fully alive are ever seeking that to which it is akin – God; and are ever longing to hear... about Him."[1] "I say nothing new, only what has been believed through the ages. God is good and beautiful and blessed with all good things, in the highest degree of goodness and beauty; but if, as is asserted, he comes down to man, he must change, and change from good to evil, from beauty to shame, from blessedness to misery, from supreme good to the lowest depths of evil. Now who would choose such a change? It is indeed the nature of a mortal being to be changed and moulded afresh, but of the immortal to remain ever the same, unchanging."[2] "God made nothing mortal, but all things immortal are the works of God, and mortal things the work of them. And soul is a work of God, but the nature of body is different. And herein there is no difference between the body of a bat or a worm or a frog or a man; for the fundamental substance is the same and the corruptible part of them is alike."[3] And a long section follows to show that God has no greater love for man than for the animal creation. It is clear from these few quotations how Celsus regarded the doctrine of the "Word made flesh". It was impossible to his mind that God should take man's nature upon Him, and to say that He only did so in appearance was to impugn His moral character.[4] To say that God has come to save sinners implies that He is unjust.[5] "What harm is there in not having

[1] I. 8.
[2] IV. 14, cf. VIII. 21.
[3] IV. 52, cf. IV. 65-9.
[4] IV. 18.
[5] III. 63, cf. III. 70-1, 78.

sinned?"[1] "What in the world is the preference of sinners?... Blasphemy of God and lies."[2]

There is no meaning for Celsus in the restoring of God's children by their Father.[3] Righteousness has to be earned and won: to change nature by love is impossible. "I imagine, it is clear to everyone that no one, even by punishment, could completely change those who by nature and habit are given up to sin, much less by pity; for to change nature completely is extremely difficult, but the sinless have a share in a better life."[4] The reality of the power of the spirit of Jesus in men's lives was not understand or counted by Celsus. He attacks the resurrection fiercely on historical grounds,[5] but mainly because it shows a mortal and material idea of God.[6] Are men so bound up with the body? He cannot endure that God should be described by such "anthropomorphic" terms or limited, even in thought by time and space. There is a touch of the sarcasm of Elijah, taunting the priests of Baal, in the bitter language which Celsus uses to condemn these doctrines, "unworthy" of God.[7] Even when he does not understand, he attacks always vital points: for Jesus came to teach and prove by his life and death and resurrection that God loves and desires the hearts of men, "like as a father pitieth his own children"; and this knowledge of God, which came as a new and radiant burst of sunshine even to the Jews, whose prophets had foreseen and foretold and hoped,

---

[1] III. 62.
[2] III. 64, cf. II. 71.
[3] IV. 3, 67.
[4] III. 65.
[5] II. 63, III. 22.
[6] VII. 27-34, 36, VIII. 49, cf. II. 77, V. 14, VI. 72, VII. 32.
[7] VI. 51-3, 60-6, 69, 81, VII. 12, 14.

brought an even greater shock to the pagan world, whom Paul described in a strong phrase "without hope and without God."[1] Further it was in the risen, living Christ that his followers found their power to rise above their past sins and present hindrances. It was in this power that the fame of "ἀγραμμάτοι"[2] spread through the city of Jerusalem, so that all men "knew they had been with Jesus". When Celsus attacked the resurrection,[3] he attacked the stronghold of a great spiritual fact, visible every day in the growth of the early church and the life of early Christians.[4] So in the person of Christ, who revealed the Father and by the power of His risen life gave energy to men, Celsus found the central point for attack.

His aristocratic feelings were offended on the intellectual side, because to him the Christians seemed to stand for irrational methods. "Do not examine, but believe", and to scorn all learned and educated men.[5] He treats at great length the origin of Christianity in Judaism[6] and pours scorn on "the Jews grovelling in some corner of Palestine, entirely uneducated,"[7] contrasting them with other eastern nations and characterising their sacred books as "incredible legends without any literary grace."[8] Children, silly women and fools are, in his mind, the only people with whom such

---

[1] Eph. 2.12

[2] ["uneducated", cf. Acts 4.13. – GPB]

[3] II. 45.

[4] III. 12, 14, 39, V. 64, VIII. 12, 14.

[5] I. 9, III. 49, VI. 11-12.

[6] I. 21, 23-4, 26, III. 1, 5, 7-8, IV. 20-3, 31-3, 36, 38, V. 6, 25, 41, VI. 78, 80.

[7] IV. 36.

[8] ib.

"ἰδεωτίκοι λόγοι"[1] as Jewish and Christian writings can find favour.[2]

On the social side also he has no respect for Christian converts: "the scum of the earth"[3] he often calls them, and speaks with ineffable scorn of the "gatherings in the fuller's shop or the cobbler's shop."[4] He collects stories about the lowly origin of Jesus, and his birth from the union of Mary and a Roman soldier.[5] It is a testimony to Paul's claim for the universal equality of Christians, "neither Greek nor Jew, bound nor free", that Celsus should complain of the conversion of slaves, but it would be interesting to know how far the followers of Christ in the aristocratic circles of Rome were marked out and recognised by the other members of society. Yet even if Celsus did know Christians of that type, he had ample proof in the body of Christian converts for the charge, which was to him a degrading blot and to Christians a glory and a triumph – Christ is for every man.[6]

The conception of a fellowship, which could transcend nationality and unite men of different nations, in the bonds of one union was to Celsus so impossible as to be ridiculous.[7] The Greek must always remain a Greek, the Scythian a Scythian and obey the Gods and laws of his own country. Patriotism and the service of the Roman Empire is

---

[1] ["clumsy words" – GPB]

[2] I. 27, cf. III 18, 68.

[3] I. 61-2, II. 46, III. 73.

[4] III. 57.

[5] I. 28, 32, 39.

[6] III. 44.

[7] VIII. 72.

the plain duty of every Roman:[1] therefore to Celsus the teaching of Christianity was as abhorrent in its practice as in its ideas, because it did not produce good citizens.[2] It was one of those "secret associations" which caused so much trouble in the first two centuries of the Empire, and its members seemed to Celsus to deserve none of the privileges of a community, whose duties they would not share.[3] "Theirs is the language of sedition, of those who wall themselves off and tear themselves away from other men."[4] The last few paragraphs of the book are a straightforward exhortation to good citizenship: "Help the king with all your strength, and labour with him for justice and fight on his behalf, and join in the expeditions, if he need you, and help him to lead his armies[5]... Take part in the government of your country, if it is necessary to do so to preserve the laws and fulfil the demands of religion."[6] Celsus saw Rome and civilization threatened by barbarians; his demand is sincere patriotism, like Browning's "Home Thoughts from the Sea":

> Nobly, nobly Cape St. Vincent
> to the North-west died away
> Sunset ran, one glorious blood red,
> reeking into Cadiz Bay;
> Bluish 'mid the burning water, full in face
> Trafalgar lay;
> In the dimmest North-east distance
> dawn'd Gibraltar grand and gray;

[1] VIII. 69, 71.
[2] I. 1, VIII. 17.
[3] VIII. 55.
[4] VIII. 2.
[5] VIII. 73, cf. VIII. 68.
[6] VIII. 75.

"Here and here did England help me:
how can I help England?" say,
Whoso turns as I, this evening turn to God
to praise and pray,
While Jove's planet rises yonder, silent over Africa.

Whether a Christian should serve his country as a soldier was a matter for sore heart-searching in the second century as in the twentieth, but for Celsus at least the issue was plain. He was a Roman, he loved Rome, and summoned all Romans to protect her power.

Before Celsus speaks for himself, a word must be said about his book from the literary point of view, though criticism must be tempered by the fact that we possess the work in Origen's quotations, and not as Celsus meant it to be read. Origen charges him frequently with tautology and repetition of the same argument. This, as Patrick observes,[1] is almost inevitable from the form in which Celsus chose to throw the book. It was a masterly stroke to represent the Christians as rebel Jews, by introducing a Jew who addresses Jesus, 'converts from Judaism', and Gentile converts in turn, but naturally a certain number of his points are used again, when Celsus, later in the book, accuses in his own person. For the rest, the True Word is a precise, scholarly production; the style is terse and expressive; the argument is given point by the brilliance and sarcasm of the writer. Behind every word there is the force, which comes from a man, who is earnest and determined to strike with deadly effect. This fierceness gives an added clearness to Greek which is already lucid. He is quick to see a weak point in his

[1] Op. cit. Part I, pp.16-17.

opponent's armour and to make the best possible use of it.[1] "If Jesus really wished to manifest power of God, he ought to have appeared to those who had ill-treated him, and to him who pronounced sentence, and to all men everywhere."[2] He is equally quick to try to prove Jesus inconsistent, and His followers also, in their attitude to daemons.[3] His description of the vulgar nature of Christianity stands out as one of the most characteristically sarcastic passages.[4] There are many others, but to understand Celsus fully, it is best to read his own words.

Translation of the quotations from the *True Word* of Celsus, given by Origen in his treatise *Against Celsus*

(The text is that of Koetschau; the square brackets indicate a word or two inserted, to piece together fragmentary quotations).[5]

The Christians enter into secret associations with one another contrary to what is allowed by law, saying of associations, some are public and these are in accordance with law, while others are private and maintained without the sanction of law... [Celsus slanders] the love feast of the Christians,

---

[1] I. 6, II. 8, 75, VII. 18.

[2] II. 63.

[3] I. 6, II. 49, VIII. 28.

[4] III. 50, 55, 59. cf. V. 52, VI. 34, 51, 53, VII. 9.

[5] [The text contains many signs of Celsus' acquaintance with OT and NT Scriptures. I have supplied Bible references to a few direct quotations by Celsus, and to a few of the apparent allusions which feed into other debates. The reader will recognize many further allusions– GPB]

which takes its origin from the common danger and is more cogent than any oath.[1] The system of teaching is barbarous in its origin... barbarians are very clever at discovering such systems, but the Greeks are better at adjudging, confirming and practising the discoveries of barbarian nations with a view to moral improvement.[2] The Christians practise and teach secretly what is pleasing to themselves... and they do this to some purpose in that thereby they thrust aside the penalty of death, which overhangs them and their dangers [are like] those dangers which were encountered for the sake of philosophy by such men as Socrates.[3] [Their] system of ethics [is] shared with other philosophers and is not anything worthy of honour or a new teaching.[4] They do not believe images made with hands to be gods because it is not in accordance with reason that images made by workmen, who are morally worthless and wicked, should be gods, since also they are often provided by the unrighteous... [the saying] of Heraclitus "Those who draw nigh to lifeless objects as gods act like any who might converse with houses"... The Persians are of this opinion... Herodotus is the authority for the fact.[5] The Christians seem to possess power through the names and incantations of certain daemons... The Saviour by means of sorcery obtained power to accomplish the miraculous works which he appeared to perform, and foreseeing that others were likely to gain the same knowledge and perform the same wonders, boasting that they do them by the power of God, for this reason Jesus drives out such men from His

---

[1] I. 1.
[2] I. 2.
[3] I. 3
[4] I. 4.
[5] I. 5.

Kingdom[1]... if there is a just cause for excluding them, while He Himself is guilty of the same actions, His character is unworthy of respect, but if He is not proved unworthy by doing such things, neither are they who act like Him.[2] The system [of teaching] is secret.[3] I do not say that the man, who is attached to a good system, ought to desert it or feign desertion or openly deny it, if he is likely... to risk danger from his fellow-men... There is something in man better than the element of earth, akin to God... they in whom this element is fully alive, are ever seeking that to which it is akin – God, and are ever longing to hear and be reminded about Him.[4] [We ought] to adopt our opinions by following reason and a guide possessed of reason, since deceit is frequently the reward of one who agrees with any system without taking this course. Those who believe without the guidance of reason [are like] the Metragyrtae and soothsayers and Mithrae and Sabbadians and to anything else a man may chance upon, and the phantoms of Hecate or any other female daemon or daemons. [These lead men astray] so also it happens among the Christians... And some do not wish either to give or receive reason about the things wherein their faith is set, but take refuge in, "Do not examine but believe" and "Thy faith will save thee"... and, "The wisdom of the universe is a bad thing, foolishness good."[5] So then if they would be willing to answer me, not as if I were making first trial of it (for I know the whole story by heart) but as one who takes an equal interest in all, it would be

---

[1] [Perhaps alluding to Matthew 7.22-23 – GPB]
[2] I. 6.
[3] I. 7.
[4] I. 8.
[5] I. 9. [cf. 1 Corinthians 1.20-21 – GPB]

well. But if they will not and keep on saying, as they generally do, "Do not examine," and so on, they must explain to me both the nature of what they say and its origin [etc.].[1] Among many of the nations there is kinship with the same spirit of reason... There is an ancient account from the beginning to which, as is well-known, the most learned nations and cities and scholars have given constant attention... the Egyptians, Assyrians, Indians, Persians, Odrysians, Samothracians, Elevsinians.[2] The milk-eaters of Homer and the Druids of the Gauls and the Getae also are most learned and ancient nations, for they discuss [resemblances to the Jewish traditions]... Linus and Musaeus and Orpheus and Pherecydes and the Persian Zoroaster and Pythagoras discussed these topics and committed their opinion to books and the actual words are preserved to this day.[3] The universe is uncreated... for from all eternity there have been many conflagrations and many deluges and the flood, which recently occurred in the time of Deucalion is comparatively modern... also the conflagration in the time of Phaethon.[4] The Greeks believe this to be ancient history, because owing to deluges and conflagrations, they have not witnessed (nor do they relate anything more ancient).[5] Moses, having understood the teaching current among the learned nations and men famed for wisdom, obtained a divine reputation.[6] It [circumcision] came from the

[1] I. 12.
[2] I. 14.
[3] I. 16.
[4] I. 19.
[5] I. 20.
[6] I. 21.

Egyptians.[1] There followed Moses, who led them, herdsmen and shepherds whose minds were deluded by empty stories of unlearned men, so that they believed that God was one[2] named either the Highest or Adonai or the Heavenly or Sabaoth or by one of those other names, which they delight in giving to this world of ours: and they knew nothing more... It makes no difference whether we call the God who is over everything by the name Zeus, which is current among the Greeks or that name (what is it now?) used by the Indians, or that Egyptian one, which escapes me at the moment.[3] They [the Jews] worship angels and are addicted to sorcery, wherein Moses was their instructor... later I will explain about the Jews, how through ignorance they were deceived and led into error... a few years ago he began this teaching being deemed by the Christians to be the Son of God... they were deceived and accepted a teaching, which does harm to the life of men.[4] It is unworthy of respect from a thinking man and therefore had power only with common, unlettered people… there are among them some men, quite up to the average, of good and lovable character, intelligent and capable of understanding allegory.[5]

Jesus invented his birth from a virgin... he was born in a village of Judaea of a poor woman in that neighbourhood who earned her bread by spinning... she was turned out of doors by her husband, a carpenter by trade, being convicted of adultery... after being cast off by her husband and wandering about in disgrace she gave birth to a bastard, –

[1] I. 22.
[2] I. 23.
[3] I. 24.
[4] I. 26.
[5] I. 27.

Jesus; he because of poverty hired himself out as a servant in Egypt and there learned some wonder-working powers, on which the Egyptians pride themselves, and returned home very much elated because of them and by their means proclaimed himself to be God.[1] The child's father was a soldier named Panthera.[2] The star appeared at the birth of Jesus.[3] [Celsus compares the fables] of Danae and Melanippe and Auge and Antiope.[4] If, as you will say, the mother of Jesus was beautiful it was, I suppose, on account of her beauty that God had intercourse with her, He whose nature it is not to love a corruptible body... it was not likely that God would be in love with her, for she was not rich or of kingly birth, since no one knew her, no not even one of her neighbours... when she was hated by the carpenter and turned out of doors, God's power did not save her nor did her story find credence. Such things as these have nought to do with the reign of God.[5] When you were bathing in the presence of John, you say that the appearance of a bird from the air alighted upon you... What trustworthy witness beheld this appearance? Or who heard a voice from heaven recognising you as Son of God? There is no proof but your own assertion and another suborned by you of those who have been punished with you.[6] [The Jew in the dialogue said] But my prophet once declared in Jerusalem that the Son of God will come, a judge of the righteous and chastiser of

---

[1] I. 28.
[2] I. 32.
[3] I. 34.
[4] I. 37.
[5] I. 39.
[6] I. 41.

the wicked.[1] Why should it be you rather than those thousands of others, who existed after the prophecies, to whom the predictions were applicable?... Some in a mood of enthusiastic frenzy, others gathering crowds, say the Son of God has come down from on high... The prophecies applied to the story of his life may fit other events too.[2] [The Saviour] was not helped by the Father and could not help himself.[3] If you say that every man born according to the providence of God is a Son of God, how would you differ from another?... People, thousands of them, will convict Jesus, asserting that the prophecies spoken of him were intended to apply to them.[4] Chaldaeans are mentioned by Jesus as having been stirred up to come at his birth, that they might worship him, while yet an infant, as God, and they told this to Herod, the tetrarch; the latter sent and killed all the boys born about that same time; thinking that he would secure the death of Jesus among the others, that he might not by any chance live to a sufficient age to obtain the throne.[5] But if it was in order that you might not grow up and reign instead of him, why, since you actually did grow up, do you not reign as king, instead of begging your bread miserably, hiding from fear and wandering about up and down in destitution, you who are the Son of God?[6] Jesus attached to himself ten or eleven persons of infamous character, tax-gatherers and sailors, the worst he could find and with them he fled like a runaway slave from one place to another,

---

[1] I. 49.
[2] I. 50.
[3] I. 54.
[4] I. 57.
[5] I. 58.
[6] I. 61.

picking up his living in a disgraceful and mean manner... they had not even the elements of education.[1] What need was there for you to be taken to Egypt, while still a babe, to escape murder? For it does not seem very likely that God should fear death. But an angel came from heaven commanding you and your parents to flee, lest you should be left behind in the city and perish. So then I suppose the great God, though he had already sent two angels on your account, was not able to guard you safely there, you – His own son. [He mocks at the blood of Jesus on the Cross, saying] It was not "ichor such as flows in the veins of the blessed Gods."[2] The old myths which attributed divine origin to Perseus, and Amphion, and Aeacus, and Minos (not that we believed them of course) set forth their great and marvellous deeds truly beyond man's power, that they might not seem incredible. But, I ask you, what have you accomplished noble or wonderful either in deed or word? You have shown us nothing, though they challenged you in the temple to give some clear sign that you were the Son of God.[3] All the statements about his cures, or resurrection, or the few loaves which fed vast numbers and from which many fragments were left and all the other stories of marvels, which the disciples recorded... Well, let us believe that you actually accomplished these works. [Celsus compares them to] the tricks of jugglers, who profess to do still more wonderful things and the accomplishments of those who have learnt from the Egyptians and in the middle of the market-place for a few obols give away their wonderful sacred learning and drive demons out of men and blow away diseases, and

[1] I. 62.
[2] Homer, Il. V. 340, I. 66
[3] I. 67. [Jn 2.18 tells of a demand for a sign *made in the Temple* – GPB]

invoke the souls of heroes and exhibit costly banquets and tables and sweetmeats and dainties which are not real, and set in motion, as if alive, animals which are not really live animals but possess only the semblance of life. Since then those men do these things, will it be necessary for us to think they are sons of God? Or are we to say that they are the practices of wicked men, possessed by an evil spirit?[1] Such a body as yours could not have been God's... the body of God would not have been begotten as you were begotten, Jesus.[2] The body of God is not fed in such a way either... the body of God does not use that kind of voice or that kind of persuasion.[3] This was the teaching of a person hated by God, a villainous sorcerer.[4]

To the converts from Judaism... What came over you, my fellow-countrymen, that you abandoned the law of our fathers, and letting your minds be enchained by him with whom we have just conversed, were most ridiculously deceived and deserted from us to another name and another life? Yesterday and the day before when we punished this man who cheated you, you revolted from the law of our fathers... How can you take your origin from our worship, and yet, when you have gone some way, cease to respect it, though you have no beginning for your doctrine other than our law?... For if anyone foretold to you that the son of God should really come to men, that prophet was ours and a prophet of our God.[5] [Jesus] sinned and was punished by the Jews... trite and stale is the teaching about a resurrection of

[1] I. 68.
[2] I. 69.
[3] I. 70.
[4] I. 71.
[5] II. 4.

the dead and a judgment of God and honour for the righteous and fire for the wicked... no new teaching.[1] Jesus kept all the Jewish customs even to the sacrifices observed among them... we ought not to believe in him as son of God.[2] To those willing to be deceived many others would have appeared such as Jesus was... this charge is brought against the Jews by these who believe in Christ, that they have not believed in Jesus as in God... How should we, who have made known to all men that there will come from God one who is to punish the wicked, dishonour him when he came?... Why did we dishonour him whose coming was proclaimed? Was it that we might be punished more than the others?[3] How are we likely to believe he is God, who not only, as the report went, performed none of his other promises, but when we had convicted and condemned him, deeming him deserving of punishment, was caught trying to hide himself and run away in a most disgraceful manner and who was betrayed by those whom he called disciples? And yet he, being God, could neither flee nor be bound and led away, and least of all could he be abandoned and betrayed by those, who had lived with him, had shared everything with him, had looked up to him as teacher, even him who was deemed saviour, and Son of the greatest God and an angel.[4] A good general, a leader of many multitudes has never been betrayed, nay more, not even a wicked brigand, a captain of the very scum of the earth whom his comrades deemed valuable; but Jesus, was betrayed by those under him, and neither ruled as a good general nor, when he had deceived

[1] II. 5.
[2] II. 6.
[3] II. 8.
[4] II. 9.

his disciples, did he even produce in them a feeling of goodwill (if I may so call it) such as a brigand chief would win.[1] I could say a great deal about the events of Jesus' life – true and not like the records of the disciples, but I purposely pass it over... [The Jew does not believe] Jesus foreknew everything which befel him.[2] The disciples of Jesus, having no sure foothold in clearly evident fact, devised the statement that he foreknew everything.[3] Just as if anyone in saying that a man is righteous shows him to be unrighteous, in saying he is holy, proves him to have committed murder, or immortal and yet at the same time dead, adding to all this the statement that he had fortuitously predicted it... For you do not even say this – "He seemed to wicked men to endure these sufferings, but did not endure them in reality." No, you acknowledge that he actually and openly suffered... How is the foretelling credible?... How could the dead man be immortal?[4] What God or divine spirit or prudent man, seeing that such things were coming upon him, would not avoid them, if he could, but he threw himself into that which he knew beforehand.[5] How is it that if Jesus mentioned beforehand the man who would betray him and the man who would deny him, they did not fear him as God, even to the point of desisting the one from his treachery, the other from his denial... But they actually betrayed and denied him without any thought or care for him.[6] For generally, I imagine, if a man who is the object of a plot comes to know

[1] II. 12.
[2] II. 13.
[3] II. 15.
[4] II. 16.
[5] II. 17.
[6] II. 18.

of it beforehand and tells the conspirators, they are turned from their design and are on their guard. Not then because these events were predicted, did they come to pass, for it is impossible, but their very occurrence has proved the prediction of them false; for it is altogether impossible that these who were warned beforehand, should continue their design of betraying and denying.[1] He predicted these things, being God, and the prediction must altogether come to pass. So then God led his own disciples and prophets, with whom he ate and drank, to the point of becoming impious and unholy, God, who ought above all others to do good to men and especially to those with whom his daily life was passed. Could a man share the table of a fellow-man and not plot against him, but when he has banqueted with God, become a conspirator? And what is still more absurd, God himself plotted against those who sat at meat with him, making them traitors and villains.[2] If he had resolved to do this and was chastised in obedience to the Father, it is clear that through his very Godhead and willing submission, that which was done in accordance with his own decision was neither painful nor distressing.[3] Why does he lament and mourn and pray to escape the fear of destruction, in such phrase as this: "O my Father, if it be possible, let this cup pass from me?"[4] Even though you tell lies, you were not able to give a plausible covering to your fictions.[5] Some of the believers like those whom drink drives to lay hands on themselves, have changed the Gospel from its original written form,

---

[1] II. 19.
[2] II. 20.
[3] II. 23.
[4] II. 24. [Matthew 26.39 – GPB]
[5] II. 26.

threefold, fourfold and to still further degrees, and have remodelled it that they may be able to contradict objections.[1] The Christians use the prophets, who proclaimed beforehand the events of Jesus' life... the prophecies can be made to fit ten thousand others more credibly than Jesus.[2] Great and powerful and lord of all the earth and all the peoples and all armies do the prophets declare him to be, who is to dwell among men... they did not announce a plague like this man.[3] From such signs and misinterpretations and from such worthless proofs no one can establish him firmly as God and the son of God... For as the sun, which gives light to all the rest of the world makes himself visible at the beginning, so ought the Son of God to have done.[4] They are guilty of sophistry in saying that the son of God is the actual Logos... when we declare the Logos to be the Son of God, we show not a Logos pure and holy, but a mortal man led away to a death of shame and scourged... If for you divine reason is the Son of God, we also give our assent to this.[5] Those men were filled with pride and boasting, who made Jesus in the genealogies to be descended from the first man and the kings of the Jews... the carpenter's wife would not have been ignorant of the fact, if she had happened to be of such illustrious descent.[6] But what noble deed did Jesus perform, such as befits God? Did he pour contempt on men and laugh them to scorn and make a sport of what happened to him?[7]

---

[1] II. 27.
[2] II. 28.
[3] II. 29.
[4] II. 30.
[5] II. 31.
[6] II. 32.
[7] II. 33.

There are the words in the Bacchae of Euripides – "Whene'er I wish, the God Himself will set me free"[1]... But even the man who condemned him, suffered no ill, like the madness or tearing in pieces of Pentheus... men mocked him and put on him a purple robe, and a crown of thorns, and in his hand a reed... he wept shamefully.[2] Why does he not at least now, if not before, give some proof of his divinity and save himself from this disgrace and take vengeance on those who insult both himself and his father?[3] What is there in the crucified body? Ichor such as "flows in the blessed Gods"?[4] The vinegar he rushed with gaping mouth to drink and did not endure thirst as any ordinary man you meet often endures it.[5] So then you, O ye holders of the true faith, accuse us, because we do not believe in this man as God nor agree with you that he endured these sufferings to help men, in order that we also may despise punishment.[6] He won no one to his side while he lived, no not even his own disciples, but he was punished and endured such sufferings as you describe.[7] He certainly did not prove himself to be pure of all evil.[8] He was not blameless.[9] Surely you will not say of him that when he had failed to win over those here he was sent to Hades to gain the people there?[10] If you imagine that by devising absurd defences, wherein you have been ridiculously

[1] V. 498.
[2] II. 34.
[3] II. 35.
[4] Homer II. VI. 340. II. 36
[5] II. 37.
[6] II. 33.
[7] II. 39.
[8] II. 41.
[9] II. 42.
[10] II. 43. [A possible allusion to 1 Peter 3.19? – GPB]

deluded, you are making a true defence, what is there to prevent your regarding others also, who have been condemned and perished miserably as greater and more divine messengers... for anyone who was similarly devoid of shame could say of a robber and murderer, who had been punished, that he was not a robber at all but a god: for he told his confederates beforehand that he would endure the sufferings which actually did befall him.[1] In the next place his comrades during his life, who listened to his words and followed him as teacher, when they saw him enduring punishment and dying, did not die with him or for him, nor were induced to think punishment a light thing, but even denied they were his disciples: but now you die with him.[2] While here he only gained ten sailors and tax gatherers, the very scum of the earth, and not even all of those... Living he won over no one, after his death any who wish win crowds – surely this is the height of absurdity?[3] By what reasoning were you induced to believe on him as Son of God? [Celsus makes the Christians answer] we were brought over to him because we know that his punishment was endured for the slaying of the father of evil... Well now, have not many others been punished, and with no less dishonour?[4] [Celsus makes the Christians answer] we believe him to be the Son of God because he healed the lame and blind... And, as you say, he raised the dead.[5] O light and truth, with his own voice he distinctly declares, as you yourselves have recorded, that there will come to you others also, using

---

[1] II. 44.
[2] II. 54.
[3] II. 46.
[4] II. 47.
[5] II. 48.

similar wondrous works, evil men and sorcerers, and he calls anyone who uses such tricks, Satan. So even Jesus himself does not deny that these practices are not divine at all but the acts of wicked men: but being compelled by truth, he at the same time unmasked the proceedings of others and condemned his own acts. Surely then it is contemptible reasoning to consider from the same works one man a god and the rest sorcerers? Why then, as far as these acts are concerned, should the others be accounted wicked rather than he, since they have his witness? For he himself has confessed that these works at least are the marks not of the nature of God but of certain deceivers and worthless characters.[1] What won you over except that he foretold he would rise from the dead?[2] Come then, let us assume that he did foretell it. How many others practise similar tricks in order to win over simple listeners, from whose errors they make profit? Zamolxis, they say, did this in Scythia, the slave of Pythagoras, and Pythagoras himself in Italy and Rhampsinitus in Egypt: the latter "played dice" in Hades with Demeter and came back to earth with a gift from her, a golden napkin; and Orpheus too among the Odrysians and Protesilaus in Thessaly and Heracles on Taenarus and Theseus acted in the same way. But the point in question is whether anyone, who had really died, ever rose again with an actual body; or do you imagine that the statements of the others are myths in essence and in seeming, while you have discovered a turning-point and climax for the drama, which is fitting and credible, in the voice on the cross, when he was breathing his last, and the earthquake and the darkness? You

[1] II. 49. [cf. Matthew 24.24 – GPB]
[2] II. 54.

say that while alive he gave no help to himself, but when dead he rose again and showed the marks of his punishment and how his hands were pierced – but who saw this? A woman driven half-mad, as you assert, and possibly some other of the same society of frauds, who had either dreamed it because of some psychological bias and influenced by an erring idea had imagined facts to be as he wished them (and this has happened to thousands); or, (and this is more likely) he wished to create a sensation among the others by this marvel and by such a lie to afford a foundation for other impostors.[1] If Jesus really wished to manifest the power of God, he ought to have appeared to those who had ill-treated him and to him who pronounced sentence and to all men everywhere.[2] For he certainly no longer feared any man after his death, especially since he was, as you say, God, nor was he sent for this end, to be hidden.[3] Further if this helped in the very least to prove his divinity, he should certainly have vanished instantly from the cross.[4] What messenger sent forth ever hides himself, when he ought to speak out the message given to Him?... While he was disbelieved in the body, he preached to all continuously, but when he might have produced a strong faith by rising from the dead, he showed himself only to one woman and to the members of his own inner circle secretly... So then while being punished everyone saw him, but after he was risen, one only; whereas the opposite should have occurred.[5] He will lead the God-

---

[1] II. 55.
[2] II. 63.
[3] II. 67.
[4] II. 68.
[5] II. 70. [Matthew 28.9f and John 20.15ff record resurrection appearances to women; but only John says that "one woman" saw Jesus – GPB]

fearing into the light and will have mercy on the sinners or those who have repented.[1] If he wished to be hidden, why was the voice from heaven heard proclaiming him to be the son of God? If he did not wish to hide, why was he punished, or why did he die?[2] His having wished by the punishments which he endured to teach us also to despise death demands that, when he was risen from the dead, he should call all men to the light and teach them why he had come.[3] You have all these statements taken from your own writings and we ask no other additional witness; for you are your own undoing.[4] O mighty one from Heaven, what God finds men disbelieving when he comes to them? Or why, I should like to know, is he not recognised by men who have been expecting him for so long?[5] He threatens and reviles lightly saying, “Woe unto you”, and “I tell you beforehand”. For by these words he clearly acknowledges that he cannot persuade men, and this would not happen to God or even to a sensible man.[6] We certainly hope that we shall rise again in the body and possess life eternal and he who is sent to us will be our pattern and leader in this, showing that it is not impossible for God to raise up a man with his body... Now where is he? Let us see him and believe.[7] Did he come for this purpose, that we should not believe him?[8] Therefore he was man and of such character as the very truth shows him to be and

[1] II. 71.
[2] II. 72.
[3] II. 73.
[4] II. 74.
[5] II. 75.
[6] II. 76.
[7] II. 77.
[8] II. 78.

reason proves.[1] Christians and Jews have a most foolish controversy with one another; there is not a pin to choose between their discussion about Christ and what is called proverbially "the fight about an ass's shadow", there is nothing demanding respect in the questions agitated among the Jews and Christians for they both believe that by the spirit of God it was prophesied that one should come and dwell on earth, a saviour to the race of men, but they do not yet agree as to whether the prophesied saviour has come or not.[2] Asclepius helped men and foretold the future to whole cities, dedicated to him, such as Tricca and Epidaurus and Cos and Pergamum, Aristeas of Proconnesus too and a certain man of Clazomenae and Cleomedes of Astypalaea.[3] The Jews, being Egyptians by race, have abandoned Egypt, after revolting against the Egyptian government and despising the custom in Egypt with regard to religious worship; as they treated the Egyptians, so they in their turn were treated by these who followed Jesus and believed in Him as Christ and in both cases the cause of the new departure was rebellion against the state.[4] Being Egyptians, the Hebrews date their beginning from the rebellion; in the days of Jesus others, being Jews, rebelled against the Jewish government and followed Jesus.[5] A revolt was originally the beginning of the Jewish nation and later of Christianity.[6] If all men should desire to be Christians, they would not wish

[1] II. 79.
[2] III. 1.
[3] III. 3.
[4] III. 5.
[5] III. 7.
[6] III. 8.

it.[1] In the beginning they were few and of one mind, but when they spread and became numerous they were divided and split up and wished each to have his own individual sect, for this was their desire from the beginning.[2] Being thus separated because of their numbers they refute one another in argument, still sharing one (is that a paradox?) name, if indeed they do still share it. And this alone they are in spite of everything ashamed to abandon; other points are settled in different ways by different sects.[3] It is true that their unity is the more wonderful, the more it can be proved to hold together on no substantial foundation. But still rebellion is a substantial foundation as also are the advantages, which come from it and the fear of external foes. These things make their faith strong.[4] [They gather] legends of every kind and [invent] terrors. May neither they nor I nor any other man ever cast away the belief that the wicked will be punished and the righteous deemed worthy of honourable rewards... weaving together errors of ancient lore you sing them forth and din them into the ears of men, as the priests of Cybele clash the cymbals around the Corybants.[5] [Like] the Egyptians, for among them, as you approach, you see glorious parks and groves and gateways, tall and beautiful and wonderful temples and all round surpassing buildings and ceremonies overflowing with reverent and mystic worship, but when you go in and reach the inmost shrine, you behold as object of worship – a cat, or an ape, or a

[1] III. 9.
[2] III. 10.
[3] III. 12.
[4] III. 14.
[5] III. 16.

crocodile, or a goat, or a dog.[1] They give out an impression to those who understand these things, that they are not initiated to no purpose. They drive away all the wise from the teaching of their faith and summon only fools and slaves.[2] They make fun of the Egyptians, though they offer many mysteries, which are by no means to be despised, when they teach that such rites are the worship of eternal verities and not, as most men imagine, honours paid to animals, creatures of a day; they are absurd, for they introduce in their accounts of Jesus nothing more impressive than the dogs and goats we find among the Egyptians.[3] The Dioscuri and Heracles and Asclepius and Dionysus... they cannot endure to call gods because they were men, men first and last,[4] though they showed much nobility in the cause of mankind; but Jesus, they say, was seen after death by his own circle of followers.[5] Of Asclepius, [it is said that] a great number of Greeks and barbarians declare that they frequently have seen and do still see, not a mere phantom, but the man himself healing and doing good and foretelling the future.[6] Aristeas of Proconnesus, who disappeared in such a strange supernatural fashion from among men and was seen again so clearly and many times afterwards visited many parts of the world, brought wonderful news, yea, though Apollo himself enjoined the Metapontines to hold him a god, yet no one still believes that this Aristeas is a

---

[1] III. 17.
[2] III. 18.
[3] III. 19.
[4] κὰι πρῶτοι (text doubtful)
[5] III. 22.
[6] III. 22.

god.[1] No one believes in Abaris, the Hyperborean as God, though he was powerful enough to dash along like an arrow.[2] Do they not say that the soul of the Clazomenian often left his body and flitted about, bodiless? And yet men did not believe in him as God.[3] Cleomedes of Astypalaea hid in a chest and, being shut into it, was yet not found inside, but he flew out by means of some divine fate, when some people cut the chest in two in order to catch him.[4] And one could mention many others of the same kind... In worshipping one, who was taken and put to death, they act like the Getae, who worship Zamolxis, and the Cilicians, who worship Mopsus, and the Acarnanians who reverence Amphilochus, and like the Thebans who do the same to Amphiaraus and the Lebadians to Trophonius.[5] Take the favourite of Hadrian – his honours are no whit less than those paid to Jesus. A band of sorcerers paying court to the bidding of a king or the command of a ruler, seem to make him a god.[6] If you compare him with Apollo or Zeus, they will not endure it.[7] Faith takes possession of their minds [Christians] first and forces this agreement of theirs about Jesus.[8] They believe that Jesus, being God, was of mortal body and imagine it is a reverent belief[9]... his mortal flesh, even more corruptible than gold and silver... Well, but when he has laid aside this flesh, will he then be God: why not Asclepius instead and

[1] III. 24.
[2] III. 31.
[3] III. 32.
[4] III. 33.
[5] III. 34.
[6] III. 36.
[7] III. 37.
[8] III. 39.
[9] III. 41.

Dionysus and Heracles?[1] They laugh at those who worship Zeus, when they point out his tomb in Crete, and yet worship the man from the tomb and understand not the ways and reasons which the Cretans have for it.[2] Listen to the rules laid down by their wise men – let no one come, who is educated, no one learned, no one intelligent: for all these things are held among us to be evil; but all the ignorant, all the fools, all the uneducated, all the simple, let them come with good confidence. So acknowledging out of their own lips that such people are worthy of their God, they show clearly that they are willing and able to win over only the silly and low-born and foolish and slaves and women and children.[3] For why in any case is it an evil to be educated and to have studied the best literature and philosophy and to be and to appear wise? Why is this a hindrance to knowing God? Why should it not rather be a help and a means whereby a man might more readily attain truth?[4] No, we certainly see that even those who give shocking performances in the market-places and gather crowds, would never enter an assembly of intelligent people, nor dare to exhibit their shows to them, but wherever they see boys and a mob of slaves and a crowd of brainless fools, there they push themselves in and show off their tricks.[5] We see, as you know, in private houses the woolworkers and cobblers and fullers and the uneducated and uncultured not daring to say a word in the presence of their elders and more learned masters; but whenever they get hold of the children by

---

[1] III. 42
[2] III. 43
[3] III. 44.
[4] III. 49.
[5] III. 50.

themselves and certain women, fools also, they relate all sorts of wonderful stories, and tell them that they ought not to heed their father and their teachers, but believe and obey them; they say if you please that the former talk nonsense and are stupid and can neither know nor do anything really worthy of admiration, since they are preoccupied with empty trifles; they themselves, on the other hand, alone know how men ought to live and if children obey them, they will be happy themselves and bring happiness to their home. And with these very words in their mouth, if they see one of the children's teachers coming or someone more learned or even the father himself, the more cowardly of them are afraid, while the more pertinacious egg the children on to rebel, whispering this kind of thing – "While your father and teachers are here, we neither will nor can explain to you anything good, for we detest their fatuity and stupidity – people utterly corrupt and hopelessly degraded and given to punishing us: but if you want to hear, you must run away from your father and teachers and come with the women and your playfellows to the women's rooms or the cobbler's or fuller's shop, to gain the perfect." So they talk and win them.[1] That I bring no accusation more bitter than truth forces me to make, anyone may infer from the following. Those who summon to the other mysteries make this proclamation: – "Whosoever is clean of hand and wise of tongue", and again others say "whosoever is pure of all stain, and whose soul is conscious of no evil and whose life has been good and righteous." So they proclaim, who promise cleansing from sins. Let us hear whom these Christians invite. "Whosoever," they say, "is a sinner, whosoever hath

[1] III. 55.

no understanding, whosoever is childish," and, to put it in a word, any miserable wretch, him will the kingdom of God receive. Now do you not call him a sinner, who is unjust and a thief and a burglar and a poisoner and a temple robber and a tomb breaker? What others could a robber call, if he made a proclamation?[1] They say that to sinners has God been sent... Why now was he not sent to the sinless? What evil is there in not having sinned?... [They assert that] God will receive the unrighteous man, if he humble himself because of his wickedness, but the just man, even though he look to him with moral purity from the beginning, him God will not receive.[2] Men who preside properly at a trial make those who bewail their evil deeds cease their cries of pity and lamenting, that sentence may not be passed on them from compassionate feelings rather than regard for truth; but God then, you say, judges not with regard to truth but to flattery... This is apparently true that it is somehow the nature of men to sin... So then all without distinction should be invited, seeing all are sinners.[3] So then, what in the world is the preference of sinners?... They blaspheme God and speak lies.[4] So they talk to turn sinners, since they can gain over no man, who is really honourable and just, and therefore open their gates to the most abandoned and worthless of rogues... Yet, I imagine, it is clear to everyone that no one, even by punishment could completely change those who by nature and habit are given up to sin, much less by pity, for to change nature completely is extremely difficult; but the

[1] III. 59.
[2] III. 62.
[3] III. 63.
[4] III. 64.

sinless have a share in a better life.[1] Unlearned [stories].[2] [Celsus objects to] God will be able do everything… He will not desire to do anything wicked.[3] [Celsus assumes] like those who are the slaves of pity, God, enslaved to pity, lightens the punishment of the wicked, who excite his pity and cast off the good, who do nothing of the kind – which is unjust.[4] [Celsus puts in the mouth of Christians] wise men reject what we say, being led astray and ensnared by their wisdom.[5] Ridiculous… no wise man is convinced by the word, being driven away by the multitudes who adhere to it.[6] Their teacher seeks the unintelligent.[7] The teacher behaves like one who promises to cure people's bodies, but prevents them from consulting skilled doctors, because his own lack of knowledge is exposed by them... they take refuge with the childish and with unlettered idiots, saying to them, "Shun doctors" – "See that none of you lays a finger on knowledge" – "knowledge is bad" – "knowledge is a stumbling block to men and deprives them of soundness of soul"... "Give heed to me" – "Those who are really doctors destroy those whom they promise to cure".[8] Their teacher acts like a drunken man, who comes into a party of drunkards and accuses the sober of being drunk.[9] The teacher is like a man with ophthalmia, who in a company of men

---

[1] III. 65.
[2] III. 68.
[3] III. 70.
[4] III. 71.
[5] III. 72.
[6] III. 73.
[7] III. 74.
[8] III. 75.
[9] III. 76.

similarly afflicted accuses the sharp-eyed of being blind.[1] I bring these charges and (not to enumerate them one by one) others of the same kind, and I say that they are entirely out of harmony with right for they insult God, they may lead on wicked men by vain hopes and persuade them to despise the better way, declaring that if they keep from it, they will attain more good.[2]

Jews and certain Christians assert, the latter that there has come down, the former that there will come down to earth a certain God or Son of God, a Judge of the dwellers on earth – this is a contemptible assertion and its refutation does not call for many words.[3] What is the intention of such a descent, on God's part?... To learn what goes on among men?.... Does he not know everything?... Is it then that he knows, but does not help them, since he cannot uplift men by his divine power?... So then, is it impossible for him to regenerate the earth by his divine power, except by sending someone specially to do it?[4] It follows from "God Himself will come down to men" that He has left His dwelling... if you were to change even the least one of things on earth, everything will be overthrown and perish.[5] But really if God were unknown among men and because of this appeared to be in an inferior position, would He not desire to make himself known and to make trial of those who believe and those who do not, like the "nouveaux riches" among men, who are eager for display? So they testify to a great and an

[1] III. 77.
[2] III. 78.
[3] IV. 2.
[4] IV. 3.
[5] IV. 5.

exceedingly mortal love of honour on the part of God.[1] God does not desire to be known for His own sake but for salvation desires to give knowledge of Himself, that those who accept it may become good and be saved, but those who refuse it may be proved wicked and punished... So then only after so many ages did God remember to bring righteousness to man, having cared nothing about it before?[2] It is perfectly clear that they chatter about God without reverence or respect... to astonish the ignorant... like these in the Bacchic mysteries, who introduce phantoms and terrors.[3] The idea has came upon them from a misunderstanding of accounts of these things that after long periods of time and returns and meetings of stars, conflagrations and floods occur, and that after the last flood in the time of Deucalion, the period, in accordance with the alternation of everything demands a conflagration; this made them assert (though it is an erroneous idea) that God will come down, bringing fire like a torturer.[4] But let me take up the argument from the beginning again with more proofs. I say nothing new, only what has been believed through the ages. God is good and beautiful and blessed with all good things in the highest degree of goodness and beauty, but if, as is asserted, he comes down to men, he must change and change from good to evil, from beauty to shame, from blessedness to misery, from superlative good to the lowest depths of evil. Now who would choose such a change? It is indeed the nature of a mortal being to be changed and moulded afresh, but of the immortal to remain ever the same, unchanging. So then God

[1] IV. 6.
[2] IV. 7.
[3] IV. 10.
[4] IV. 11.

would never accept this change.[1] Either God really changes, as they say, into a mortal body (and we have already declared that it is impossible) or he does not really change, but makes the beholders imagine it and deceives them and lies. Deceit and lying are wholly evil and would only be used as medicine if you were trying to cure sick friends and madmen, or against enemies by one who was planning escape from danger. But no sick man or madman is a friend of God, nor does God fear anyone, that he should fly from danger by leading him astray.[2] The Jews say that life being filled with all kinds of evil needs one sent from God that the wicked may be punished and all things made clean, as it happened in the case of the first flood... Christians add to this.[3] In similar manner to the flood, which cleansed the earth... occurred the overthrowing of the tower... Moses who wrote the story of the tower, perverted the story of the sons of Aloeus and applied it to the account of the tower... and the account of Sodom and Gomorrah... and their destruction by fire because of their sins... is like the story of Phaethon.[4] And the Christians, adding to the stories of the Jews, say that because of the sins of the Jews the Son of God has already been sent, and that the Jews by punishing Jesus and giving him gall to drink have drawn down on themselves wrath from God.[5] The whole race of Jews and Christians is like a flight of bats or swarm of ants coming out of a granary or to frogs in council round a mud pool or worms holding their assembly in the corner of a dung hill and quarrelling with

---

[1] IV. 14.
[2] IV. 18.
[3] IV. 20.
[4] IV. 21.
[5] IV. 22.

one another as to which of them are greater sinners; and they declare that God shows and announces everything to us beforehand, and leaving the whole universe and the ways of the heavens and passing over the vast earth, He dwells as a fellow-man with us alone and to us alone gives his messages and never ceases sending and seeking how we may be with him for ever... like worms, who declare that God is and then that after Him we were made by Him in every way like unto Him, and all other things are made subject to us, earth and water and air and stars – for our sakes are they all and appointed to be our slaves... saying, "Now since some among us err, God will come or send His son to burn up the wicked, and that we, the remnant, may possess eternal life with him?... This wrangling, is more bearable among worms and frogs than Jews and Christians.[1] The Jews were run-away slaves from Egypt, who never did anything worthy of note and were never held in esteem or reputation;[2] though the loved of God.[3] They tried to trace their origin back to the first race of sorcerers and impostors, bringing forward as testimony dark and ambiguous sayings, veiled in darkness; these they twisted into wrong interpretations to the unlearned and unintelligent, and that too when there had never been any ambiguity about the passages for centuries before.[4] Nations have claimed antiquity, such as the Athenians and Egyptians and Arcadians and Phrygians, who say there have existed among them men sprung from the earth and bring detailed proof; then the Jews grovelling in some corner of Palestine, entirely uneducated and unaware that this theme

---

[1] IV. 23.
[2] IV. 31.
[3] IV. 32.
[4] IV. 33.

had been sung by Hesiod and thousands of other inspired poets long ago, put together incredible legends without any literary grace – that a man was moulded by the hands of God, who breathed into him life, and a woman from his side; legends of commands of God, and a serpent who fought against them and was victorious against God's command: so they tell old wives' stories, most impiously making God weak even from the beginning and unable to win over even one human being, whom He moulded Himself.[1] The more reasonable of Jews and Christians are ashamed of these stories and try somehow to allegorize them.[2] They talk of a flood and a strange ark, with everything inside it, and a dove and a crow as messengers, falsifying and treating recklessly the story of Deucalion; for I do not imagine they expected that it would come to light, but merely invented stories for young children.[3] Absurd and unreasonable is the begetting of children... the plots of brothers... a father's sorrow... treachery of mothers... if God live close to these men and shared their life, it is absurd... that God should give His sons asses and sheep and camels.[4] God also gave wells to the righteous.[5] Lot and his daughters are more immoral than the crime of Thyestes.[6] The hatred [of Esau]... brothers selling... a brother sold... a father deceived.[7] The dreams [of the chief butler and baker] and their explanation, from which Joseph was brought out [of prison]... and though his brothers had

[1] IV. 36.
[2] IV. 38.
[3] IV. 41.
[4] IV. 43.
[5] IV. 44.
[6] IV. 45.
[7] IV. 46.

sold him the one who had been sold treated them kindly when they were hungry and had been sent with their asses to buy food... the recognition... Joseph, who had been sold as a slave, was set free and came with a procession to his father's tomb: and by him the glorious and divine nation of the Jews, having increased to great numbers in Egypt, was commanded to settle somewhere outside and feed their flocks in districts of no reputation.[1] They do not admit an allegorical interpretation.[2] But are clearly foolish legends.[3] Indeed the allegorical explanations of them, which appear to have been written, are much more disgraceful and absurd even than the stories themselves, for they try to harmonize with wondrous but altogether senseless madness things which can never be made to fit.[4]

This is the nature, as I well know, of the dialogue between one Papiscus and Jason, which deserves pity and hatred rather than mirth. However it is not my purpose to refute all those statements; for, I imagine, everyone can see it for themselves, especially if they could have patience and endure to read the books themselves. Rather I wish to explain one thing clearly, the nature of the Universe – that God made nothing mortal, but that all things immortal are the works of God and mortal things the work of them. And soul is a work of God, but the nature of body is different. And herein there is no difference between the body of a bat or a worm or a frog or a man; for the fundamental substance is the same and the corruptible part of them is alike.[5]

[1] IV. 47.
[2] IV. 49.
[3] IV. 50.
[4] IV. 51.
[5] IV. 52.

Animals, not endowed with reason, are more beloved by God than we and have a purer conception of the divine.[1] Common is the nature of all the bodies mentioned before, and single, going and returning again through the same cycle of change.[2] No product of matter is immortal... on this point I have said enough... if anyone is able to give further hearing and research, he will know.[3] The sum of evil in the world was never formerly, and is not now, nor will be in the future greater or less; for the nature of all things is one and the same and the generation of evil is always the same.[4] What is the origin of evil it is difficult for one without philosophy to understand, but it is enough for most people to say that evil does not come from God, but has its foundation in matter and its abode among mortal things; the revolving course of mortal existence is the same from beginning to end, and in accordance with the appointed cycles it is necessary that the same things should always be, things past, things present, things to come.[5] Neither have visible things been given to man, but each for the preservation of the whole comes into existence and perishes according to the change, which I mentioned above, from one thing into another:... God does not need to correct his work and make it fresh... nor like a man, who has made an imperfect design and executed it unskilfully, does God correct the universe, cleansing it by flood or conflagration.[6] Even if something seem to you evil, it is not by any means certain that it is so; for you do not

[1] IV. 58.
[2] IV. 60.
[3] IV. 61.
[4] IV. 62.
[5] IV. 65.
[6] IV. 69.

know what is of advantage either for yourself or for another and for the world.[1] [Celsus ridicules] words of anger. and threats.[2] Anger is a passion on the part of God... they ascribe to God the passions of men and hold impious views about him and err in the accounts they offer of him.[3] How is it not ridiculous – that a man who was angered with the Jews slew them all, root and branch, and burned their city (so utterly powerless were they), whereas, God, the Mighty One, as they say, being angry and indignant and uttering threats sent his son and met with the treatment we all know... But, not to speak of the Jews alone, (for that is not my intention), but of the whole of nature, as I promised, I will make clearer what I have already said.[4] They say that God made all things for man... no more for the sake of man than for the irrational animals were all things created... Why should they exist for the nourishment of human beings rather than for plants and trees and herbs and thorns?[5] Thunder and lightning and rain are not the works of God... if anyone were to grant that these are the works of God, they exist no more for the sustenance of us men than for plants, trees, herbs and thorns... even if you say that these things are created for men, why will you assert that they are rather for men than for irrational animals, the very wildest?[6] We indeed by toil and suffering gain with difficulty a scanty living, but for them all things grow "unsown and unploughed".[7] But if you quote the words of

[1] IV. 70.
[2] IV. 71.
[3] IV. 72.
[4] IV. 73.
[5] IV. 74.
[6] IV. 75.
[7] IV. 76.

Euripides: "To mortal men the Sun and night are slaves"[1] why should they be our slaves rather than slaves of the ants and flies? For to them is the night given for rest and the day for light and work.[2] If anyone were to call us lords of the beasts, because we hunt the other animals and feast upon them, we should say, "Why were not we rather created for them, since they hunt us and devour us? Further, we need spears and weapons and many people to help and dogs for the chase; but to them immediately and spontaneously has nature given weapons, which easily subject us to them.[3] With regard to your assertion that God has given us the power to capture and use wild animals, I would say that probably, before cities existed and arts and society as we know it, before weapons and snares were invented, men were caught and eaten by wild beasts, while the wild beasts were seldom caught by men.[4] In this way God rather subjected men to wild beasts.[5] There is no difference between a man and ants or bees; if men appear to differ from irrational animals because they have built cities and make use of political constitutions and government and leadership, this is nothing to the purpose, for ants and bees do the same. Bees actually have a leader, who has a retinue and attendants and wars and victories, and[6] capture of the conquered and cities and suburbs too, and succession of labours and judgments passed on the idle and wicked: for the drones they

---

[1] Phoenissac V. 546.
[2] IV. 77.
[3] IV. 78.
[4] IV. 79.
[5] IV. 80.
[6] αἱρέσις (text doubtful)

drive away and punish.[1] The ants help one another with their loads, when they see one wearied by them... the ants set apart the grains which sprout, that they may not swell and grow, but remain for their food through the year.[2] When ants die, the living set apart a special place for them. And that is their ancestral tomb... and when they meet one another, they converse, and therefore never miss their way; so they have abundance of reason and common ideas on certain general topics and a voice and occurrences and expressions.[3] Come now, if anyone were to look down to earth from heaven how would he think our actions differed from the ants and bees?[4] There is sorcery among the irrational animals... if men pride themselves at all on their knowledge of sorcery, even in this serpents and eagles are wiser than they; for they certainly know many charms and simples and also virtues of certain stones for the preservation of their young, which if men chance upon, they think they have found something wonderful.[5] The writings of the Jews and Christians are very simple and ordinary and those who allegorize them do violence to the meaning of the writers.[6] If, because man has laid hold on conceptions of God, he is considered superior to the other animals, let those, who affirm this, know that many of the other living creatures will lay claim even to this; and with good reason – for what could anyone call more Godlike that to foreknow the future and to foretell it? So men learn this from the other animals and especially from birds; and all

[1] IV. 81.
[2] IV. 83
[3] τυγχάνοντα καὶ σημαινόμενα (text doubtful). IV. 84.
[4] IV. 85.
[5] IV. 86.
[6] IV. 87.

who listen to their information, are prophets. If then birds and other prophetic creatures are given foreknowledge by God and teach us by means of signs, by so much do they seem nearer by nature to communion with God and to be wiser and more loved by Him. But the wise among men say that they have gatherings, clearly more sacred than ours and that they know what is said there and give proof that they know, when having stated previously that the birds have said they will go away somewhere or do this thing or the other, they prove their assertions by the fact that the birds do go away and act as they have foretold. And there seems to be nothing more faithful than elephants, or more devoted to ideals of God, solely, I imagine, because they have knowledge of Him.[1] Storks are more devoted to duty than human beings. who, in their turn, bring food to their parents... the Arabian creature, the phoenix, after many years goes to Egypt and carries its dead father, buried in a ball of myrrh and places it in the precinct of the sun.[2] Everything was not made for man, any more than for the lion or the eagle or the dolphin, but that this world might, being God's work, be complete and perfect in every detail. To this end all things have been arranged not in relation to one another but [...][3] to the whole. And God cares for the whole and His providence never leaves it or deteriorates; nor does God after a time bring it back to Himself, nor is He angered on account of men any more than for apes or flies, nor does He threaten these creatures, each of whom in its station has received its lot.[4]

---

[1] IV. 88.
[2] IV. 98.
[3] (text unintelligible.)
[4] IV. 99.

O Jews and Christians, no god or Son of God has ever come down or could come down. But if you mean that certain angels came, what do you say they are? Gods, or some other race? Another race, I suppose – daemons.[1] The first point about the Jews to excite wonder is that they should worship the heaven and the angels in it, but should neglect its most holy and powerful parts, the sun and moon and the other heavenly bodies, fixed stars and planets; as if it were possible that the whole could be God and its parts not divine; or to treat with great honour those who are said to appear to those in darkness somewhere; blinded by crooked sorcery, or dreaming with shadowy phantoms, while those who prophesy so clearly and gloriously to all men, through whom rain and heat and clouds and thunder (which they worship) and lightning and fruit and all kinds of offspring are given, by whom God is revealed to them, the brightest heralds all above, those who are truly heavenly angels – these are to be regarded as of no value.[2] It is folly on their part to imagine that when God brings fire, like a cook, all the rest of the human race will be roasted to death, while they alone will remain, not only the living, but also those who have long been dead, rising from the earth with that same flesh they wore long ago; it is a very hope of worms. For what soul of man would still desire a mouldering body? Yes, for this teaching of yours is not shared by some of the Christians, nor do they agree with its exceeding vileness and loathliness and impossibility of proof. For what body having been entirely corrupted can return to its original nature and that very first self-same condition, whence it was dissolved? Having no

[1] V. 2.
[2] V. 6.

answer to give they take refuge in a most ridiculous statement – all things are possible with God. But yet God cannot do what is base nor does he will what is contrary to his nature; nor if you, according to your natural wickedness, desire anything evil, will God be able to do it, nor must you even believe that it will instantly occur. For not of clashing desire or of erring disorder but of upright and just nature is God the ruler and governor. To the soul He could give eternal life, "But corpses" as Heraclitus says, "are more worthless than dung." But flesh certainly God neither will nor can contrary to reason declare to be immortal, for it is full of what it is not seemly even to mention; for He Himself is the reason of all things; so He is not able to act contrary to reason or contrary to Himself.[1] Since the Jews became a peculiar people and ordained laws according to their dwelling-place, and maintain them among themselves even up to the present day and preserve a way of worship, which, whatever else it may be, is at any rate handed down by their fathers, they do in these respects behave like the rest of mankind, because each nation follows its ancestral customs, whatever they may be. This method seems to be advantageous not only because it has occurred to some nations to hold different opinions and it is necessary to protect what is ordained for the public weal; but also because probably the quarters of the earth were in the beginning all allotted to different guardian spirits, and being divided among different governing powers were controlled in that way. And further whatever was done in each nation in this way would be rightly done, if it was what pleased the people, while it was impious to destroy what had been appointed

[1] V. 14.

among districts from the beginning.[1] [Later] let the second come forward and I shall ask them whence they came and who is the author of their ancestral customs. No one, they will answer, because they too spring from the same source and take their teacher and master from no other origin; yet they have revolted from the Jews.[2] One might take the evidence of Herodotus on this point, when he says: "For the people of the city of Marea and Apis, who dwell in the parts of Egypt bordering on Libya, considering themselves Libyans and not Egyptians, and being angered at the sacrificial worship wished not to be cut off from cow's flesh; so they sent to Ammon, saying they had nothing in common with the Egyptians, for they dwelt outside the Delta, and they wished to be allowed to partake of all kinds of food. But the god did not allow them to do this, saying their country was in Egypt, which the floods of the Nile watered and that all were Egyptians, who dwelt to the south of the city of Elephantine and drank from the river."[3] Such is the statement of Herodotus. But Ammon is no worse ambassador for the thoughts of God than the angels of the Jews, so there is no wrong in each nation worshipping after its own customs. Truly we shall find the differences between the nations very great and yet each considers its own belief the best. The Ethiopians, who dwell in Meroe worship Zeus and Dionysus only, Arabians Ourania and Dionysus only, all Egyptians Osiris and Isis, Saites Athena, while the Naucratites quite recently have named Serapis a god, and the rest worship each according to their own laws. And some refrain from eating sheep, worshipping them as sacred, and others from

[1] V. 25.
[2] V. 33.
[3] Herod., II. 18.

crocodiles, others from cows, and loathe the flesh of swine. The Scythians actually hold it a good thing to feast upon human beings; there are some Indians too, who in eating their fathers, think they are performing a sacred duty. And somewhere Herodotus already quoted, mentions it. I will quote his actual words again for the sake of credibility; this is what he writes: "If anyone were to make a proposal to all mankind, bidding them select the best laws of all, each would after consideration choose those of his own country. For men always think the laws of their own country far superior to any other. Therefore it is not likely that any other than a madman would ridicule such things. That this is the opinion of all men regarding laws, it is possible to establish by many other proofs and especially by the following evidence. Darius, during his reign, summoned the Greeks who happened to be there at the time and asked at what price they would be willing to eat their dead fathers; they answered that nothing would induce them to do it. After this Darius summoned those Indians called Callatians, who eat their parents, and asked them in the presence of the Greeks, who understood what was being said through an interpreter, at what price they would take their dead fathers and burn them with fire; they shouted aloud and bade him be silent. Such then is the state of mind about such topics. And Pindar seems to me right, when he says that law is monarch of all."[1] If then the Jews preserved their own law in these respects, they are not therein to be blamed but rather those who deserted their own customs and adopted those of the Jews. But if they pride themselves on it, as possessed of higher wisdom, and hold aloof from intercourse with others as not

[1] Herod., III. 38. V. 34.

equally pure, they have already heard that they hold no peculiar and special ideas about heaven, but, to pass over all the others, ideas long ago held by the Persians, as Herodotus shows somewhere. "For they have a custom" he says "of going up to the tops of mountains and sacrificing, calling the whole circle of heaven Zeus." Therefore I think it makes no difference whether you call the Highest Zeus or Zen or Adonai or Sabaoth or Ammon, like the Egyptians, or Papaeus, like the Scythians. Nor would they be held at all holier than the others, in that they practise circumcision, for this the Egyptians and Colchians did before them, nor because they abstain from swine's flesh, for this the Egyptians did too, and from the flesh of goats, sheep, oxen and fish, as well, While Pythagoras and his disciples do not eat beans or anything with life in it. But it is not likely that they are high in God's favour or loved by Him at all differently from the others, or that angels were sent to them alone from Him, as if they had been allotted some land of the blessed for we see them and of whose country they were deemed worthy. So let this sacred band depart having paid the penalty of its boasting, not knowing the Great God, but being led astray and deceived by the sorcery of Moses, of which they became disciples to no good end.[1] We pass over the refutation which can be given about their teacher and grant that he is really an angel. Is he the first and only one who came to men or were there others before him? If they were to say he was the only one, they would be convicted of lying against themselves. For they assert that others came many times, yes, sixty or seventy together, who, so they say, became wicked and were punished by being cast in chains

[1] V. 41.

under the earth, whence came the warm springs, their tears: moreover there came, so they declare, an angel to the tomb of this leader of theirs – according to some, one, to others, two – who answered the woman, saying he was risen. For the son of God, as it appears, was not able to open the tomb, but needed another to move away the rock. And on behalf of Mary, being pregnant, there came an angel to the carpenter and again another angel that they might take up the young child and flee away. But what need is there to elaborate particulars and count up all the angels said to have been sent to Moses and others of them? If others were sent, it is clear that he came from the same God. But let us consider him to have a more important message; for instance suppose the Jews were sinning or corrupting their religion or acting impiously; for all these things are suggested by obscure hints.[1] So he is not the only one who is related to have dwelt among the human race, as even those who under the pretext of teaching the name of Jesus have revolted from the Creator as being inferior and have came over to some superior God, the father of him who came to live on earth, declare, saying that before him certain beings from the Creator came to dwell among the human race.[2] They and the Jews clearly have the same God... it is certain at any rate that the members of the great church admit this and acknowledge as true the accounts of the creation of the world current among the Jews about the six days, and the seventh day, on which... God rested returning to the contemplation of Himself... of the first man they give the same account as the Jews and draw the same genealogy from him as they… the same

[1] V. 52.
[2] V. 54.

conspiracies of brother against brother... the same descent into Egypt and the same flight thence.[1] Let no one think I do not know that some of them will allow that their God is the same as the God of the Jews, while others will say He is different and opposed to the God of the Jews, and that from Him came the Son... and let there be also a third class of those who call some material and other spiritual... and some who are called Gnostics... some who accept Jesus, while still wishing to live, like the majority of Jews, in accordance with the Jewish law... some sibyllists.[2] Some Simonians, who worship Helene or Helenus as teacher and are called Helenians... and Marcellians so-called from Marcellina and Harpocratians from Salome and others from Mariamne and others yet from Martha... and Marcionites, who followed Marcion.[3] Others have taken another teacher and spirit making wicked inventions and wallowing about in great darkness, more lawless and abandoned than the fellow-revellers of Antinous in Egypt... they utter terrible blasphemies against one another, utterable and unutterable; and they will not yield the smallest point for the sake of harmony for they hate one another bitterly... circles and wily agitators.[4] Some are called "cauterizings of the hearing"... some "enigmas"... some sirens, who betray mysteries and give specious arguments and stop the ears of those whom they deceive and change them into swine... You will hear all these who are so widely different and who in their disputes

[1] V. 59.
[2] V. 61.
[3] V. 62.
[4] V. 63.

argue so shamefully with one another saying, "The world is crucified to me and I to the world."[1]

How can Christians who have received any education say they know more than the Jews? Come now, if they have no foundation for their system let us examine the teaching itself; let us consider the corruptions they make through misunderstanding and ignorance, when in first principles they persist obstinately without any sense of fitness in opinions on things of which they know nothing, as follows... What the Christians say is said better and more clearly [among philosophers].[2] It has been better expressed by the Greeks without exaggeration or promises of God or the Son of God.[3] From the letter of Plato – "If I thought these ideas could be adequately described to the multitude and expressed, what nobler could I have accomplished in life than to write down so great a boon for humanity and to lead the nature of all men to the light?"[4] [Another quotation] from Plato – "through the use of question and answer light is shed on the thoughts of those who follow his philosophy."[5] The good can be known by few, since the many being filled up with unrighteous pride, with lofty and empty hope, assert, as the possessors of wonderful knowledge, that certain things are true: yet though Plato said these things before,[6] yet he does not talk of marvels nor shut the mouth of one who wishes to find out for himself what is the essence of his promises, nor does he bid them on the spot hasten to believe

[1] V. 64. [cf. Galatians 6.14 – GPB]
[2] V. 65.
[3] VI. 1.
[4] Ep. VII. 341 D. VI. 6.
[5] Ep. VII. 344 B. VI. 7.
[6] Ep. VII. 341 E.

that God is of a particular character and that He has a son of a particular character and that the latter came down and conversed with me.[1] From Plato – "It has occurred to speak still further on this point; for perhaps I might express myself more clearly than I have yet done for there is a certain true reason, opposed to the man who has dared to write anything at all on such a subject, and since I have often mentioned it on former occasions, it seems to me that I ought to mention it now. In each of existing things through which it is necessary that knowledge come, there are three elements, knowledge itself is fourth, and fifth must be placed that which is really knowable and true; of these, one is name; the second, reason; the third image; the fourth, knowledge."[2] You see how Plato, although he has affirmed that it cannot be expressed, nevertheless, to afford the appearance of retreating to an irrefutable position, adds a reason for this difficulty; for even nothing might possibly be expressed... Plato does not boast and tell lies, declaring that he is making some new discovery or come to announce it from heaven, but acknowledges the source of these statements... they say to all their hearers, "First believe that he whom I bring before thee is the Son of God... although he was shamefully bound and punished with much dishonour, and only yesterday was treated with scorn and disgrace before the eyes of all men... believe even more for this reason".[3] If they bring forward this man and others someone different, but common to all and always ready to hand is the cry, "Believe, if thou wilt be saved, or go away", what are they to do, who will truly to be saved? Are they to cast the dice to divine

[1] VI. 8.
[2] Ep. VII. 342 A.B. VI. 9.
[3] VI. 10.

whither to turn and whom to join?[1] They declare the wisdom among men to be foolishness with God... the reason of this has been stated long ago, their wish to win over the uneducated and foolish only... this statement is not original but borrowed from the wise men of Greece, who have said that the wisdom of men is different from the wisdom of God... the words of Heraclitus, "Man's character has not fixed principles, God's has"... "A foolish man listens to a daemon as a boy to a man"... the words of Plato in the Apology of Socrates: "For I, men of Athens, have obtained this name for no other reason than for my wisdom. Of what nature is wisdom? Probably the wisdom of man, for in that I venture to think I am really wise."[2] They discourse about the wisdom of God to the most uneducated, to slaves, to the most unlearned.[3]

Sorcerers... they flee headlong from the more scholarly as not being fit subjects for deception, but decoy the more unlettered.[4] About their humility... it is a misunderstanding of the words of Plato in the Laws, "God, as the ancient account tells, having the beginning and end and middle of all existing things, marches straight on his way, advancing according to his nature. There follows him always justice, the avenger of all lapses from the law of God; he who is about to attain blessedness follows her closely with humble and seemly appearance"[5]... the man of humble mind humbles himself without order, or seemliness, casting himself on his knees or falling headlong putting on raiment

---

[1] VI. 11.
[2] Plato. Ap. V. 20. D. VI. 12.
[3] VI. 13.
[4] VI. 14.
[5] IV. 7 p.715 E. ff.

of mourning or sprinkling himself with dust.[1] The saying of Jesus against rich men "it is easier for a camel to go through the eye of a needle than for a rich man to go into the kingdom of God"[2] is clearly taken from Plato and Jesus perverted the words of Plato in which he said: "It is impossible to be surpassingly good and surpassingly rich at the same time."[3] The words of Plato... "All things are around the king of all and all things exist for his sake and that is the cause of all that is fair: there is a second for second things and a third for third. The soul of man therefore is eager for knowledge of these things and their nature, looking to the things akin to itself, of which none is perfect. But as regards the king and the things of which I spoke, there is nothing of that nature."[4] Certain Christians have misunderstood the words of Plato and boast of their God above the heavens, ascending above the heaven of the Jews... from the Phaedrus "No poet on earth has ever sung of the realm above the heavens nor will ever sing in worthy manner"... for the essence colourless, formless, intangible, really existing is beheld by understanding alone, the pilot of the soul, and around it the spring of true knowledge has its home."[5] Seven heavens... souls can make their way to earth and from earth through the planets."[6] These mysteries are obscurely indicated in the accounts of the Persians and the rites of Mithras, which are celebrated among them. For in the latter there is a representation of the two heavenly revolutions – of

---

[1] VI. 15.

[2][Matthew 19.24 – GPB]

[3] Legg. V. 12. p.743 A. VI. 16.

[4] Ep. II. 312 E. VI. 18.

[5] Phaedrus XXVII. 247 C. VI. 19.

[6] VI. 21.

the fixed stars, and of that assigned to the planets and of the way of the soul through them. It is like this: there is a ladder with seven gates and on it an eighth gate; the first gate is of lead, the second of tin, the third of bronze, the fourth of iron, the fifth of a mixed metal, the sixth of silver, the seventh of gold. The first they assign to Saturn showing by lead the slowness of the Star, the second to Venus, likening her to the dazzling brightness and softness of tin, the third to Jupiter, firm and solid bronze, the fourth to Mercury, for both Mercury and iron are enduring of all kinds of toil and money-making and are hard-working, the fifth to Mars, being unequal and varied in appearance because the metal is mixed, the sixth of silver to the Moon, the seventh of gold to the sun, imitating their colour... this order is shown by symbols in the names of the rest of matter... musical reasons… and a second explanation connected with musical ideas.[1] [The Christian ideas] call for any silly listeners, slaves... [and are taken] from the Persians and Cabiri.[2] Anyone wishing to examine the Christian rites parallel with the Persian ones, placing them beside one another and stripping the Christian ceremonies bare will see in this way the difference between them... the diagram.[3] In the diagram were depicted ten circles distinct from one another but united by one circle... the diagram was divided by a thick black line and this was said to be Gehenna, which is also Tartarus.[4] He who sets the impress of the seal is called father, he, who is sealed, is called young man and son, who answers: "I have been anointed with white ointment from the tree of life"...

[1] VI. 22.
[2] VI. 23.
[3] VI. 24.
[4] VI. 25.

mentioned by those who give up the seal, seven angels, who stand on either side the soul of the dying body, the one being called "of light", the other "of rulers" and the ruler of those called "rulers" is called God accursed. They say the God of the Jews is accursed, God who sends rain and thunder, the Demiurge of the universe.[1] The Christians call God, the Creator, accursed... the God of the Mosaic cosmogony... is of such a character and deserving of curses according to those who hold these opinions about Him, since He cursed the serpent, who introduced the knowledge of good and evil to the first human beings.[2] What could be more foolish or mad than this senseless wisdom? How did the Jewish law-giver blunder? And how can you accept his cosmogony for yourself by means, as you say, of a kind of type and allegory, and the law of the Jews too, while you are reluctant, most impious of men, to praise the Creator of the Universe, who has promised everything to them, to increase their race to the ends of the earth and to raise them up from the dead with the same flesh and blood, who gave His spirit to the prophets, and again you pour abuse on Him? But when you are pressed by these facts, you acknowledge that you worship the same God; but when your teacher Jesus and the Jewish Moses give contrary laws, you seek another God instead of Him and the Father.[3] The seven ruling daemons... the first shaped like a lion... the angel of the Creator… the lion-like....the second in order a bull... the third an amphibious kind of animal hissing frightfully... the fourth had the form of an eagle.... the fifth had the face of a bear... the sixth is said by them to have the face of a dog... the

---

[1]VI. 27.

[2] VI. 28.

[3] VI. 29.

seventh has the countenance of an ass and was named Thaphabaoth or Onoel.[1] Some people return to the shapes of these rulers, so that some become lions, others bulls, and others snakes, or eagles, or bears, or dogs... in the diagram... a square pattern.[2] They continue to add one thing to another, words of prophets and circles on circles and effluences from an earthly church and circumcision, and power flowing from one Prunicos, a virgin, and a living soul and a heaven slain to live and earth slaughtered with the sword, and many men slain to live, and death ceasing in the world, when the sin of the world dies, and a way again narrow and gates that open of their own will. And everywhere there is the tree of life and a raising up of the flesh from the tree, because, I imagine, their teacher was nailed to a cross and was a carpenter by trade. So that if he had chanced to be hurled from a precipice or cast into a pit or hanged in a noose, or had been a worker in leather or stone or iron, there would have been above the heavens a precipice of life or a pit of resurrection or a rope of immortality or a blessed stone or an iron of love or a holy leather. Now what old woman would not be ashamed to whisper such stories even in singing lullabies to put a child to sleep?[3] That is not the least of their marvels, for they interpret certain writings between the upper circles – above the heavens – especially two words, a greater and a less – meaning the Son and the Father... they make profession of a kind of magic sorcery; and this is the sum of their wisdom.[4] Those who use magic and sorcery and call on the barbarous names of certain daemons, act like those who

[1] VI. 30.
[2] VI. 33.
[3] VI. 34.
[4] VI. 38.

on the same foundation perform marvels for those who do not know that the names of daemons are different among the Greeks and Scythians... In Herodotus... the Scythians call Apollo Gongosyrus, Poseidon Thagimasada, Aphrodite Argimpasan, Hestia Tabiti[1]... I have seen in the hands of some of their elders barbarous books with the names of daemons and marvellous works. These elders make no good profession, but act altogether for the harm of men.[2] – A certain Dionysius, an Egyptian musician, met me and told me with reference to magic that it is only with the uneducated that it has power and with men of corrupt moral character, while it is not possible to work any miracles with philosophers because they take careful thought to live in a healthy way.[3]

And some of their most impious errors are due to this excessive ignorance of theirs, wherein they have wandered away from the meaning of divine mysteries, setting up an adversary to God and calling him the devil and naming him in the Hebrew tongue Satan. Now it is absolutely certain that all these statements are of mortal invention and unworthy of being stated, namely, that the mightiest God, wishing to do good to men, has an adversary and is helpless before him. In that case the Son of God is conquered by the devil, and being punished by him teaches us also to despise the punishments which he inflicts; telling us beforehand forsooth that Satan, having appeared in the same way as he himself, will show great works and wonderful deeds, claiming as his own the glory of God. But men ought not to be willing to err and turn aside to him through the influence of these works, but ought

[1] VI. 39.
[2] VI. 40.
[3] VI. 41.

to believe in himself the Son of God alone. These are clearly the words of a sorcerer, planning and taking careful thought against those who hold opposite views to him and who take sides against him...

The ancients hint at a certain war amongst the gods, and Heraclitus speaks in this way of it: "we must realise that war is universal, and strife is justice, and that everything comes into being and advances by means of strife"; while Pherecydes, who is much more ancient than Heraclitus, tells a myth of one army arrayed against another, and names Oonos as the leader of the one and Ophioneus as the leader of the other and recounts their challenges and struggles and says that they made agreements with one another that whichever party of them should fall into Ogenos should be considered conquered, while those who had expelled and conquered them should possess heaven. And he says that some such meaning is attached to the mysterious stories about Titans and giants who tell stories of battles with gods, and also the Egyptian mysteries of Typhon and Horus and Osiris... Those are not like the stories of a devil or daemon or (as he says with more truth) of an impostor who is trying to establish an opposite opinion, and Homer too refers obscurely to matters similar to those mentioned by Heraclitus and Pherecydes and those who promulgate mysteries of Titans and giants in these words which Hephaestus addressed to Hera:

> Once in your cause I felt his matchless might
> Buried headlong downward
> from the ethereal height.[1]

and in those of Zeus to Hera:

[1] Il. I. 590-1 (trans. Pope).

Hast thou forgot, when bound and fixed on high,
From the vast concave of the spangled sky
I hung thee trembling on a golden chain,
And all the raging gods opposed in vain?
Headlong I hurled them from the Olympian hall,
Stunned in the whirl and breathless with the fall.[1]

... The words of Zeus to Hera are the words of God addressed to matter, and the words addressed to matter signify that matter, which was at the beginning in discord, God took and bound together and set in order with certain laws, and that the daemons concerned with it who were rebellious, these he cast down in punishment by the way which leads hither. So Pherecydes understood these words of Homer when he said: "Beneath that region is the region of Tartarus, over which the daughters of Boreas, the harpies and the tempest, keep guard, where Zeus banishes any one of the gods who is rebellious." With some such ideas is connected the peplos of Athena, which is seen by all in the procession at the Panathenaea. For it is clear from this that some daemon without mother and without defilement is master of the daring of the earthborn.... The Son of God is punished by the devil and teaches us that we should be steadfast under punishment from him too. Such statements as this are altogether ridiculous; for I think it is the devil who ought to be punished, while those mortal men who are the victims of his devilry ought not to be threatened.[2] And the very origin of their title for him, Son of God, I can tell you. Men of old declared that this universe was born of God, being His child and His son. Now the other Son of God is

[1] Il. XV. 18-24. (trans. Pope.).
[2] VI. 42.

certainly very like this one.[1] And furthermore, their cosmogony is very ridiculous... And their story of the creation of men is very foolish... that man should be made in the image of God... that God planted paradise and that man passed his life there, and how his life was changed by accident and he was cast forth because of sin and dwelt opposite the paradise of luxury... Moses wrote this with no serious intention but in the joking spirit of the writers of the old comedy, who related "Proitus wedded Bellerophon, but Pegasus was from Arcadia."[2] Moses and the Prophets who left to us their writings knew not at all what is the nature of the universe and of man, but have patched together a story which is sheer nonsense... [Celsus accuses] the days of Creation.[3] For I do not imagine that the Creator, took light for Himself from above, like those who kindle their lamps at those of their neighbours... And if there really did exist an accursed God, an adversary to the great God, who acted contrary to His wishes, why did He lend him light?[4] With regard to the creation and destruction of the universe, and to the question as to whether it is uncreated and indestructible, or created but not destructible, or the reverse, I at present say nothing... They say that the spirit of God existed in alien things here below... Certain wicked plots, made by a different Creator, against the will of the great God and against His Spirit, require to be destroyed since the higher God tolerated them... and they say that the great God, having given His Spirit to his creator, demands it back... What God gives any gift with the intention of demanding it back? For

---

[1] VI. 47.
[2] VI. 49.
[3] VI. 50.
[4] VI. 51.

to demand a gift back is the mark of a needy person, but God stands in need of nothing... Why did He not know He was lending to an evil creature?... Why does He disregard a wicked creator who is working against Him?[1] Why does He send secretly and destroy His own creation? Why does He employ hidden force and persuasion and craft? Why does He allure those who, as ye assert, have been condemned or accursed by Him and carry them off like some slave dealer? Why does He teach them to run away like slaves from their lord, and to flee from their father? Why does He claim them for Himself against the father's will? Why does He profess to be the father of those who are not His own?... Holy and reverend indeed is the God who desires to be father of those who are already condemned by another as sinners and of men without inheritance, and, as they themselves say, of the very dregs, and who has not the power to capture and punish even his messenger who escaped him... If these are his works, how is it God created evil? How is it that He has no power to persuade and admonish men? Is it that He repents over their ingratitude and wickedness, and His own handiwork, and loathes and threatens and destroys His own offspring? Whither can He carry them away out of their universe which He made Himself?... According to them, God is the creator of evil.[2] The most foolish thing of all is the assigning of definite days to the creation of the world before days existed, for when the heaven was not yet created nor the earth laid on firm foundations, nor the sun yet revolving in its orbit, how could there be days? Further taking these points from the beginning, let us consider them.

---

[1] VI. 52.
[2] VI. 53.

Would it not be ridiculous that the first and the mightiest God should give this order? – Let this thing be created, and then again another thing, and yet a third, and, accomplishing so much on the one day, and on the second day again so much more, and on the third and the fourth and the fifth and the sixth.[1] And actually after this, like a very bad workman, He is weary and needs leisure to refresh Himself... It is not right or fitting that the first God should be wearied or work with His hands or give orders.[2] He has no mouth nor voice... God possesses nothing of which we know.[3] And He did not make man His image, for God has not man's nature nor is He like to any other form.[4] God does not partake of form or colour or motion... or even of actual substance.[5] Of Him are all things... He is not to be touched by word... He cannot be expressed by name... for He has undergone no suffering which can be described by words.... He is outside all suffering.[6]

[Celsus introduces someone saying] "How then am I to know God? – and how am I to learn the way to Him? – and how do you show Him to me? For now you cast darkness only before my eyes and I see nothing clearly"... Those who should be led out of darkness to the bright light cannot stand against its brilliance, so that their power of vision is injured and harmed and they think they are blinded.[7] [Celsus gives as Christian answer:] "Since God is great and difficult to

---

[1] VI. 60.
[2] VI. 61.
[3] VI. 62.
[4] VI. 63.
[5] VI. 64.
[6] VI. 65.
[7] VI. 66.

behold, He put His own spirit into a body like ours and sent it down here that we might be able to hear and learn from Him."[1] In saying that God is spirit, they differ not at all from the Stoic philosophers among the Greeks who assert that God is spirit-diffused through all things and containing all things in Himself.[2] Since the Son of God who existed in a human body is spirit, this very son of God cannot be himself Immortal... There is no spirit of such a nature that it can last for ever... It is necessary that God must have breathed forth His Spirit, and it follows from this that Jesus could not have risen again with his body, for God would not have received back the spirit which He had given after it had been defiled by the nature of body.[3] But if God did wish to send down His Spirit, why did He need to breathe it into the womb of a woman? For since He knew already how to fashion men, He could have moulded a body even for this man too, and need not have cast His own Spirit into such defilement, and in that case he would not have met with as much disbelief if he had derived his origin straight from above.[4] [Celsus speaks:] Of Marcion... How shall he who was punished in such a manner be proved to be Son of God unless it was foretold of him?... There are two sons of gods, one of the Demiurge and the other the son of Marcion's god... and single combats... battles of gods which the fathers relate are like battles between quails, or the fathers being themselves incapacitated by old age and doddering interfere with one another but allow their sons to fight it out.[5] Since the spirit of God was in

[1] VI. 69.
[2] VI. 71.
[3] VI. 72.
[4] VI. 73.
[5] VI. 74.

a body, the body must certainly have been entirely different from others, either in grandeur or beauty or strength or voice or impressive appearance or persuasive grace, for it is impossible that he to whom more of God was given than to others should not differ from others, whereas this person differed in no way from another, but was, as they say, small and ill-favoured and of mean appearance.[1] Well now, even if God really did wish, like Zeus in the comedy, on awaking from long slumber, to rescue the race of men from evil, why on earth did He send this spirit of whom you speak to one corner only? He ought to have breathed His Spirit in the same way into many bodies and sent them out over all the earth. Now the comic poet, who was writing to give amusement in the theatre, represented how Zeus woke up and sent Hermes to the Athenians and Lacedaemonians. But do you not really think that you have made the Son of God an object of ridicule in having him sent to the Jews?[2] From the beginning the nation most inspired of God was the Chaldaeans... and the Magi also... the Egyptian people too... the Persians are an inspired race... and the Indians... but the Jews are about to meet utter destruction.[3] God, although He is all-knowing, did not know that He was sending His son to wicked men who would be sinful and inflict punishment on him... but they say that all these things were prophesied long ago.[4] Let as see how they will find a defence; for those who introduce a second god have none, while those who recognise the same god always say the same thing, and a clever thing too: “It had to came to pass in this way and this

---

[1] VI. 75.
[2] VI. 78.
[3] VI. 80.
[4] VI. 81.

is the reason – it was predicted long ago".[1] They set no value on the predictions of the Pythian priestess or of the priests of Dodona or Clarus or Branchidae or Ammon and thousands of other seers, by whose advice the whole earth has been duly colonised. But these sayings which were uttered, or even not uttered, in Judaea after the manner of the Jews as even to this day the dwellers in Phoenicia and Palestine are wont to prophesy, these they consider marvellous and unchangeable.[2] There are many kinds of prophecy… There are many even nameless people who assume this so-called inspired action without any difficulty on the slightest cause within or without temples gathering crowds and going again and again to cities or camps. Each is wont to cry glibly: "I am God, I am the Son of God, I am the Spirit of God. I am come, for already the universe is perishing and you, O mortal man, through your unrighteousness are as the dead. But I wish to save you, and you shall see me again coming with the power of heaven. Blessed is he who now gives me homage. On all the rest I will send down everlasting fire, both cities and lands, and men who know not their punishment shall repent in vain and weep bitterly; but those who believe me I will keep safe for evermore"… To these threats and promises they add next strange, mad and entirely unintelligible words, of which no intelligent person could find the meaning: for they are obscure and of no value, but to every fool or impostor they give an opportunity of supporting his statements on any subject he wishes.[3] Why, those prophets to whom I have listened with my own ears, when challenged, actually confessed what was their true aim

[1] VII. 2.
[2] VII. 3.
[3] VII. 9.

and acknowledged they were making up ambiguous words.[1] Those who defend the case of Christ from the prophets, can give no pertinent answer about the statements in them which appear to attribute evil or shame or impurity to God.[2] God acts in a most disgraceful way and is most disgracefully treated... God is a servant of evil... For that God should eat the flesh of sheep and drink vinegar or gall was nothing else but sheer feeding on filth.[3] Tell me now, if the prophets foretell that the great God (I will not put it more baldly) should be a slave or be ill or die, will it therefore be necessary that God should die or be enslaved or ill, because it has been foretold? Must He die to prove that He is God? But the prophets would never have uttered such predictions; they are wicked and irreverent. Therefore the question is not whether a thing has or has not been predicted, but whether or not the action is worthy of God and honourable. We must not believe in the evil and base, even if all men in a fit of madness seem to foretell it. How then can the story of this man's life be reverent or right as applied to God?[4] If these prophecies were uttered about the God who is over all, are we then bound to believe such statements about God just because they occur in prophecy?[5] Will they not take this further point into consideration? If the prophets of the God of the Jews foretold that this man would he His son, how could He through Moses give them laws bidding them grow rich and powerful and fill the earth and slaughter their enemies root and branch and put whole nations to the sword

[1] VII. 11.
[2] VII. 12.
[3] VII. 13.
[4] VII. 14.
[5] VII. 15.

– which He actually did in the eyes of the Jews, as Moses says, and further threatens them that if they do not obey His commands He will definitely treat them as enemies; while, on the other hand, His son, the Man of Nazareth gave laws entirely opposite, saying that no one can come to the father, who is rich or loves power or seeks after wisdom or glory, that men should take no more anxious thought for food and stores than the ravens and for clothing less than the lilies, and that to him who has struck them once they should offer themselves to receive a second blow? Did the father, who sent this Jesus forget the commands He gave to Moses? Or did he condemn His own laws and change His mind and send the messenger to bring about a different purpose?[1] They say that God is corporeal in His nature and has a body like a man.[2] Where do they expect to go? What hope have they?... To another land better than this?... Inspired men of long ago have told stories of a blessed and happy life for the blessed. Some called it the islands of the blest, others the Elysian plain from the loosing of earthly evils, as Homer says:– "But the immortals will send thee to the Elysian plain, where is a life of perfect rest."[3] Plato, who believed in the immortality of the soul, distinctly called the place whither it is sent a land, in these words: "It extends far and we dwell in a small part only from Phasis to the pillars of Heracles along the seashore, like ants or frogs around a marsh and many other men dwell in other similar places elsewhere. For everywhere all over the earth are hollows of different kinds, varying in shape and size into which have flowed water and mist and air, but the land which is really pure lies in the purity of

[1] VII. 18.
[2] VII. 27.
[3] Od. IV 563-5.

heaven."[1] It is not easy for everyone to understand what Plato means by these words, unless he can understand the saying "Because of our weakness and slowness we are not able to reach the heights of the air" and "If our nature were capable of bearing the contemplation, we should understand that there is the true heaven and the true light".[2] They teach the doctrine of the resurrection through a misunderstanding of metempsychosis.[3] And even when they are entirely worsted and refuted they return again, as though they had not listened at all to the same question, "How are we to know and see God? And how are we to go to Him?"[4] They expect to see God with their bodily eyes and hear His voice with their ears and to touch Him with their visible hands.[5] Those who are seeking God should go to the oracles of Traphonius and Amphiaraus and Mopsus, where gods are seen in human form... not lying phantoms but real visions... Anyone can see them not just once after which they slip away like this deceiver, but always communing with those who desire it.[6] They will ask again, "How can we know God, if we do not comprehend Him by our senses? How is it possible to learn apart from sense-perception"... The voice is not the language of a man or of the soul, but of the flesh. Still, let them hear if men so miserable and so devoted to the body can do so; if, silencing the senses you look upward with the mind and turning away from the flesh, awake the eyes of the soul, in this way only you will see God. If you seek a guide in this,

---

[1] LVIII. p.109 A.B. VII. 28.
[2] Phaedo LVIII. P.109 D.E. VII. 31.
[3] VII. 32.
[4] VII. 33.
[5] VII. 34.
[6] VII. 35.

shun all deceivers and sorcerers and those who seek after phantoms, that you may not excite the worst possible ridicule, by blaspheming the other recognised gods as idols, while you worship one who is even more wretched than real idols and not even an idol at that, but a dead man and you seek a father like to Him.[1] Such then is the delusion and so great and wonderful are the counsellors and so inspired the words, which you address to the lion and the amphibious creature and the being like an ass and others and those divine doorkeepers, whose names you learn off with such trouble, ye wretched creatures, going crazy and suffering death at the stake.[2] They should follow... so as not to lack guides of antiquity and holiness... inspired poets and wise philosophers… from whom they can hear much wisdom of God.[3] A more effective teacher... is Plato... in the Timaeus... "The maker and Father of this universe it is hard to find and even having found Him it is impossible to speak of Him to all."[4]... You see how the way of truth is sought by men inspired of God and how Plato knew that it was impossible for all men to walk therein. But since wise men have discovered it for this purpose that we should gain some idea of Him, who is inexpressible and first, an idea showing Him to us either by synthesis of other things or by analysis of them or by analogy; if I wished to explain what is absolutely incapable of being expressed in words, I should be surprised if you were able to follow, being entirely bound up in the flesh and beholding nought that is pure.[5] Real existence can

[1] VII. 36.
[2] VII. 40.
[3] VII. 41.
[4] Tim. V. p.28 C.
[5] VII. 42.

be known; becoming can be seen; with existence is truth, with the other error; with truth then is knowledge concerned; with error opinion, the intelligible is the object of understanding, the visible of sight. Mind perceives the intelligible, the eye the visible. As then among visible objects the sun is not the eye nor sight but for the eye the cause of seeing, for vision the cause of existing by its means, for things visible the cause of being seen, for all sensible objects the cause of existence and finally the actual reason of its own visible appearance, so among things intelligible that which is neither mind not intelligence nor knowledge, but to the mind the cause of thinking, to the intelligence the cause of existence and to knowledge the cause of knowing and to all intelligible things, to truth itself, to existence itself the cause of being, and being above them all it is by some inexpressible power intelligible. This is said for men who possess understanding. But if ever you understand anything of it, it is well for you. And if you think that a spirit coming down from God announces the things of God, it must be the spirit who proclaims these truths, with whom men of old were verily filled when they gave many messages of good; but if you cannot understand, be silent and conceal your own ignorance and do not say the clear-sighted are blind or those, who run, are lame, when you yourselves are utterly lamed and mutilated in your souls, and living only in the body, which is dead.[1] How much better it would have been for you, since you are so very anxious for novelty, to spend your zeal on one of the noble dead, who could be the subject of a god-like myth? Why, even if Heracles and Asclepius and those who received honour of old time did not please you, you had

[1] VII. 45.

Orpheus, whom all acknowledged to be possessed of the divine spirit and who died a violent death too. But perhaps others had taken him before you. At any rate there is Anaxarchus, who being cast into a mortar and terribly beaten showed a fine contempt for his punishment and said, "Beat, beat the shell of Anaxarchus, himself you do not beat," – words of a spirit which surely came from God. But even here some have been before you and followed him – physicists. Well, try Epictetus; when his master was twisting his leg, he said smiling without any agitation: "You will break it", and when he had broken it, "Did I not tell you you would break it?" Did your God say anything to equal this while he was being tortured? But you would have been more reasonable, if you had put forward the Sibyl, in whom some of you believe, as the child of God. But as it is you have dared to make many impious additions to her writings and set up as God one whose life was infamous and his death most pitiable. Would not Jonah under the gourd or Daniel saved from the wild beasts have been more suitable for you, or others even more full of marvels than these?[1] They have a command to this effect, that they should not defend themselves against the aggressor: "If you are struck", he says, "on the one cheek, turn the other also."[2] This is very old and has been excellently expressed before, but they have reported it in less polished language. For Plato has portrayed Socrates conversing with Crito as follows – "So then we must never wrong anyone?" Certainly not". "And must we not then retaliate, according to conventional ideas, when wronged, since we must never do any wrong at all?" "I think

[1] VII. 53.
[2] [Matthew 5.39 – GPB]

not". "But tell me why?" "Ought we to do evil, Crito, or not?" "Certainly not, I imagine, Socrates". "Well then, is it right or not right to retaliate when wronged, according to the conventional standards?" "It is wrong." "Yes, for I suppose there is no difference between doing evil to a man and wronging him." "That is true." "So then we ought never to retaliate with wrong or do evil to any man, whatever evil we may suffer from him." So Plato speaks and adds: "Consider then please very carefully whether you agree with me and share my opinion and whether we can start from this consideration that it is never right to do evil or to return evil or even if you have been harmed to return the bad treatment in self-defence: or do you disagree and not share the first principle? It has been my opinion for a long time now and is still."[1] Such was Plato's view and the opinion was held even before by men of God. But let this suffice as an example of the way in which they borrow and pervert this and other truths. Anyone who likes to look for more of them will find them.[2]

Let us pass from that. They cannot endure seeing temples and altars and statues, but then neither can the Scythians nor the Nomadic Libyans nor the Seres who worship no god nor any other of the most impious and lawless tribes, and that the Persians hold this opinion Herodotus tells us in the following words: "I know that the Persians have the following laws. They do not consider it lawful to set up statues and altars and temples, and they accuse of folly these who do so because in my opinion they believe that the gods have not men's nature as the Greeks do."[3] Heraclitus too declares: "People who

[1] Crito X. 49 B.E.

[2] VII. 58.

[3] Herod. I. 131.

pray to these images are like people who converse with the walls of houses, not knowing who the gods or heroes are." And at any rate what have they to teach us wiser than Heraclitus? He certainly implies quite plainly that it is foolish to pray to statues unless a man knows who the gods and heroes are. That is the opinion of Heraclitus; but they give no honour at all to any statues. If it is for the reason that stone or wood or bronze or gold which someone or other wrought into a statue cannot be God, then their wisdom is ridiculous, for who in the world unless he is an absolute fool considers that these things are gods and not just offerings to gods and their images? But let us grant (as the Persians think) that we must not take these for the images of God because God's form is different, then without knowing it they have convicted themselves in their words: "God made man His own image and gave him a form like Himself." They will admit, however, that these images are made for the honour of someone, whether unlike or like them in form, but they will say that the beings to whom they are dedicated are not gods but daemons, and that a man who honours God ought not to serve daemons.[1] First I will ask why we ought not to serve daemons. Surely all things are ordered according to the will of God and all providence is from Him, and everything which happens in the universe, whether it be the work of God or angels or other daemons or heroes – does it not all obey the law of the most high God? And is not one who has been deemed worthy set over each with power assigned to him? Therefore will not the man who worships God be right in serving those who have received their authority from Him? No, he says, for it is not possible for the

[1] VII. 62. [cf. 1 Corinthians 10.20-21 – GPB]

same man to serve many lords.[1] This is the language of sedition, of those who wall themselves off and tear themselves away from other men... Those who say this ascribe as far as they can their own personal feelings to God, and amongst men it holds true that he who is in the service of one master cannot well serve another, because the service which he renders to the one interferes with that which he owes to the other, and no one who has already engaged himself to the service of one must join the service of another because it is harmful. And it is a reasonable statement that it is not possible to serve at the same time different heroes or daemons; but with regard to God upon whom no loss at all or any suffering can came unaware, it is absurd to be on our guard against serving too many gods as though we were dealing with men and heroes and other spirits of that kind. He who serves many Gods, by honouring one of the things which belong to the Most High; pleases him in this very act... It is not right to give honour to any to whom God has not given honour, therefore he who honours and worships all the beings who belong to God is not grieving God to Whom all belong.[2] And indeed the very man who says that one is called Lord when he is speaking of God is guilty of impiety in dividing the Kingdom of God and raising a sedition, implying that there is faction and one who leads opposition against God.[3] If this people really served one God alone and no other they would perhaps have had a strong argument against the others; but as it is they give excessive worship to that man who has appeared but lately, and yet think they are committing no sin towards God if they worship His Servant

[1] VII. 68.
[2] VIII. 2.
[3] VIII. 11.

also.[1] If you were to teach them that Jesus is not the Son of God though God Himself is the Father of all, and that Him alone they should truly worship, they would not be willing to do so if they did not also worship Jesus who is the leader of their sedition; and they actually call him Son of God, not because they have great reverence for God, but because they wish to give Jesus great honour.[2] That I may not hazard a casual opinion I will use their own words, for I believe it is in "the heavenly dialogue" somewhere that they speak as follows: "If the son is stronger than God and the son of man is His lord (and who else could rule over God Who is over all?), how is it that while so many go round about the well no one goes down into it?[3] Why are you afraid when you have gone so far on the way? [Answer,] you are mistaken, for I have both courage and sword." Is not this just the opinion attributed to him, to honour the God above the heavens, (but the god whom they suppose is father of this man on whose account they have formed their society,) in order that under the form of the great God they may worship this Jesus alone, whom they put forward as the son of man, whom they assert to be stronger than God and lord of the God who is lord of the universe. And therefore they have that command not to serve two lords that they may be on their guard against rebellion from this one.[4] They shrink from raising altars and

---

[1] VIII. 12.

[2] VIII. 14.

[3] ["The heavenly dialogue": Celsus is quoting from a text from the Ophite Gnostic sect. cf. The Gospel of Thomas, logion 74: "(A man said to Jesus) Lord, there are many round the cistern, but nobody in the cistern." Meaning: many people approach wisdom, but few dare to embrace it. – GPB]

[4] VIII. 15.

statues and temples... the pledge of a secret and forbidden society.[1] Yet God is to be shared in by all alike. He is God; He stands in need of nothing; He is raised above jealousy. What then hinders those who are most devoted to Him from taking part in public feasts?[2] If these idols are nothing, what is there so terribly wrong in taking part in a high festival? If on the other hand they are daemons, it is certain that they too belong to God and that we must believe in them and sacrifice to them according to the laws and pray to them that they may be gracious.[3] If it is actually in accordance with ancestral tradition that they refrain from the flesh of sacrificial victims of this kind, they ought entirely to abstain from all animal food as Pythagoras thought who thus honoured the soul and all its organs. But if, as they say, they abstain that they may not feast along with daemons, I congratulate them on their wisdom in having discovered at last that they are always eating with daemons, and then you see they only avoid doing so when they are looking upon a sacrificial victim, but whenever they eat food and drink wine and taste fruit and drink actual water and breathe in air, do they not then receive each of these things, from some daemons to whom have been assigned the care of these different provinces?[4] Therefore we must either not live at all or not come into this life, or if we have come into this life we must do so on these conditions – that we give thanks to the daemons who have been set over the affairs of the world and offer them first fruits and prayers as long as we live that we may find them

[1] VIII. 17.
[2] VIII. 21.
[3] VIII. 24.
[4] VIII. 28.

kindly to men.[1] The satrap of a Persian or a Roman monarch and a governor or general or ruler, yes, and even those who hold lesser offices or positions of trust or service could do great harm if they were neglected. Will then the satraps and ministers of the air and the earth do little harm if they are insulted?[2] If anyone call them by name in a barbarous tongue they will have power, but not if he speak in Greek or Latin.[3] [Celsus represents Christians saying:] "Behold, I stand outside a statue of Zeus or Apollo or any other god you like: I blaspheme it, I beat it and it takes no vengeance on me."[4] But do you not see, my friend, that anyone can stand beside your daemon, and not only blaspheme him but banish him from all the earth and the sea, and bind you yourself who are dedicated like an image to him and lead you away and fasten you to a stake, and the daemon, or as you call him Son of God, takes no vengeance on the man who harms you.[5] The priest of Apollo or Zeus... says: "The mills of God grind slowly" and... "to their children's children who may live after them."[6] You revile the statues of these gods with impurity[7], but if you had reviled Dionysius himself or Heracles in person you would not perhaps have got off so easily, while those who tortured and crucified your god have not been punished at all for their action either at the time or throughout their lives. What new thing has happened since then to make anyone believe that he was not a human

[1] VIII. 33.
[2] VIII. 35.
[3] VIII. 37.
[4] VIII. 38.
[5] VIII. 39.
[6] VIII. 40.
[7] [*sic.* Should be "impunity" – GPB]

impostor but the son of God? And did he who sent His son to bring a certain message actually allow him to be thus savagely treated so that his message perished with him and, although so long a time has gone by, has paid no attention to him at all? What father was ever so unnatural? Perhaps, as you say, he endured insults because he wished to suffer whatever happened, but of those whom you revile it is possible also to say that they too had this wish, and that therefore they endured reviling. For it is best to treat both sides impartially, but these gods at any rate punish the blasphemer severely so that he either flees on that account and hides himself, or is caught and killed.[1] What need is there to make a list of all the oracular sayings uttered with the voice of God not only by prophets and prophetesses, but by others who were inspired, both men and women, all the wonders which have been heard from the shrines themselves? – all the revelations given by sacrifices and victims to those who use them, and from other miraculous signs? To some, visible forms have appeared. The whole of life is full of them. How many cities have been raised by the advice of oracles and have driven away disease and famine? How many colonies have neglected them and perished miserably? How many colonies have been sent out and by obeying their commands have flourished? How many people, eminent or obscure, have by this lost good or evil? How many who bewailed their childlessness have obtained their desires? How many have escaped the wrath of daemons? How many have had crippled bodies healed? How many again, who have violated temples, have been instantly punished – some being overcome by madness on the spot,

[1] VIII. 41.

others confessing openly their crime, others having put an end to themselves, others being the slaves of incurable disease? Some even have been destroyed by a terrible voice from the inmost shrine.[1] Exactly as you, my friend, believe in eternal punishments, so also do those who interpret the sacred rites of other religions, and initiate and lead men into their mysteries. The threats of punishment which you hold over others, they hurl at you. Which of them has the greater truth and power, we can inquire; for in argument both sides assert firmly the truth of their own contention; but, if we demand proofs, the priests of other religions produce many which are convincing, wonders performed by certain daemonic powers and oracles, collected from all kinds of divination.[2] Surely it is very inconsistent of you to set so much affection and hope on the body, that you expect it to rise again, as if we possessed nothing more valuable or precious, while at the same time you expose it to tortures as though it were without value. But with men who hold this view and are so wedded to the body, it is not worth while to discuss, for they are in this and other respects rough, impure and victims of the disease of revolt without any reason. But I will converse with those who hope to possess eternally with God their soul or mind, whether they choose to call it spiritual, or intelligent spirit, holy and blessed, or living soul, or the heavenly immortal offspring of a divine, incorporeal nature, or whatever name they prefer to give. And in this at least their ideas are right – that those who have lived good lives shall attain the happiness of the blest, while the wicked shall be entirely captured by eternal punishments. And from

[1] VIII. 45.
[2] VIII. 48.

this belief neither they nor any other men should ever be led away.[1] Since men are born fettered to a body, whether for the sake of the order of the universe or as a punishment for sin, or because the soul is weighed down by certain sufferings until it be cleansed by the appointed periods of time – for we must, according to Empedocles, be wanderers from the abodes of the blest for 300,000 seasons – the soul taking during this time every possible mortal shape: so we must believe that they are entrusted to certain keepers of this prison-house.[2] There is a choice of two alternatives. If they refuse to give due worship to the gods and respect to those who are set over it, they must not grow up or marry wives or have children or take any share at all in the affairs of life, but must depart with all speed, leaving no posterity behind, that such a race may become extinct from the face of the earth. But if they take wives and have children and taste the fruits of the earth and share the joys of life and endure its appointed sorrows, (for it is the essence of nature that all men should taste sorrow; for sorrows must exist and there is no other place for them), then they must pay due honour to those who are set over these provinces of life and discharge the proper duties of life, until they are released from its chains, that they may not seem thankless towards those beings. For it is wrong to take a share of what they offer and make no contribution in return.[3] Anyone can learn from what the Egyptians say that even the very smallest thing is entrusted to the power of some daemon. The body of a man is divided into thirty-six parts and daemons or spirits of the air are appointed to its care, each having charge over a

[1] VIII. 49.
[2] VIII. 53.
[3] VIII. 55.

different part – though some make the number much larger. And they know the names of the daemons in the language of the country, for instance – Chnonmen, Chnachnoumen, Cnat, Sicat, Bion, Erou, Erebiou, Ramanor, Reianoor and other Egyptian names. Moreover, they call upon them and are healed of diseases in different parts of the body. What I ask prevents a man from honouring them and others, if he wishes to be well rather than ill, and prosperous rather than unsuccessful and as far as possible to escape tortures and punishments?[1] Care must be taken, however, lest anyone by association with these matters should became engrossed with the care of them, and through love of the body should turn his mind away from higher things and be sunk in forgetfulness. For perhaps we ought not to disbelieve wise men who certainly say that most of the earth daemons are busied with "becoming" and wallow in blood and odours and sweet songs, and being bound by other such things they are unable to do anything more than heal the body and foretell to men and cities the fortune which is coming upon them, and other such practices as concern the life of mortals – these they know and are able to perform.[2] It is a better opinion that daemons need nothing nor do they desire anything, but rejoice in those who act piously towards them... We must never in any way lose our hold on God, neither by day nor by night, in public or in private, in any word or deed, but – apart from these actions or with them let the soul ever be fixed upon God... but if this is so, how is it wrong to gain the goodwill of the rulers on earth, whether they be human princes and things or other beings? For it is through the

---

[1] VIII. 58.
[2] VIII. 60.

strength of daemons that human men gain their power here.[1] If, however, a man who honours God should be ordered either to be irreverent or say any wicked word, he must in no wise obey, but rather endure all kinds of torture and suffer all manner of death rather than say or even think anything unworthy about God... But if anyone command you to sing praises to the sun or to glorify Athena devotedly with a beautiful hymn, you will if you sing praise to them seem to give still greater honour to the great God, for the worship of God becomes more perfect if it extends through all things.[2] If anyone command you to swear by a human king there is nothing wrong in it, for to him have been given the things upon earth, and whatever you receive in this life you receive from Him.[3] We must not disobey the ancient writer who said long ago; "Let one be king to whom it was given by the son of Cronos crooked in counsel."[4]... If you disregard this maxim the king will naturally punish you, for if everyone were to act like you there would be nothing to prevent his being left alone deserted and the affairs of the earth would fall into the hands of the most savage and lawless barbarians, and there would no longer remain among men the glory of your worship and true wisdom.[5] Surely you will not say that if the Romans were persuaded by you to neglect their customary duties to gods and men, and call upon your most high or whatever you like to call Him, that He would fight for them and that there would be no need of any other force? For even before this same God promised this and much more

[1] VIII. 63.
[2] VIII. 66.
[3] VIII. 67.
[4] Hom. Il. II. 205.
[5] VIII. 68.

than this to those who follow Him, as you yourself say, but in spite of His promises you see how He has helped them and you; for they, instead of being masters of the whole world have not a single clod of earth or a hearthstone left to them, and as for you, if one of you transgresses even in secret he is sought out to be punished by death.[1] Surely it is intolerable for you to say that if our present rulers are won over by you and defeated by the enemy, you will still be able to persuade those who rule after them, and if they too are captured you will persuade their successors, and so on until, when all who have yielded to your persuasion have been taken, some single wise ruler will arise, and foreseeing what is going to happen, will destroy you all root and branch before destruction comes from you.[2] If it were possible that all the inhabitants of Asia and Europe and Libya, Greeks and barbarians of the uttermost ends of the earth should join together in harmony of mind under one law... anyone who thinks this possible knows nothing.[3] Help the king with all your strength, and labour with him for justice, and fight on his behalf, and join in the expeditions if he need you, and help him to lead his armies.[4] Take part in the government of your country if it is necessary to do so to preserve the laws and fulfil the demands of religion.[5] [I will write:] another treatise after this to teach those who wish it how to live, if they are open to persuasion.[6]

---

[1] VIII. 69.
[2] VIII. 71.
[3] VIII. 72.
[4] VIII. 73.
[5] VIII. 75.
[6] VIII. 76.

CHAPTER IV
ORIGEN AND THE REPLY TO CELSUS

The reply of Origen to the True Word extends to eight long books, which almost defy synopsis or generalization. It is impossible to sum up either one book or the whole treatise in a short space, indicating the main lines of argument and literary construction. In fact, we have not in this apologetic of Origen any attempt at literary art or any desire to produce a complete whole, save in so far as fullness of argument and defence against the attack on Christianity are concerned. We have here a book written with a definite purpose, which entirely subordinates all other conditions of literary effort to itself. It is clearly and in every line of it the work of a teacher, of a University lecturer, and of a lecturer too, whose aim is not to lecture but to teach. Every book is given unity by the personality of its writer and the strength of Origen's character is seen in none of his writings more clearly than in the answer to Celsus, but it is the power and insight of Origen, the teacher, his familiarity with the minds of students and the fundamentals of education which alone can give unity to the loose construction of this Apology, illuminating its style its methods and its plan. At the beginning of the fifth book he states the purpose of the whole refutation and shows how he is trying to effect it:

> If I could only enter with my words into the conscience of everyone, who comes across the treatise of Celsus, and pull out every shaft that is wounding him, who is not completely fenced about with the panoply of God, and if I could lay on the ointment of reason to cure the wound made by Celsus, a wound which saps the

> healthy faith of those who give heed to his words – I would certainly have done so. But this is God's work – to visit unseen according to His own Spirit with the spirit of Christ those, with whom He judges it right to dwell; but for me, who am trying by means of arguments and treatises to establish men's faith, the task is set to do everything in my power to win the reputation of "a workman, who need feel no shame, who is an honest teacher of the word of truth"... May God grant to my mind and reason not to approach my task, bare and empty of God's spirit, so that the faith of those for whose help I pray, may not "be in the wisdom of men", but that I may win the mind of Christ from Him who alone can give it, even His Father and that I may be strengthened by my share in the wisdom of God to pull down "all loftiness, which exalts itself against the knowledge of God", and destroy also the intention of Celsus, who lifts himself up against us and against our Jesus, and against Moses too and the prophets: so that when He who gives "a word to those who preach the Gospel with mighty power" supplies it to me also and gives me this mighty power, faith may live in those, who shall pick up my book, in the word and power of God.[1]

Throughout the book we realise that Origen as he writes, is thinking of those who will read his words and therefore his argument is not academic but always turned to meet the difficulties of human minds, "weak in the faith".[2] It is no pen and ink victory against a dead opponent for which Origen

---

[1] V. 1.

[2] Introd. 6.

strives. He is facing not Celsus but the buzzing life of Alexandria, as he knew it and Ambrosius knew it – especially on its student side. Indeed, Celsus seems to come into the book always as the third person. Origen never even uses the literary form of addressing him, but always refers to him as an example on which he is commenting to a class. Once or twice he likens Celsus to "a lad at school accusing someone with the help of a string of commonplaces,"[1] or refers to "some headlong fellow, who after attending a philosopher's lectures for three days, looks down on other people."[2] He was evidently familiar with all kinds of pupils. He tells Ambrosius, as we have seen, that he is sorry that he cannot deal personally with the difficulties and uncertainty of each individual, who has been perplexed by the arguments of Celsus: as this is impossible, he is compelled to send out his book in faith that it will meet individual demands, though doubtless, as he composed it, he must have often had in mind the students who were under his instruction for so many years in Alexandria. The teacher's characteristics show themselves in small but definite ways. Now and then in the midst of argument comes a word of direct admonition or practical exhortation. Celsus says, "even if a thing seem to you evil, it is not yet certain that it is evil: for you do not know what is advantageous to yourself or another or the whole universe." Origen replies that on this basis evil would not be wholly evil, and even if God, who preserves free will in man, can deal with evil in the administration of the world, let "no-one make this an opportunity... to commit sin", on the ground that by it he will be of use to the whole.[3] There

---

[1] V. 58.

[2] IV. 29.

[3] IV. 70. cf. I. 52 (ad.fin.) II. 11 (ad.fin.), VI. 7 (ad.fin.) VII. 51 (ad.fin).

are numberless apparent digressions in the argument, yet they are hardly digressions. Origen, like all teachers of deep and abundant learning, will often establish a point with several (even alternative) proofs, will pile up evidence and information and elaborate details, always going beyond the immediate refutation of Celsus, if it seems necessary, in order to elucidate other important questions, which are involved. Sometimes he anticipates difficulties, sometimes he only continues his explanation, but it is the mark of a man, who has been wont to fit his discourses to the minds of his hearers rather than to make set speeches to them. Both ways are open to the lecturer but only one to the teacher. He goes, for instance, into a detailed explanation of the nature of names,[1] refers often to his conversations with learned Jews and gives his own theory of the apportioning of the earth among men[2] and his ideas on spiritual temples.[3] Sometimes he stops himself,[4] when he is about to digress, sometimes he apologises for the digression, but always his attitude is that of a man, who will spare no pains to throw light on the subject in hand. "Since we are on the question of Peter, and the teaching of Christianity to the circumcised..."[5] is the preface to one digression, and the others are all made in a similar way.[6] Perhaps even the line-by-line and word-by-word method of refutation, which Origen chose to use against Celsus, is in part due to his teaching instinct. He wishes to leave nothing unanswered and to answer every

[1] I. 24-5.
[2] V. 29-32.
[3] VIII. 19-20.
[4] e.g. IV. 60.
[5] II. 2.
[6] cf. I. 26-7, 35-6, 45-8, 55. III. 38. IV. 32, 92-5.

point. He explains it in the preface as being partly due to lack of time. "Let my preface apologize for beginning my answer to Celsus on one plan and continuing it on another. For at first I intended to indicate the heads of the argument and then, shortly, the answers; after that to make a systematic treatise. But afterwards the stress of circumstance suggested to me, being pressed for time, that... I should in the rest of the book struggle with the charges of Celsus as I went along."[1] Even if literary coherence was lost by this method, the power of the apologetic was not weakened for those, who found every single objection of Celsus considered. Even on later readers, who are not always interested in the points immediately at issue, the constant reiteration of vital facts produces a strong effect. It is a tribute to the value of the subject-matter that the book has triumphantly survived the cumbrous and somewhat confusing form in which it is written.

The actual style of Origen in this treatise is varied and in certain characteristics reflects himself and his profession. The main impression which his language leaves, is on the whole unsatisfactory. There is no pungency or grace about his Greek; his sentences are often long and badly balanced, the whole effect is unwieldy and a trifle confused. Here again can he traced the mark of the teacher, the elaboration of thought at the expense of style, and the sacrifice of lucidity of expression to fullness of statement and argument. There is absolutely no attempt at literary effect. On the other hand, though Origen's written style lost distinction from his profession, it gained a stamp of brilliance from his unique personality. There are passages, which break the level of the

[1] Introd. 6.

rest of the exposition, and show a literary beauty and ordered style, combined with strength. In them the feud between philosophy and poetry is momentarily at least subdued, and depth of feeling has lifted even the words of argument to a high level of literary achievement. It is enough to take one example:[1]

"καινὸν οὖν γέγονεν, ἐξ οὗ πέπονθε χρόνου ὁ Ἰησους, κἀκεῖνο, λέγω δὲ το κατὰ τὴν πόλιν καὶ πᾶν τὸ κατὰ τὸ ἔθνος καὶ τὸ κατὰ τὴν ἀθρόαν γένεσον ἔθνοος Χριστιανῶν ὡσπερεὶ τεχθέντος εἰσάπαξ καινὸν δὲ καὶ τὸ τοὺς ξένους "τῶν διαθηκῶν" τοῦ θεοῦ καὶ ἀλλοτρίους τῶν ἐπαγγελιῶν τοὺς μακρὰν τῆς ἀληθείας δυνάμει τινὶ θείᾳ παραδέχεσθαι αὐτήν. ταῦτα δε οὐκ ἀνθρώπου γόητος ἦν ἀλλ' ἔργα θεοῦ, πέμψαντος τῶν αὐτοῦ ἀγγελματων ἕνεκα τὸν αὐτοῦ ἐν τῷ Ἰησοῦ λόγον ὠμῶς κολασθέντι, ὡς τὴν ὠμοτήτα κατηγορεῖσθαι τῶν ἀδικως αὐτὸν κολασάντων, καὶ ἀνδρειότατα ὑπο μείναντα καὶ μετὰ πάσης πραότητος· οὐ διέφθειρε δὲ ἡ κόλασις αὐτοῦ τὰ τοῦ θεοῦ ἀγγέλματα ἀλλ', εἰ δει οὑτῶς ὀνομάσαι, εἰς γνῶσιν αὐτὰ ἤγαγεν ὡς καὶ αὐτὸς ἐδίδαξεν ὁ Ἰησοῦς λέγων· "ἐὰν μὴ ὁ κόκκος τοῦ σίτου πεσὼν εἰς τὴν γῆν ἀποθάνῃ, αὐτὸς μόνος μένει· ἐὰν δὲ ἀποθάνῃ, πολὸν καρπὸν φέρει." ἀποθανῶν οὖν "ὁ κόκκος τοῦ σίτου" Ἰησοῦς "πολὺν καρπὸν" ἤνεγκε, καὶ ἀεὶ ὁ πατὴρ προνοεῖ τῶν ἐκ τοῦ θανάτου τοῦ κόκκου "τοῦ σίτου" γεγεννημένων καὶ γινομένων ἔτι καὶ ἐσομένων καρπῶν. ὅσιος οὖν πατὴρ ὁ τοῦ Ἰησοῦ πατὴρ, "τοῦ ἰδίου μὴ φεισάμενος υἱοῦ ἀλλ' ὑπὲρ ἡμῶν πάντων παραδοὺς αὐτον ἀμνον ὄντα ἑαυτοῦ, ἵν' ἄρῃ τὴν ἁμαρτίαν τοῦ κόσμοῦ ὁ ὑπὲρ

[1] cf. also I. 3 (ad.fin), 4 (ad. fin), V. 35, VI. 44 (first part), VII. 44, VIII. 64.

παντὸς αὐτοῦ ἀποθνῄσκων ἀμνὸς θεοῦ δι ’ ὅν οὐκ ἀναγκαζόμενος ἀλλ ’ ἑκὼν ὑπέμεινε τὰ ἀπὸ τῶν ὑβριστῶν αὐτῷ προσαγόμενα.”[1]

Further, the intensity of Origen’s passion for truth flashes out here and there in an illuminating phrase or a short sentence, brilliant with the simplicity of clear and perfect expression:

’Ιησοῦς οὐν ἀεὶ ψευδομαρτυρειται, καὶ οὐκ ἔστιν ὅτε κακίας οὔσης ἐν ἀνθρώποις οὐ κατηγορεῖται·[2] ἐνιδεῖν

---

[1] VIII. 43. “Some new thing, then, has come to pass since the time that Jesus suffered—that, I mean, which has happened to the city, to the whole nation, and in the sudden and general rise of a Christian community. And that, too, is a new thing, that those who were strangers to the covenants of God, with no part in His promises, and far from the truth, have by a divine power been enabled to embrace the truth. These things were not the work of an impostor, but were the work of God, who sent His Word, Jesus Christ, to make known His purposes. The sufferings and death which Jesus endured with such fortitude and meekness, show the cruelty and injustice of those who inflicted them, but they did not destroy the announcement of the purposes of God; indeed, if we may so say, they served rather to make them known. For Jesus Himself taught us this when He said, ‘Except a grain of wheat fall into the ground and die, it abides by itself alone: but if it die, it brings forth much fruit.’ Jesus, then, who is this grain of wheat, died, and brought forth much fruit. And the Father is ever looking forward for the results of the death of the grain of wheat, both those which are arising now, and those which shall arise hereafter. The Father of Jesus is therefore a tender and loving Father, though ‘He spared not His own Son, but delivered Him up’ as His lamb ‘for us all,’ that so ‘the Lamb of God,’ by dying for all men, might ‘take away the sin of the world.’ It was not by compulsion, therefore, but willingly, that He bore the reproaches of those who reviled Him.” (Trs. of these passages is taken from the *New Advent* website. My initials show only that I created the footnote – GPB)]

[2] Introd. 2. [“Jesus, however, is at all times assailed by false witnesses, and, while wickedness remains in the world, is ever exposed to accusation.” - GPB]

δὲ ἔστι καὶ τῷ τοῦ Ἰησοῦ ἤθει πανταχοῦ περιϊσταμένου τὴν περιαυτολογίαν;[1] αὐτον φαμεν καὶ μέγαν ἀγονιστὴν γεγονέναι·[2] καὶ ἀεὶ δ᾽ ἐν τᾶς γνησίοις μαθηταῖς καὶ μαρτοροῦσι τῇ ἀληθείᾳ ὁ Ἰησοῦς συσταυροῦται λῃσταῖς καὶ τὴν αυτὴν αὐτοις παρὰ ἀνθρώποις καταδικην πάσχει·[3] ἐπέμφθη γὰρ οὐ μόνον, ἵνα γνωσθῇ, ἀλλ᾽ ἵνα καὶ λάθῃ. [4] It seems almost more than a coincidence that in all these phrases Origen is speaking of the heart and centre of his faith.

Another of his characteristics is to bring his sentence to an end, almost with a jerk, on a vitally important word or phrase, thus throwing nearly as much emphasis on the words as if he were speaking them. ἔστιν οὖν υἱὸς τοῦ δόντος τὸν νόμον καὶ τοὺς προθήτας θεοῦ ὁ Ἰησοῦς·[5] "ἦλθεν

---

[1] I. 48. ["For it may be observed as a trait of the character of Jesus, that He on all occasions avoided unnecessary talk about Himself" – GPB]

[2] I. 69. ["We say that He was also a great wrestler" – GPB]

[3] II. 44. ["Jesus, indeed, is ever crucified with robbers among His genuine disciples and witnesses to the truth, and suffers the same condemnation which they do among men." – GPB]

[4] II. 67. ["Yet He was sent into the world not only to become known, but also to be hid" – GPB] cf. also IV. 3. ἀρετῆς μὲν ἐὰν ἀνέλῃς τὸ ἀνεῖλες αὐτῆς καὶ τὴν οὐσίαν ["if you take away the spontaneity of virtue, you destroy its essence" – GPB]; V. 51. δείκνυται γὰρ οὐκ ἀθεεὶ τὰ τηλικαῦτα δεδυνημένος ["for it is demonstrated that He could not have accomplished such mighty works without the divine help." – GPB] VII. 12. πληκτικώτερος γὰρ ἂν ὁ λόγος αὐτοῦ ἦν καὶ πρὸς ὅ ἐβούλετο ἀνυτικώτερος ["for then his argument would have had much more force, and would have furthered his purpose much better" – GPB] VII. 66. οὐδὲν γὰρ νόθον χρὴ ἐνυπάρχειν ἐν τῇ ψυχῇ τοῦ ἀληθῶς εἰς τὸ θεῖον εὐσεβοῦς. ["For there is no falsehood or pretence in the soul which is possessed with true piety towards God."- GPB]

[5] II. 6 (ad.init.) ["*Jesus*, then, is the Son of God, who gave the law and the prophets" – GPB]

οὖν οὐχ ὑπὸ ἑνὸς προφήτου ἀλλ᾽ ὑπὸ πάντων προκηροχθεὶς Ἰησοῦς Χριστος.[1]

Finally, the style of the Reply to Celsus is unstudied and without ornament. If passion raises him, Origen can write prose worthy of his subject or flash out vivid phrases, but in the main his language is unpretending and instruction his first thought. Indeed, his own views on this point of literary style are clearly expressed in answer to Celsus' attack on the language of Scripture, which he compares very unfavourably with the writings of philosophers. "I assert that if the purpose of ambassadors of truth is to help as many people as they can and to lead to truth, as far as possible, through their love to men everyone without exception not only the clever but the stupid also, not only Greeks but also barbarians... it is obvious then that in their speaking they must devise a style, which helps all alike and can win a hearing from everyone. But all those, who dismiss the uneducated, as slaves unable to understand the sequence of careful phrasing and ordered sentences, and think only of those who have moved in literary and learned circles, have narrowed their ideas of public service into a very strait and limited view... For our prophets and Jesus and His Apostles were careful that the style of their speaking should not only embrace the truth but also have power to win over the common herd, until attracted and led inwards, each according to his capacity, they advance to the mysteries hidden in words which seem quite simple. And – if I may venture to say it – the style of

[1] II. 79 (ad.fin.) ["*Jesus Christ* therefore came announced beforehand, not by one prophet, but by all" – GPB] cf. also II. 81 (Koetschau p.272.1.6) IV. 28 (K.p.297.1.28), V. 46 (K.p.50.1.19), 48, (K.p.53.1.11). VI. 13 (K.p.84.1.1) 66 (K.p.136.1.28) VII. 17 (K.p.168.1.23), 39, (K.p.189.1.9).

Plato, beautiful and polished as it is, and of those, who write like him, has given help to very few... while, on the other hand, the style of those who taught and wrote more simply and practically, aiming at what most people want, has been useful to a great many... I say this without meaning to blame Plato (for he too has served the vast world of men); but I want to explain the meaning of the words, 'And my word and my preaching was not in the persuasive words of man's wisdom, but in the revelation of the spirit and of power, that our faith may not exist in the wisdom of mortal men but in the power of God.' God's word declares that the spoken word is not enough, even if it be true in itself and worthy of trust, to reach the heart of man, unless a power from God be given to the speaker and grace bloom upon his words, and this comes only to successful speakers through God."[1]

To summarize the contents of Origen's Apology is even more baffling than to estimate its literary character. It can be done only by collecting statements and arguments from all the different places in the treatise where they occur, and this method of course takes away their individual setting: we know what Origen said, but unless we read his answers in their context, we cannot know exactly how and why he said it. A full analysis of the book is not attempted here,[2] but only a sketch of its chief characteristics, illustrated by certain specimens of the argument, together with a short statement of the defence made against the fourfold attack of Celsus on the religious, intellectual, social and political position of

---

[1] VI. 1-2.

[2] Patrick (op. cit. Part II) gives a complete synopsis of Origen's defence under five [*sic*] heads: – the Scriptures, the Incarnation, the Person and Work of Christ, the Church and its Adherents, Christianity and the Empire, Counter-attack on Hellenic philosophy and religion.

Christians. The dominating feature of Origen's apologetic is that the final basis of his argument is always in fundamental fact. Again and again is reiterated the proof which rests on the character of Jesus, on the wonder and unique value of His life and death, on His influence, which affected not only His own disciples but others, changing their lives completely and producing a new factor in the world – Christian character. To this power, which made itself manifest in the early Church, Origen returns with ever-fresh wonder, pointing out the marvellous growth of the Church and the devotion of the apostles to their mission in spite of all danger and opposition, emphasising constantly the universality of the Christian message, which is free and open to every human being. That is the keynote of the book, and it is a note of victory – not of victory to be achieved but of victory, certain and assured, instinct with the life which thrills through the plain history of the Acts of the Apostles.

There is the answer to what Celsus (in the person of the Jew) says against the poverty and mean birth of Jesus. Origen speaks first of the help which birth and influence can give a man in his career, quoting Plato's story of Themistocles and the Seriphian and continuing thus: "But our Jesus is reproached with being born in a village and not even a Greek village at that, nor of any nation well-known in the world's eyes, and was despised for being the son of a poor peasant-woman, and for leaving His own country to work for hire in Egypt because he was so poor... and yet He has been able to shake the whole inhabited world not only far beyond the power of Themistocles, the Athenian, but of Pythagoras also and Plato and of any of the world's great men, be they sages, kings or soldiers."[1] Celsus attacks the character of Jesus, alleging that He was not irreproachable. "Let him produce his evidence," says Origen, "I, seeing continually fulfilled what He foretold before it happened – that the Gospel should be preached in the whole world – that his disciples should go to all nations to take the message of His word – further, that they should be brought before governors and kings for no other cause than His teaching – I am lost in wonder at Him, and day by day my faith in Him grows firmer."[2] "Perhaps," he continues "Celsus does not understand the sufferings of Jesus, wishing Him to be subject to no human weakness. But Jesus through what He suffered did not cast discredit on the faith we have in him, but rather won approval among those who are willing to pay attention to manly courage, and among those who learnt from Him that the real and actual happy life is not here and now, but in what is called in His words 'the world that is coming', while life in what is called 'the present world' is the sport of circumstance, or a struggle – the first and greatest of the soul"[3] The worship of Jesus seems to Celsus on a par with barbarian deifications of men, and Origen points out the essential difference between barbarian rites and the homage Jesus compelled from men, in that He led them to God, the Father. "We are lost in wonder at Jesus, who has turned our mind from all that we perceive with our senses... and has led us up to worship with an upright life God, who is over all, and with prayers which we bring to Him, as through one, who is mid-way between the nature of the uncreated and the nature of all created things, who brings us the good gifts of

[1] I. 29.
[2] II. 42.
[3] ib.

the Father, and like a High priest conveys our prayers to God supreme."[1] And again, "And we alone when we show pure truth, unmixed with falsehood, to be in the teaching of Jesus Christ, do not commend ourselves but our teacher, to whom witness was borne by God supreme through many men and the prophetic writings of the Jews and the very clearness of the facts: for it is plain that He could not have done what He did without God."[2] Perhaps the must eloquent of all is the passage (already quoted in Greek), in which Origen refutes Celsus' repetition of the taunt, "He saved others, Himself he cannot save." "If you had reviled Dionysus or Heracles... you would not have escaped scot-free."[3] Origen begins with one of his favourite ideas – that the Jewish people suffered dispersion and conquest as punishment for the death of Jesus, and then goes on, "So then, something new has come about since Jesus suffered – I mean what has happened to the city and to the nation as a whole, and the simultaneous rise of a 'nation' of Christians, as though they had been suddenly born all together. It is a new thing also that the strangers to God's covenants, alien from His promises, far from truth, should now by some power from Him receive the truth. This is not an impostor's work, but the work of God, who sent to give His message His own word in Jesus, who was cruelly tortured, so that the very cruelty arraigns those who tortured him: but He endured His sufferings with the greatest bravery and gentleness of spirit and they did not harm the messages of God, but, if I may so put it, rather made them known: even as Jesus Himself taught us, saying, 'Unless a grain of wheat fall into the ground and die, it abideth by itself alone;

[1] III. 34.
[2] V. 51.
[3] VIII. 42.

but if it die, it bringeth forth much fruit.'[1] So then the grain of wheat – Jesus – died and brought forth much fruit and the Father is ever looking forward for the fruit of the death of the grain of corn, fruit in the past, fruit even now present and fruit to come. A tender and good father then is the Father of Jesus, even though He spared not his own son, but gave Him up for us all[2] – His own lamb – that so He may take away the sin of the world, the Lamb of God, who dies for all."[3]

The argument of the changed lives of Christians and the influence of Jesus on character occurs almost incessantly. The Jew is made to say, "The prophets did not predict such a plague." Origen does not waste many words in his answer: "Neither Jews nor Celsus nor any other can with proof establish that a 'plague' turns crowds of men away from the flood of evil to a life in accordance with nature, marked by self-control and the other virtues."[4] The same facts are used very effectively in Origen's defence of the miracles of Jesus. "I would say that, as Jesus promised, His disciples have done even greater works than the miracles of Jesus, which the senses could perceive. For, there are ever opened the eyes of the blind in soul, and the ears of those who are deaf to words about virtue hear eagerly about God and the happy life with Him; and many, who are lame in the feet of what Scripture calls the "inward man", are healed by the word and not only leap, but leap as the hart (an animal which hates serpents and is stronger than the poison of vipers). And these cripples, at any rate, who have been cured, receive from Jesus power to

[1] John 12. 24.
[2] Rom. 8.32.
[3] VIII. 43, cf. I. 68, II. 10, 35, 78, III. 23, 28, 33-6, V. 3, 51, 53, 62, VI. 11, VIII. 12.
[4] I. 29.

tread down with the feet, that were lame, the serpents and scorpions of evil and, to put it simply, all the power of the enemy; and when they tread, they are not hurt, for even they have become stronger than all evil and the poison of daemons."[1] In a discussion as to the relative truth of Christianity and the pagan mysteries, Origen can make this strong point, "I should say that those speak the truth, who have the power to make their hearers live as though what they heard was true:"[2] elsewhere too he can claim that the Gospel of Jesus has so changed men's character that "the Churches of God, which are followers of Christ, when they are examined side by side with the civil assemblies of the districts where they are situated, are as beacons in the world."[3] The example of the first disciples was copied: "from the beginning then, this teaching of Jesus has especial weight with those who heard Him – that they should despise the life which most people follow eagerly, but be eager to live like the life of God."[4]

The devotion of the disciples to the spread of the Gospel is a sure witness to the fact of the Resurrection. "One may wonder how it came about that the disciples – if, as those who decry Jesus say, they did not see Him after He rose from the dead and were not convinced that there was something from God in Him – should not be afraid to suffer what their Master suffered and to meet danger face to face and to forsake their own lands in order to teach, as Jesus willed, the word which He entrusted to them. For I think that

---

[1] II. 48.
[2] VIII. 48.
[3] III. 29.
[4] II. 45, cf. I. 9, 26, 27, 29, 30, 43, 47, 62, 63-4, II. 44, 50, III. 30, 59-71 (conversion and philosophy) V. 57. VI. 15.

anyone who examines the facts with an open mind, will not say that these men gave themselves up to a hazardous life for the sake of the teaching of Jesus, without a deep conviction of its truth which He wrought in them."[1] In another place he says: "I hold the efforts of His disciples to be a clear and obvious proof (of the resurrection); they devoted themselves to a teaching, full of risk to their lives and they would not have spread this teaching so courageously, if they invented the rising of Jesus from the dead."[2] Origen is never tired of pointing to the marvellous spread of the Church as a proof of the Divine Spirit therein. "For although from the beginning all things opposed the spread of His teaching throughout the world... yet it conquered, being the Word of God, whose nature cannot be withstood and becoming stronger than all its numerous antagonists, it won mastery over the whole of Greece and much of barbarian countries and turned many thousands of souls to worship God, as He taught."[3]

The universality also of the Christian religion is emphasised frequently by Origen as part of its unique claim. "Jesus... wished not to heal men in one corner of the world only but as far as in Him lay, men everywhere: for He came as saviour of all men."[4] "Now for the sake of sinners everywhere that they may abandon their sin and entrust themselves to God, is Jesus proclaimed to have dwelt with men."[5] Jesus "has given light and announced to all men the road to the worship of God."[6]

---

[1] I. 31.
[2] II. 56.
[3] I. 27, cf. I. 43, 46, 62, 67, II. 39, 42, 77. VII. 35. VIII. 47.
[4] IV. 4.
[5] IV. 28.
[6] VII. 41. cf. III. 17.

This then is the general tone of Origen's apology – certainty of fundamental fact, which could bear the burden ultimately of all his vital reasoning. In the end he always came back to that argument, which, as he said in his preface, made all arguments unnecessary – "the power of Jesus, which is clear for anyone to see."[1]

There are other strongly-marked characteristics of his work, among which one of the most notable is his use of Scripture. It is not only that he defends the antiquity and the style[2] of the Jewish scriptures as well as New Testament writings, not only that he defends the ideas of God and man set forth therein, claiming for them a deeper inspiration of God's spirit than was given to Greek philosophers. In addition, he manifests quite plainly his own conviction about the Bible, which was based on profound knowledge; for Origen was not only a Biblical scholar, but also a student of the Bible from a human point of view. His attitude to the scriptures (apart altogether from the question of allegorical interpretation) is that of a man, who knows and believes that he has really found "the Word of God". He turns to the Bible instinctively for the knowledge of God and God's will, for light on the path of man's life and for a standard wherewith to test all wisdom and all humanity. He is full of indignation against those who assert that the Bible is not for the learned, declaring that they have not even begun to understand the mysteries, which lie hidden in its words.[3] In the Old Testament he finds a prophecy of Christ, though he does not use it simply as a storehouse of proof-texts for His

[1] Introd. 3.
[2] e.g. II. 4.
[3] cf. VI. 7.

Messiahship.[1] The whole Bible is essentially for him a book of life and he quotes from it with an eloquence, which is unsurpassed. His mind seems to range like lightning over all the Scriptures. To take one example out of many there is a remarkable passage in the fifth book of the Apology, where he is answering the charge of not worshipping the sun, moon and stars. The passage is too long to give in full. He begins by quoting from Deuteronomy the Mosaic law against the worship of the host of heaven, passing on to God's promise to Abraham that the chosen nation shall be as the stars of heaven for number: "having the hope that they would became as the stars of heaven, they were not likely to worship them." Then he goes on to quote Daniel and Paul on those, who are to share in the resurrection and "shine as the stars" with their differing glory. Was it likely, he asks, that those who had learnt to ascend above created things and had heard "Ye are the light of the world" and "Let your light so shine before men that they seeing your good works, may glorify your Father who is in heaven" and had attained the eternal spiritual light, was it likely that they would worship the mere visible light of sun, moon and stars? "God is light, and in Him there is no darkness at all." The Son of God is "the true light which lighteth every man that cometh into the world", He who said "I am the light of the world." Not, indeed, that sun, moon and stars are regarded as of no account. They are the works of God and summon men to worship God, who made them. "But if Celsus had read all our thousands of passages about sun and moon and stars and especially "Praise Him, all ye stars and light" and "Praise Him, ye heavens of heavens", he would not have said of us

[1] VII. 7-8.

that we assert such mighty beings, who mightily praise God, to be nothing. And Celsus does not know the passage; "For the earnest expectation of the creature waiteth for the manifestation of the Sons of God. For the creature was made subject to vanity, not willingly but by reason of him who hath subjected the same in hope; because the creature itself also shall be delivered from the bondage of corruption into the glorious liberty of the children of God."[1] This is a typical illustration of the way in which Origen confirms his meaning, gives point to his discussion and beauty to his argument from the wealth of his knowledge of the Bible.[2]

Of all the Biblical writers the Apostle Paul seems to have been the man to whom Origen's mind was most drawn. It is not only or even primarily that he admired the conversion and wonderful work of Paul, calling him "the founder after Jesus of Churches in Christ,"[3] but he discovered in him spiritual vision, which pierced through the things of sense and sought the deep mysteries of God. His was a mind akin to Origen's own, a mind which knew that in "the fulness of Christ" (the "riches of Christ" as he sometimes expressed it), was the completion of all human knowledge, there and there only the perfection of wisdom. It is possible to see how Origen venerated Paul even from the manner and frequency

---

[1] V. 10-13 (passages from the Bible quoted therein – Deut. 4.19-20. 1 Pet. 2.9. Gen. 15.5. Deut. 1.10. Dan. 12.1-3. 1 Cor. 15.40-2. Matt. 5.14 amd 16. 1 Jn 1.5. Matt. 19.17. Deut. 6.13. Ps. 107.20. Matt. 28.20. John 1.26-7. Jer. 23.23-4. Rom. 8. 19-21. Ps. 148.3.)

[2] cf. III. 45-8 (wisdom and wise men), IV. 13 (God and fire), IV. 28(God loves all living things), VI. 5 (light), VII. 29 (the city of God).

[3] I. 63.

of his quotations,[1] but there is one passage also where he gives the Apostle's writings no measured praise. Celsus has been ridiculing the doctrines of Christianity as contemptible, and unworthy of comparison even with the despised superstitions of Egypt. Origen indignantly denies this, declaring that the "wisdom of the Word" is unfolded to the "complete" in Christianity; and about them, as being adequate to understand the wisdom in Christianity Paul says in his teaching, "We speak wisdom among the perfect; yet not the wisdom of this world nor of the princes of this world, who come to naught, but we speak the wisdom of God in a mystery, even the hidden wisdom which God ordained before the world unto our glory, which none of the princes of this world knew."[2] "And I say to those, who think with Celsus, 'according to you, then, Paul had no idea of a surpassing wisdom, when he promised to speak wisdom among the perfect?' And since he spoke with his characteristic daring, saying that Paul made this promise not possessing any wisdom himself, I give this answer; first, get to know well the letters of the man who made this assertion and examine carefully the meaning of each expression in them — say in the letters to the Ephesians, to the Colossians, to the Thessalonians, to the Philippians and the Romans – and then prove two things: first, that you have understood Paul's words, and second, that you can show them to be foolish or stupid. For if he give himself to attentive reading of Paul, I am quite certain that he will either marvel at the mind of a man, who wraps his mighty thoughts about with

[1] Introd. 5, I.2, 13, 57. II 3, 7, 16, 17, 24 (ad.fin.) 50, 63, 65-6, 71, III. 13, 33, 46-9, 53, IV. 18, 44, 49, 70, V. 8, 17-19, 39, VI. 19-20, 45-6, VII. 21, VIII. 21.

[2] III. 19.

ordinary words, or if he does not marvel he will himself be open to ridicule, whether he state the writer's meaning as though he understood it, or whether he try to refute and overthrow what he only imagined he understood."[1] There is no other writer, pagan, Jewish or Christian, of whom Origen speaks in such terms.

Inseparably connected with Origen's use of the Bible is his theory of allegorical interpretation. It was, as has been said, a characteristic of his mental environment, of minds with practically no idea of progress, historic-development or gradual revelation. The practice of allegorical interpretation belonged to the age; Origen made it his own and adapted it to his own deep conviction of the mysterious wisdom of God and the varying capacity of man to behold that wisdom. Every word, he maintained, had three meanings and could be interpreted in three ways; the three meanings corresponded to the body, soul and spirit of man,[2] but the exact limitation of each is difficult to rediscover. This method of interpretation is to the modern mind utterly unsatisfactory and insecure, yet the remains of Origen's Biblical commentaries, which survive, show that he reached the heart and centre of Bible truth as surely as any modern reader, even though the bridge, whereby he reaches it, was different. In his apology the allegorical method shows itself chiefly in his defence of the Scriptures against Celsus' assertion that their stories and epithets are unworthy of God and often a contradiction of the Spirit of Christianity. There is one passage where Origen seems to approach more nearly the modern view of historic revelation, and compares the

[1] III. 20.

[2] περὶ ἀρχῶν ["First Principles", Origen's key theological work – GPB] IV. 11. cf. Prat: *Origène. Le théologien et l'exegète*, Liv. II.

language of Scripture to words specially adapted to young children, the words from God to a people whom He is educating; but the real way of explanation always lies for him in the deeper spiritual meaning of words, which is unperceived by the ignorant.[1] The following is a short example of one of his more obvious explanations. "In this way I understand the message in the 137th Psalm, which runs as fellows: 'O daughter of Babylon, who are to be destroyed; happy shall he be that rewardeth thee as thou hast served us: happy shall he be that taketh and dasheth thy little ones against the stones.' For the 'little ones' of Babylon, (which means 'confusion') are those confusing thoughts of evil, which grow and rise up suddenly in the soul: he who subdues them, by striking their heads against the firm and strong rock of reason and truth, is the man who 'dasheth the little ones against the stones;' and is thereby blessed and happy. Therefore God may bid men destroy completely their sins at birth, without teaching anything contrary to the commands of Christ."[2] There is also a long section in the fourth book on the figurative meanings of certain Old Testament stories,[3] illustrating this method of treating documents, which seems to modern ideas so fantastic and which was in ancient Alexandria quite usual.

Throughout the argument, which is often concerned with small and sometimes rather irrelevant details, Origen preserves that characteristic of sound and broad thinking, which has justly earned for him the title of the greatest of early Christian philosophers. It is natural that it should be

[1] e.g. I. 4, 18, II. 4, 6, 69, IV. 39-51, 71-2, 87, V. 55-6, 59-60, VII. 9-25.
[2] VII. 22.
[3] IV. 43-8.

more obvious in his theological work, περὶ ἀρχῶν,[1] but it is always present in his apology, even though his style of address is more like that of a teacher than a philosopher. It is apparent in his treatment of the origin and nature of evil, "a subject" as he says "not easy even for a philosopher to master;"[2] he calls for sane, unhurried thinking, based on accurate knowledge, before an easy theory is formulated. He appeals to reason as God implanted in man. "Everything is a part of the cosmos, but no part of the whole is God. For God must be without the imperfection of the part. Perhaps deeper thought will show that in reality, as God is not a part, so He is not the whole, since the whole consists of parts; reason refuses to accept the idea that God, who is above all, consists of parts each of which cannot do what all the other parts can."[3]

These are the outstanding qualities which colour the whole of Origen's Apology. The following is an indication in outline of the main points in his reply to Celsus' attack.

The objections, which Celsus voiced so fiercely against Christianity from the religious point of view, were mainly concerned with the ideas of God and man involved in belief in the incarnation and the Divinity of Christ. Origen's answer is given from both sides of the question, and it is throughout positive rather than negative; he proves that the Christian idea of God is right and true, and that the Christian belief in Jesus is founded on sure ground. He admits with Celsus that to know God perfectly is impossible to man, but shows that certain qualities of His character may be known.[4]

[1] ["First Principles", lit. "Concerning Beginnings" – GPB]
[2] IV. 62-70.
[3] I. 23, cf. I. 13, II. 40.
[4] II. 71, VI. 17, 63-71, VII. 42-4.

Though God is purely spirit and to be apprehended only by the rational spirit indwelling in every man,[1] yet because of man's inability to grasp at once "the things unseen, which are everlasting", God reveals Himself to man by submitting to human restrictions.[2] God suffered no change, when He dwelt on earth in the flesh: we must not think of the Divine Spirit in a local way.[3] Jesus was of compound nature, God dwelling in reality not only in appearance in a human body.[4] Further, it is only natural that God should manifest himself to men rather than to the animal creation, who are also part of his design.[5] For, "if He once look upon the source of all impulses, it is clear that He would see… the superiority of man, not only over ants but even over elephants. For, He who looks from heaven will see among irrational creatures, however large their bodies no other principle than – if I may use the word – irrationality while among rational beings He will find reason, the possession of man common also to divine and heavenly beings, and perhaps to God supreme, Himself; wherefore man is said to have been created 'in the image of God,' for the image of God supreme is in His rational mind."[6] When God is declared to have come to save sinners, it does not mean that He prefers sinners, for He alone is perfectly holy; but He comes as a good physician to the souls of men, not one of whom can say that he is entirely free from sin.[7] The existence of sin does not prove that God

[1] VI. 4, VIII. 27, 33-40.
[2] IV. 12.
[3] I. 21, IV. 5-6, 14-19, V. 12, VI. 15.
[4] I. 60 (σύνθετόν τι χρῆμα), II. 9, VI. 47-8, VIII. 12.
[5] II. 38.
[6] IV. 85.
[7] I. 9, II. 67, 73, III. 59-71.

cannot control His own work. He gave to man free-will, and "if you take away the spontaneity of virtue, you take away its essence."[1] The Divinity of Jesus and His unique claim are vindicated with great force by Origen. He can challenge Celsus to contradict from any superior authority the story of His character, His life and death, unequalled in history. He lays great stress on the moral influence, which Jesus exercised over men, using as contributory though not as main proofs the testimony of prophecy and of His miracles, pointing out the central and undeniable truth of the power of His Resurrection and the spread of the Christian Gospel. This, as has been already demonstrated, is the foundation of Origen's defence. The criticism, which Celsus levelled against Christianity in the sphere of intellect, was especially poignant to Origen. He instances the wisdom and intellectual power of many Christians, especially of Paul, declaring that many who are "complete" in Christ, are far ahead even of philosophers in speculative thought and spiritual wisdom.[2] Yet, great as is the value of education, the Gospel is for the uneducated also,[3] and it is better that their lives should be changed to upright character than that they should remain in wickedness till they have mastered the dogmas of philosophy, even supposing (which is unlikely) that they have time and ability to pursue such studies.[4] All other human actions are dependent ultimately on faith.[5] Why should not the knowledge of God be approached also in that way? As to the writings of Christianity and Judaism, which

[1] IV. 3.
[2] I. 29, III. 18-21, 44-9, 52-4, 58, 74, VI. 13-14.
[3] III. 49.
[4] I. 9, VII. 49.
[5] I. 10-11.

Celsus finds so unpolished, there are no other books which have produced such an influence on men's lives. Much of the teaching of philosophers is good and true, in so far as they too were led by the spirit of God; but in the Scriptures is a greater divine revelation, which gives grace to their simplicity of language.[1]

The reproach of the low social position, not only of the body of Christian converts but also of Jesus Himself, Origen turns into a matter for glorying – a mark of honour rather than disgrace. Apart from the fact that people of the less educated classes always outnumber the others,[2] the Gospel is for every man, rich or poor, aristocrat or low-born, slave or free.[3] If Jesus was of despised and lowly origin, then it was all the more wonderful that He accomplished His marvellous deeds on earth.[4]

In answering the charges of sedition and lack of patriotism Origen is faced by two questions: one, characteristic of pagan society only, one which the history of twenty centuries has not yet settled completely even for the so-called civilised world. The first is connected with the worship of daemons, the second with the rights of the individual conscience. It was impossible for a man to take an active part in the social or political organization of the Roman Empire, without becoming involved in heathen rites and sacrifices; this, says Origen, is inconsistent with loyal worship of God,[5] and therefore Christians cannot enter into

[1] I. 2, 18, 62, III. 39, 68, VI. 1-18, VII. 59-61.
[2] I. 27.
[3] III. 54.
[4] I. 29-30.
[5] VII. 67-70, VIII. 2-64.

public life. Celsus' doctrine of "national religions"[1] – each nation assigned to a separate daemon – destroys all absolute standards of law, morality and truth, and they become purely relative to the ways of a man's country.[2] Furthermore, in Christ all nations are one and through Him men must learn to cease from war.[3] Celsus urges the argument that men must conform to the laws of the society in which they live, and bear their share of its burdens if they accept its privileges. But what if its laws are against our highest knowledge of right and truth, asks Origen?[4] Further, he maintains that Christians are really the truest patriots and best citizens, since they wage a constant war against all evil and all daemons, praying for their country and their king and serving the one true God. If the whole Roman Empire were to become Christian, no nation, be it ever so hostile, would withstand its strength. So in the third century was the question debated, even as it has been debated down the years and still remains unsettled, indeed it has become more complicated.[5] For, ultimately, to early Christians action which involved the service of any but Christ, (that is, the service of daemons), was out of the question.

The above is the barest summary of the main points in Origen's reply. More justice can be done to his work by quoting one or two examples of the argument in full. The first is a comparison of the Christian idea of God with the Platonic conception adduced by Celsus to discredit the

---

[1] V. 26-8.

[2] V. 28. 33-40.

[3] III. 7, V. 33.

[4] VIII. 64-5, 67-75.

[5] [This was written in 1915. The writer's friends included both serving soldiers and conscientious objectors. – GPB]

Incarnation; the second is an explanation of the doctrine of the resurrection of the body:

"Next after this Celsus sends us to Plato as a more effective teacher of the facts of theology, quoting the following passage from the Timaeus – 'The Maker and Father of this universe it is hard to find, and having found him, it is impossible to speak of him to all.' Then he adds these remarks, 'You see how men inspired of God seek after the way of truth and how Plato knew that to walk therein is impossible for all. But though it has been discovered by wise men, in order that we should receive some conception of the Being, who is first and inexpressible by name, a conception revealing him either by synthesis with other things, or analysis of them or analogy, I, who am anxious to explain what is inexpressible in word, should be very much surprised, if you were able to follow this course, you who are absolutely enslaved to the flesh and behold nothing pure.' There is a grandeur worthy of all respect in this quotation from Plato. But consider – does not Scripture lead us to a God more full of love for man, in God, the Logos, who 'was in the beginning with God' and became flesh, that the Logos might be able is reach all men? This is He of whom Plato says 'when found, it is impossible to speak of Him to all.' Well, Plato may say it is hard to find the Maker and Father of this universe, meaning that it is impossible for man's nature to know God, worthily or even in a very great degree and beyond what the majority attain; but, if this were true and Plato or any other Greek had really found God, they would not have given worship and adoration or the name of God to any other object, deserting Him and comparing him to things far below the character of one so great. But I, for my part, declare that man's nature is utterly inadequate to the search for God and pure knowledge of Him, without the help of Him, who is sought; He is found of those who own, after doing all they can by themselves, that they need Him, and He shows Himself to those for whom He thinks it right that they should see Him, in so far as God's nature allows Him to be known by man and as man's soul, still being in the body, can know God.[1] Plato too, when he says 'Having found the Maker and Father of the Universe, it is impossible to speak of Him at all', does not say that He is inexpressible by word or name, but that He can be expressed in words to a few. But then Celsus, as if he had forgotten his quotation from Plato, calls God 'inexpressible' – 'It has been discovered by wise men, in order that we should receive some conception of the Being who is first and inexpressible by name.' But I say that not only is God inexpressible by words, but things also below him; these Paul is struggling to express, when he says, 'I heard unspeakable words, which a man is not allowed to utter', using 'heard' in the sense of 'understand', as in the passage, 'He that hath ears to hear, let him hear.'

"Therefore, as you know, I also say it is hard to see the Maker and Father of the Universe. But He is seen and in this way – 'Blessed are the pure in heart for they shall see God'; He is seen too according to the word of 'the image of the invisible God' – 'He who hath seen me hath seen the Father who sent me.' No one with any intelligence would imagine that in these words 'He who hath seen me hath seen the Father who sent me' – Jesus was referring to His body, seen by the senses and beheld by all men; for according to that, all those will have seen God, the Father, who shouted 'Crucify

[1] VII. 42.

Him, crucify Him!', and Pilate too who had power against the human part of him: but this is absurd. Further that these words 'He who hath seen me hath seen the Father who sent me' are not to be taken in the grosser way is clear from His words to Philip, – 'Have I been so long time with you, and yet dost thou not know me, Philip?' – He gave this answer when Philip asked 'Show us the Father and it sufficeth us.' He then who understands how we ought to apply the words 'The Word became flesh' to the only-begotten Son of God, the first-born of all creation, will see how anyone, who has seen the image of the invisible God, will know the 'maker and Father of the Universe.'[1]

"Celsus, moreover, imagines that we know God by synthesis with other things (like the synthesis of mathematicians), or by analysis from them or analogy (another mathematical term), and that anyone can really come in this way to the threshold of Supreme Good, but when the Logos of God says, 'No one knows the Father but the Son, and he to whomsoever the Son will reveal Him', He declares that God is known by a gracious gift of God, coming to the soul not without God's help but with His very presence. For it is only natural that the knowledge of God should be too high for man's nature (this is the reason why men have made so many mistakes about God); it is worthy too of God's goodness and love of men that by a gift so gracious that we can hardly believe it, a God-like gift, the knowledge of Him should come to those, whom He had taken to himself beforehand in His foreknowledge; He knew that they would live worthily of Him when they knew Him, never defacing their service to Him, even if by those who

[1] VII. 43.

knew not what is religion but give its name to everything rather than the true service of God, they be led away to die or be held worthy of scorn and ridicule.

"I think God noticed the arrogance and contempt of others which characterise those who pride themselves on knowing God and on having learnt about God from philosophy, but who still, like the uneducated, lead the way to their statues and temples and much-talked of mysteries; and so He chose 'the foolish things of this world', the simplest of Christians, who live a more self-controlled and a purer life than many philosophers, that He may 'put to shame the wise', who are not ashamed to speak to lifeless things as gods or images of the gods.

"For what intelligent man will not laugh at one, who, after learning from philosophy such grand and mighty doctrines about God or the gods, gazes at images and sends up prayers to them or by gazing at them tries to reach the spiritual to which he imagines he should ascend from the visible symbol? But a Christian, even of the unlettered sort, is convinced that every place is part of the whole universe, and that the whole universe is a temple of God; so he prays in every place, shutting the eyes of sense and raising the eyes of the soul; and he rises above the whole cosmos, he does not stop at the vault of heaven but passes in thought beyond the heaven of heavens; guided by the Spirit of God; and being, as it were, outside the cosmos he offers prayer to God – not for trifles; for he learnt from Jesus to ask for nothing small (that is, objects of sense-perception), but only what is great and truly like God – gifts which, when God gives them, help to show the way to the blessed and happy life with Him, through His son, the Logos, who is God."[1]

"Since Celsus has often made fun of the resurrection of the flesh, which is preached in the churches and is understood more clearly by the more intelligent, (I need not quote his exact words again, they are given above), come now, let me put forward and state, to the best of my power, a few points about this problem specially aimed at my readers; for I am writing an apology against an enemy of the Faith for the benefit of those who are still children, tossed to and fro and carried about 'with every wind of doctrine, in the sleight of men, in cunning craftiness'. Neither I, then, nor the Holy Scriptures assert that with the same flesh, unchanged to a better state, shall those live, who died long age, rising from the ground; these words of Celsus are a false charge against us. For I hear much scripture, which speaks of the resurrection in a manner worthy of God, but it is enough for the present purpose to quote Paul's words from the first epistle to the Corinthians; he says, 'But some man will say: How are the dead raised up? and with what body do they come? Thou fool, that which thou sowest is not quickened, except it die. And that which thou sowest, thou sowest not that body that shall be, but bare grain, it may chance of wheat, or of some other grain; but God giveth it a body as it hath pleased him, and to every seed his own body.' Note how in this passage he says there is sown 'not the body that shall be,' but from the body which is sown and cast naked in the earth (and God gives to each seed its individual body) there comes, so to speak, a resurrection; from the seed cast

---

[1] VII. 44.

into the ground there rises a stalk, as, for instance, in plants like the mustard seed or bigger trees like the olive or any fruit trees.[1]

"So God gives to each thing a body as He willed: as the seeds of plants, so those, who are 'sown' in death at the right moment receive from what is sown the body which God allots to each man according to his deserts. And we hear Scripture teaching us in many words the difference between what is sown and what rises from it, saying; 'It is sown in corruption, it is raised in incorruption; it is sown in dishonour, it is raised in glory; it is sown in weakness, it is raised in power; it is sown a natural body, it is raised a spiritual body.' Let him, who can, understand what is intended by the words, 'As is the earthy, so are they also that are earthy; and as is the heavenly, such are they also that are heavenly. And as we have borne the image of the earthy we shall also bear the image of the heavenly.' Although the apostle wished to hide the secret meaning of the passage, which was not suited to the simpler kind of people or to the common understanding of those who are led through faith to a better life, yet he was forced later (that we might not misunderstand his meaning) to say after 'we shall bear the image of the heavenly,' this also, 'I say, brethren, that flesh and blood cannot inherit the kingdom of God; neither doth corruption inherit incorruption.' Then knowing there was a secret and mystical meaning in the passage he adds (as befitted one who was leaving in writing to posterity words full of deep import) these words, 'Behold, I show you a mystery;' this is his usual way of introducing subjects of deep and mystical meaning, such as it is fitting to hide from

[1] V. 18.

the crowd; as it is written in the book of Tobit, 'the secret of a king it is good to hide', but in a manner consistent with truth and with the repute and advantage of the multitude in view, 'the works of God it is good to reveal.'

"Our hope then is not the hope of worms nor does our soul long for a mouldering body; but, even if it need a body for moving from place to place, it understands (for it has studied wisdom according to the words, 'the mouth of the righteous shall study wisdom'), one difference between the earthly dwelling, which is broken up, wherein is its sheath and the house, wherein the righteous groan, being burdened; for they do not want to take off their sheath, but to be clothed with it, that by being clothed upon, the mortal may be swallowed up by life. For, because the whole nature of body is corruptible, this corruptible sheath must put on incorruption, and its other part which is mortal and exposed to death, which follows sin, must put on immortality, so that, when the corruptible shall put on incorruption and the mortal immortality, then shall come about what the prophets foretold long ago — destruction of the victory of death – for death conquered us and subjected us to himself – and destruction of death's sting, wherewith death stings the soul, which is not perfectly protected, and inflicts on it the wounds which come from sin."[1]

[Then follow two chapters of digression to show that the eschatology of philosophers, especially of stoics with their idea of conflagration and renewal, is contemptible and far less reasonable than Christian belief.[2] Origen resumes:] "Let no one suspect from these statements of mine that I belong to

[1] V. 19.
[2] V. 20-21.

those who call themselves Christians, but set aside the doctrine of resurrection according to Scripture. For they, as far as their beliefs are concerned, cannot prove in any way that the stalk or tree, which rises from a grain of corn or any other seed, comes from it; I on the other hand, am persuaded that what is sown is not made alive, unless it die, and that there is sown not the body, which shall be; for God gives it a body as he willed, after it is sown in corruption raising it in incorruption, after it is sown in dishonour raising it in glory, and after it is sown in weakness raising it in power, after it is sown a natural body raising it a spiritual body, and in this belief I guard both the mind of the Church of Christ and the greatness of God's praise, affording proof of its possibility not by mere assertion but by reasoning: for, I know that even if heaven and earth pass away and the things therein, yet His words about each separate thing, which is as part to the whole or species to the genus, the words of Him, who is God, the word, who was in the beginning with God, shall in no wise pass away. For my will is to hearken to Him who said; 'Heaven and earth shall pass away, but my words shall not pass away.'[1]

"To resume then – I do not assert that the body, which has suffered corruption, is raised up to its original nature, as even the grain of wheat which has decayed does not return to be a grain of wheat once more. What I do say is – as on the grain of wheat there rises a stalk, so a certain rational spirit is planted in the body, which is not destroyed and from which the body is raised in incorruption. The Stoics, however, say that a body, which has been altogether corrupt, comes back to its original nature because of their opinions about fixed

[1] V. 22.

unchangeableness working by cycles, and they assert that it will assume again that very same first nature from which it passed into decay – this they establish, as they think, by dilemmas of argument. And I do not take shelter in what Celsus calls a 'ridiculous' refuge – the statement that everything is possible with God: for I know how to understand the word 'all' – as not applying to what is non-existent or inconceivable. And I declare that God cannot do anything disgraceful, for then He would be a God capable of not being God; for if God do aught disgraceful, He is not God.

"But since Celsus maintains that God does not will what is contrary to nature, I give as my opinion this, – that if anyone says evil is contrary to nature, and I say God does not will what is contrary to nature – either what comes from wickedness or lack of reason; but if they are things which happen in accordance with the will and purpose of God, it follows at once and of necessity that they cannot be contrary to nature; for nothing which God does is contrary to nature, even if it be incredible or seem to someone incredible. And, if I must press the force of a word, I will say with reference to the generally accepted view of nature that there are some things beyond its sphere, which God could do at any time; for example, He lifts up man above his nature and makes him change to a better nature, more like Himself and keeps him therein, as long as the man He guards shows by his deeds that he wishes it.[1]

"I have said once that God wills nothing inconsistent with Himself, for that destroys His existence as God; I will add that if a man yielding to his wickedness desires aught

[1] V. 23.

abominable, God will not be able to grant it. So in no spirit of controversy do I approach Celsus' statements, but with a longing for truth I examine them and agree with him that God is not a God of clashing desires or of error and disorder, but of an upright and just nature, since He is the source of all good. And we admit that He has the power to provide life everlasting for the soul and not only has the power but uses it. So because of these statements, the saying of Heraclitus, quoted by Celsus, that corpses are to be thrown away as more worthless than dung, troubles us not at all: and yet on this point one could say that while dung ought to be cast out as refuse, yet human bodies, because of the soul which dwelt in them, especially if it were noble, ought not to be thrown away. For, according to the laws of decency, they are deemed worthy of burial with the honour suited to such a rite; so that we may not insult, if we can avoid it, the soul which dwelt therein, by casting forth the body, when the soul has left it, like the bodies of animals. So let God's will be (and let reason admit it) not to declare the grain of corn immortal, but rather the stalk springing from it, and the body also, which is sown in corruption, mortal, but that, which is raised from it in incorruption, immortal."[1]

These two passages are fair examples of Origen's style of argument, of his attitude to Celsus and his way of explanation, which was designed to meet the need of a known audience. That Origen was a fair and just adversary is clear. In spite of professed contempt for his opponent,[2] his criticism of the tautology and lack of arrangement in the

[1] V. 24.
[2] e.g. I. 49, 63, 71, II. 1, 3, 12, 20, 21, 36-7, III. 22, 76, IV. 30. VI. 74.

True Word, his antagonism to the spirit of Celsus, which "did not know how to speak well of honest men",[1] he owns that Celsus is sometimes right – "φίλη γὰρ ἡ ἀλήθεια".[2] The best ending for any account of his treatise and the best witness to the spirit in which it was written are the words, which he wrote himself in the last chapter: "Here, honoured Ambrosius, you have the end of the book you asked me to write, at least as much as the power given me at present can do. I have treated in eight books everything I thought relevant as an answer to that book of Celsus, entitled "True Word". It lies now with the reader of his treatise and of my reply to judge which of the two breathes most of the true God and of the way to worship Him and of truth which comes to men and gives them sound beliefs to lead them to the best life.

"You know, however, that Celsus promised to compose another treatise after this, wherein he promised to instruct those who wished to accept his opinions in the way to live. If he has not kept his promise of writing a second "Word", then I shall be very glad that these eight books I have written in answer to the first are enough; but if he began and finished the second book, please get hold of it and send it to me; that I may answer it, as the Father of truth gives me power, and either overthrow the wrong ideas in it or, laying aside the controversial spirit, testify my admiration of whatever truth is in it."[3]

---

[1] VII. 57.

[2] III. 16, ["for truth is precious" Origen writes, explaining that he will not fail to praise Celsus where he is correct – GPB] cf. I. 14, 53 (ad. fin.) VII. 46.

[3] VIII. 76.

CHAPTER V
ORIGEN AND EARLIER APOLOGISTS

Origen's work in the sphere of apologetic can be better realised after an examination of the writings of earlier Christian apologists. With the exception of Tertullian and Clement of Alexandria, they belong mainly to the earlier part of the second century, and in spite of incidental differences they possess enough characteristics in common to justify their being classified in one group. The Apologies of Justin Martyr, of Athenagoras and Aristides, Tatian's address to the Greeks, the letters from Theophilus to his friend Autolycus, and the anonymous "Epistle to Diognetus" are typical of a period of transition in the history of the Christian Church. In the early days most men had to prove their certainty of the truth in Christ by dying for Him – and they proved it; but, as time went on, the why and how of the Faith were tentatively sought by thinking Christians, who were being driven by persecution or by inquirers from without to state the content of their "illicit" religion. Towards the end of the second century the True Word was written, and evidence has been collected to prove that it was a counterblast to the Apology of Aristides;[1] another scholar maintains that "The Preaching of Peter" was the Christian book, which roused Celsus' attack.[2] Anyhow, there are a considerable number of points emphasised both by the Preaching and by Aristides which are common also to Celsus, and which indicate the first clash

[1] Rendel Harris in *Texts and Studies* (ed. Armitage Robinson) Vol. I, pp.19ff.

[2] Armitage Robinson *Texts and Studies* Vol. I Appendix pp.98-9.

of argument, heralding the battles in the next few centuries for a philosophically-expressed creed.

The purpose of all the early apologists is to explain themselves and their position clearly and to demand the right to exist. They write as men, who have seen the sun, might speak to Plato's cave-dwellers. They have found the Truth, and their aim is to open the eyes of the blind that they also may see. "O man, thou dost breathe His breath, but Himself thou knowest not,"[1] says Theophilus to his sceptic friend. Tatian puts it even more scornfully: "Ye seek who is God and what are the things around you, but ye are ignorant; gaping up to the heaven, ye fall into bottomless pits."[2] All the apologies begin with an appeal for justice and right treatment based on knowledge of the real belief and actions of this persecuted people. Justin makes an address and petition to the Emperors, Senate and Roman people, "On behalf of the men of every race who are hated and persecuted unjustly... I myself being one of them."[3]

It follows from this that the apologists should deal mainly with ordinary life as affected by their faith: they had to repel the ordinary charges brought against them and explain, as far as they could, why they took the hated name of Christian. Christians were accused of atheism because they neither had temples nor worshipped acknowledged gods; they were accused of feasting on children and of excessive sexual indulgence. The answer was given by a plainly-stated contrast between the Christian belief in God and the pagan

---

[1] Theophilus – Letters to Autolycus I. 7. ἄνθρωπε τούτου τὸ πνεῦμα ἀναπνεῖς, τουτὸν ἀγνοεῖς.

[2] Tatian. To the Greeks XXVI. ζητοῦντες τίς ὁ θεός, τίνα τὰ ἐν ὑμῖν ἀγνοεῖτε. κεχηνότες δὲ εἰς τὸν οὔρανὸν κατὰ βαράθρων πίπτετε.

[3] Justin Ap. I. 1.

myths and philosophies: there is no sparing of words in the condemnation of the latter. Aristides gives all the first part of his apology to proving that the Egyptians, the Chaldaeans and the Greeks "wandered very far astray;"[1] "all the gods of the nations are idols", but Christians "take their genealogy from the Lord Jesus Christ. He is the Son of God, the Highest. He lived on earth and was crucified of his own free will "κατ' οἰκονομίαν μεγάλην."[2] He left twelve disciples, who taught "His mighty character".[3] "And these are they, who beyond all the nations of the earth have found the Truth for they give heed to God, Founder and Creator of the Universe in His only Son and Holy Spirit, and no other God except Him do they worship."[4] So this is the way of truth which guides men who follow it to the "kingdom that lasts forever."[5]

It is because of their faith in Jesus, who taught them to serve the living God, that Christians live pure lives, and this, as Athenagoras affirms, is sufficient answer to the charges of immorality; they simply are not true. Justin quotes Christ's teaching on chastity, philanthropy, unworldliness, patience, readiness to help others, freedom from anger, truthfulness, to show that the follower of Christ really puts on a new life.[6] "Words came from Him, terse and concise; for He was no sophist, but His word was the power of God."[7] Theophilus

---

[1] Aristides Ap. XIII.
[2] ["according to the great plan" – GPB]
[3] μεγαλωσύνην
[4] Aristides Ap. XV.
[5] ib. Ap. XVI.
[6] Justin Ap. I. 15-17.
[7] ib. Ap. I. 14. βραχεῖς δὲ καὶ σύντομοι παρ' αὐτοῦ λόγοι γεγόνασιν οὐ γὰρ σοφιστὴς ὑπῆρχεν, ἀλλὰ δύναμις θεοῦ ὁ λόγος αὐτοῦ ἦν.

too points out the impossibility of men, who obey Christ's teaching, being guilty of such infamous charges, ending with a triumphant picture of Christian life and character. "With Christians dwells sanity, they inure themselves to self-control, they are careful to have one wife only, they jealously guard purity, they drive evil from its stronghold, they root out sin, they practise righteousness, law guides their social life, they act on their professed religion, they confess their belief in God, Truth is their standard, Grace watches beside them, Peace is round about them, the Holy Word is their guide, Wisdom their Teacher, Life their Judge, God their King,"[1] Here too the apologists did not shrink from emphasising the contrast with pagan morals and pagan society. All sin, wrong ideas and false gods are, they assert, the work of daemons, whose power is only broken in the personality of Jesus Christ. A large part of the apologies is taken up with the denunciation of daemons and their worship and with theories of their origin; and this is perfectly natural for the lives of early Christians were lived in an environment, penetrated through and through not only with a belief in daemons but with daily evidence of their power in the possession of human beings.[2] Justin compares pagan ideas and rites with Christian belief and worship to show daemons perverted the latter. There is no thought in these early apologists of concession or compromise with any portion of paganism: they are viewing it from the stand-point of everyday life, and there it was a war to the death. All of them prefer facing death itself to surrendering the truth in Christ, though Justin claims fair and reasonable toleration

[1] Theophilus Ep. to Autolycus III. 15.
[2] cf. Glover "The Daemon Environment of the Primitive Christian", Hibbert Journal Oct 1912; Warneck *The Living Forces of the Gospel.*

from " εὐσεβεῖς" and " φιλοσόφοι"[1] while he also plainly warns those, who put Christians to death, that punishment from God who is wholly righteous awaits them.[2] The most striking element in them all is their individual testimony, obviously springing from personal experience. For that reason it is worth while glancing at their writings one by one.

Justin Martyr was among the first who attempted apology, and his work is typical.[3] He belongs to the earlier half of the second century and, before he became a Christian, was a Platonist: he kept his touch with educated society and appealed to the sense of reason and justice among philosophers and all sensible people, in order to secure at least toleration for his fellow Christians. He wrote two apologies. The first, and by far the longer, begins with a defence of Christian conduct in ordinary affairs, supported by quotations from Christ's teaching: then follows a collection from pagan mythology of analogies to the story of Christ as given in the Gospels. All this first part of the apology is a disconnected statement of various facts, evidently as answers to certain objections with which Justin was familiar: the rest of the treatise is an ordered proof of three points, first, that Christianity is true – the proof of this is the steadiness of Christians in persecution and their pure lives; second that Christ was uniquely son of God – this proof rests on the argument from the fulfilment of prophecy,

---

[1] Justin Apol. I. 2. ["the pious" and "philosophers" – GPB]

[2] ib. Apol. II. 9 and 12.

[3] cf. Blunt *The Apologies of Justin*, introd. p.xii, "His writings were well-known and freely used by later authors such as Tatian, Athenagoras, Irenaeus, Tertullian. He was one of the first who tried to reconcile Christian Theology with philosophy, and to justify Christianity to the ordinary world of Greek culture."

which is here given at great length (with the caution that Divine foreknowledge does not take away the responsibility of human free-will); third, that heathen myths are due to daemons – this last is proved by examples of the way in which daemons have anticipated and altered Christian doctrines by myths, as, for example, the doctrine of the Spirit by the myth of Kore; or Christian baptism by heathen lustrations. An account is given both of Baptism and the Eucharist with the belief associated with them; the apology ends in a blunt demand for respect for the story, if it appears true; if not, let it be treated as nonsense, but let not these be put to death, who do no wrong. There follows Hadrian's rescript to Fundanus.

The second apology is very short and is really a protest, addressed to the Roman Senate, against the treatment and death of a Christian martyr. It is not that Christians fear death, for they know the true God and Jesus, His son, but it is only right that their persecutors should know their true teaching and be saved from punishment. "Yet our teaching is seen to be mightier than all the other teaching among men."[1] Even if those who knew the Logos fragmentarily before were punished, "no one was persuaded by Socrates to die for this belief; but Christ... not philosophers or sages only obeyed, but artisans also and men completely without education, despising glory and fear and death; for He is the power of the Father who is beyond all words, and no invention of man's mind."[2] Even when I was a Platonist, Justin tells us, I used to disbelieve the popular charges against the Christians, because their lives and their readiness

[1] Justin Ap. II. 10.
[2] ib.

for death seemed inconsistent with those accusations. But, if Christians did the acts alleged against them, they might call them mysteries of Cronos or Zeus, and show that their conduct is only like what pagans do openly.[1] Then comes his own declaration of faith, wherein he triumphantly scorns all daemonic falsehoods about Christianity, asserting, "I confess to being found a Christian both in prayer and in the fight which I wage with all my powers."[2] Here is his commendation of the Christian teaching to all who may read his apology.

Tatian, the Assyrian, was a pupil of Justin, who about the middle of the second century wrote a treatise called, "To Hellenes".[3] He had been educated in their learning and found it insufficient for the knowledge of God, and now he challenges them with their contempt for barbarian ideas. Starting from a defence of Christian citizenship and Christian ideas of God and the world, philosophically stated, he goes on to pour fierce ridicule on all Greek religion, philosophy and social customs. A statement of his own experience follows, which by its very simplicity makes his former indictment more scathing. "Therefore, having made trial of all your mysteries and religious rites, I was thrown on my own resources and was seeking in what way I might discover the truth. And as my mind was busy with high thoughts, I chanced to come across certain barbarian writings, more ancient than Hellenic philosophy and nearer the divine than its errors: and it befel that I was convinced of their truth through the wonder of the words, and the

---

[1] ib. Ap. II. 12.
[2] Justin, Ap. II. 13. χριστιανὸς εὑρεθῆναι καὶ εὐχόμενος καὶ παμμάχως ἀγωνιζόμενος ὁμολογῶ.
[3] cf. I. 16.

spontaneity of the writers, and the simplicity of their conception of the Universe, and their foreknowledge of the future, and the unique nature of the precepts and the idea of one ruling power. So my soul was taught by God and I understood that He is the giver of judgment, but that He puts an end to Slavery in the world, by delivering us from the grasp of many rulers and thousands of tyrant powers, while He offers to us not what we have never received, but what we were prevented from holding fast by our errors."[1] He next proceeds to a long chronological proof of the priority of Christian doctrine (i.e. of Hebrew Scripture) to Greek philosophy, ending with the statement: "For you, O Greeks, have I written this treatise, I, Tatian, taught philosophy by barbarians, born in Assyria, educated first in your learning and then in this teaching, which I feel a mission now to proclaim."[2]

Athenagoras, the Athenian, was another follower of Justin Martyr; he was a philosopher, and about 177 A.D. addressed his "Plea for the Christians" to Marcus Aurelius and Commodus, as Emperors, "but especially as philosophers".[3] He asks why Christians should be condemned for their name alone and not first convicted of crime, and then proceeds to reply to the three stock charges of atheism, cannibalism and immorality, giving nearly all his space to the first. His defence is very much on the lines of the quotations already given from Aristides, though Athenagoras gives rather more explanation of the belief which Aristides only states. His treatise is really only a plea for recognition, but in several

[1] Tatian. To the Greeks XXIX.
[2] ib. XLII.
[3] Athenagoras. Plea for the Christians, pref.

places it rises to literary beauty through the passion of his conviction.[1]

Aristides was another Athenian philosopher, whose apology was presented to an Emperor – probably Antoninus Pius. The main points of his argument have been already given – God is the Maker and Ruler of all, the gods of the nations are either the work of God or not gods at all, Jesus Christ came and taught men to serve the living God. "The writer" says Rendel Harris, "is more of a child than a philosopher, a child well trained in creed and practised in ethics, rather than either a dogmatist defending a new system or an iconoclast destroying an old one: but this simplicity of treatment, so far from being a weakness, adds often greatly to the natural impressiveness of the subject and gives the work a place by the side of the best Christian writing of his age."[2]

The letters of Theophilus, bishop of Antioch, and the authorless epistle to Diognetus do not come under the heading of definite apology. They are informal answers to questions and, as such, show what was in the minds of pagan inquirers. Theophilus writes three letters to his friend Autolycus, showing a keen desire for him to become a Christian, though he exhorts him to faith in God, without laying much emphasis on reasons and causes of belief.

The first letter is devoted to exhortation to believe in the Creator of the World, with whom are contrasted the heathen gods. The resurrection of the dead (evidently a stumbling block to Autolycus) is possible, if you believe in God. Theophilus ends on this note of "Be not faithless but

[1] ib. 7, 13, 16, 22 (music and ships), 24 (beauty of the world).
[2] Rendel Harris op. cit. introd. p.3.

believing," with the assurance that he himself had once been a sceptic, but now, having weighed the proofs and studied the prophets, he believes. In the second letter is a comparison of fabulous myths about God and the creation of the world with the account in the Old Testament; it contains a beautiful passage, where the teaching of truth preserved by the churches is compared to fair islands, where those tempest-tossed on the sea of the world may take refuge, while the teachings of heresy are waterless rocks, against which ships are dashed to pieces.[1] The last letter is an answer to Autolycus' objection that the Scriptures are fabulous and of recent date; after contrasting Christian and heathen morality, Theophilus proceeds to a detailed chronological proof of the ancient date of Hebrew Scriptures, at the same time urging him to read them and possess "a counsellor and pledge of truth".[2]

The Epistle to Diognetus is an answer to three questions about Christianity; first, "why do Christians face martyrdom and refrain from pagan and Jewish rites?" second, "what is the nature of Christian love?" third, "why did Christianity come so late into the world?" The unknown writer answers these questions in a short explanation of the Christian faith, so beautiful in its own way that it is unfair to summarize or quote it in part. The chief point he makes is the knowledge of God taught by Christ; this shows paganism to be irrational, Judaism incomplete, and gives strength to the martyr. God waited to show men His love until they knew their own need, but his love is from the beginning. Christian love is the response in man to this love of God, and its

---

[1] Theophilus ad Autolycum II. 14.

[2] ib. III. 30. σύμβουλον καὶ ἀῤῥαβῶνα, τῆς ἀληθείας

imitation by man; it is spiritual; Christians are the "soul of the world." The letter ends with a setting forth of the Christian Gnosis – the Logos, who is revealed in history to the world and is even now active in the Church and the souls of men, the Church wherein are united the power of knowledge and the power of life, sealed by the beauty of seemly worship and praise.

The style of this section of Apologetic literature does not call for much comment. It is simple, plain and straightforward, without pretence to adornment. They knew what they meant to say and said it. "ἑώς ὧδε ὁ πρὸς δέ μου λόγος, βασιλεῦ, ὁ ὑπὸ τῆς ἀληθείας ἐν τῷ νόί μου ὑπαγορευθείς."[1]

Those are the words of Aristides and they are typical of all. The surroundings and the purpose of these early apologists are so different from those of Origen that they can only be compared as archaic statues can be placed beside finished sculpture. They were Origen's predecessors, and he was the master, who went far to complete their first beginnings. They all strive in different ways to make clear the new knowledge, which Christ had given them of the character of God. The note of the letter to Diognetus is present in all. They are only just beginning dimly to feel their way to a philosophical statement of its truth; their apologies are more a vehement assertion that it is true, and a call to look upon the contrast of pagan religion and society. They do not give constructive teaching; their purpose is not

[1] Aristides, Ap. 17. ["Thus far, O King, extends my discourse to you, which has been dictated in my mind by the Truth." The story of the rediscovery of the text of the Apology of Aristides is complex. Mrs Pym is quoting from the version preserved in the Life of Barlaam and Josaphat – GPB]

primarily to make converts but to secure a bare foothold for their faith among thinking people. For Origen and those who came after was the task reserved of stating in the language of philosophy the fact (which had been certain in experience from the earliest days) of the Divinity of Christ, and the full content of the Christian idea of God. With Origen, apologetic could become aggressive, but Justin and the rest had fought its first battles.

From Carthage towards the end of the second century came the apology of Tertullian, unique as its author. Tertullian's personality left a vivid touch on everything he wrote, but he wrote nothing more brilliant than this short apology.[1] To mention him on the same page as Origen, is to suggest instantly antithesis and contrast; but, for the reason which Vincent de Lérins put into an oft-quoted sentence – nam sicut ille apud graecos, ita hic apud Latinos princeps[2] – the comparison is necessary. The city of Carthage was fiercer and more barbarous in its ways even than Alexandria of the many nations. The Roman element there was strong, and the spirit of African subjects of Rome was always passionate and even cruel. The story of the Carthaginian Church is a story of amphitheatres, wild beasts, and Roman legionaries; martyrs there were, as we know, in Alexandria too, but even martyrdom could not alter the pursuits of scholars and philosophers. Tertullian in his apology, as in his other writings is true to the character of his own city and church.

---

[1] cf. Jerome Ep. 83 [*sic.* Should be Ep. 70] quid Tertulliani eruditius, quid acutius? ["Can anything be more learned or more pointed than the style of Tertullian?" – GPB]

[2] ["For as he (Origen) holds by far the first place among the Greeks, so does Tertullian among the Latins" – GPB]

The argument falls into four main sections – a preface, a refutation of the chief accusations brought against Christians, a refutation of various minor points, a declaration that Christianity is not a school of philosophy.[1] In the preface Tertullian attacks the injustice, which does not even give Christians the advantage, accorded to ordinary tribunals, of being heard before they are condemned. Even the name of Christian is used as a charge; even the innocent are faced by unjust laws, enacted only by the worst emperors, while Romans who profess to honour so greatly the institutions of their ancestors, do not hesitate to repeal the laws, which are a barrier to luxury. People who accuse Christians, accuse us of "occulta facinora" and "manifestiora facinora".[2] Rumour alone vouches for these "secret horrors"; they are impossible to Christians, but you pagans commit them. "Haec in vobis esse si consideraretis, proinde in Christianis non esse perspiceretis."[3] The "open crimes" are sacrilege and disloyalty; the first is refuted and then counter-attacked by a statement of what Christian belief really is, and an onslaught on heathen gods. Christians do not worship heathen gods, because they were once mortal, have created nothing, commit crimes, and are dishonoured by their worshippers, who multiply their number, cheat them in their rites, laugh at them in literature and in the theatre, and commit sins in their temples, "nescio ne plus de vobis dei vestri quam de

---

[1] This outline is based on the analysis given in Bindley's edition.
[2] ["Secret crimes" and "open crimes" – GPB]
[3] Tertullian Ap. IX. (ad.fin.) ["If ye would consider that these things exist among you, ye would perceive forthwith that they exist not among the Christians" – trans. C. Dodgson, Library of the Fathers 1842, p.24.]

Christianis querantur. Certe sacrilegi de vestris semper apprehenduntur."[1]

There are certain erroneous statements about the God of the Christians: we do not worship an ass's head, but you worship all kinds of creatures: if we pay homage to the cross, well, so do you: supposing we worshipped the sun, we should only be like the Persians. At this idea of an "ass-born God" we laugh. In reality we worship one God, Creator of the Universe, invisible, incomprehensible, to Whom nature and the conscience of man bear witness. He, that we might draw nearer to Him, has sent us His written Word and teachers inspired by His Spirit. Our Scriptures are older than heathen writings: their divinity is quite plain: every day their prophecies are fulfilled. The Jews held Christ to be only a man; we acknowledge in Him the Incarnate Son of God, who lived a wonderful life and was crucified, as the prophets and He Himself foretold. He rose on the third day after His death and afterwards went up to Heaven. If He is really divine, no other religion can be true. There are evil spirits called daemons, who hinder men from knowing the true God. Your Gods are daemons, and they own it when a Christian adjures them in the name of Christ. So it is you, who are proved by your own gods to be irreligious. Everyone should have religious liberty. Christians alone are not allowed to worship their God. Your great empire is not the result of all your religious rites: it is prior to them. The One, True, Supreme God controls kingdoms that wax and wane. Therefore "pro fide conscientiae nostrae"[2] we will not sacrifice to gods, who

[1] ib. XV (ad.fin.) ["I know not whether your gods may not complain more of you than of the Christians. Certainly the committers of sacrilege are ever found to be of your party" ibid. p.35]

[2] ["on the strength of (i.e. on the basis of) our conscience" ibid. p.66]

are not gods. The daemons deceive you; but "illos nunquam magis detriumphamus quam sum pro fidei obstinatione damnamur."[1]

You say that we are disloyal to the emperor, but you honour him above your gods, so why sacrifice to them in his behalf? We pray for him to the True God who can alone answer prayer, and who is above all emperors. Our Scriptures bid us pray for kings and even persecutors. We do not desire the downfall of the empire, for then the end of all things will come. We swear by the safety, not the genius of the Emperor, for he holds his power under God. Therefore we honour him the more. The title "Lord" belongs only to God. We will not keep the emperor's festivals like the licentious mob. The disloyal are not Christians but men of your own religion. They are called Romans; we are denied the name, though we show kindliness to all. We never retaliate for our injuries, though we are numerous enough to do so. Our meetings are not seditious. We ought to be recognised by law.

There are some other objections to answer; our gatherings are not unseemly, but quiet and religious: all public disasters are not our fault: your idolatry causes them, while our prayers mitigate their severity: it is ridiculous to call us commercially profitless, for we have human needs; of course we cannot give to your gods and to the poor, nor encourage evil trades. You cause loss to the state by condemning so many innocent men, whose religion is the only moral force to support your laws. Though we have answered all charges and shown the goodness and truth of Christianity, you still

---

[1] ib. XXVII (ad. fin.) ["Never do we triumph over them more, than when we are condemned for steadfastness in our faith". ibid. p.68]

say we are only a school of philosophy. Why then do you not treat us as you treat philosophers – tolerantly? Really we differ from philosophers in wisdom and in purity of life. They have borrowed and corrupted the ideas of our scripture. You approve of their ideas (e.g. transmigration of souls), but torture us for teaching the resurrection of the body: yet it is a practical belief and innocent of evil. We are willing to suffer, for thereby Truth conquers. Continue, if you will, your injustice and cruelty to us. "Nec quicquam tamen proficit exquisitior quaeque crudelitas vestra; illecebra est magis sectae. Plures efficimur quotiens metimur a vobis; semen est sanguis Christianorum;... inde est, quod ibidem sententiis vestris gratias agimus. Ut est aemulatio divinae rei et humanae, cum damnamur a vobis, a deo absolvimur."[1]

No analysis can give the impression which Tertullian's arguments really produce, set forth in telling order, and hammered home with two and three-fold blows from his forceful Latin. All his training and skill as a lawyer Tertullian used in this apology; it may be named a defence, but it is a defence made effective on all sides by merciless attack. It is the relentless prosecution of an advocate, who is convinced, beyond any powers of argument, of the righteousness of his cause. The structure of the apology is close-knit and effective; the opponents' side is displayed in the worst possible light: all their objections are demolished

[1] ib. L. ["Nor yet doth your cruelty, though each act be more refined than the last, profit you anything. It is rather the allurement to our sect. We grow up in greater number as often as we are cut down. The blood of the Christians is their harvest seed... Therefore it is that we, at the same time that we are judged, thank you for your judgment. Such enmity is there between the things of God and the things of men; when we are condemned by you, we are absolved by God." ibid. pp.105-6.]

by double and treble arguments; their charges are made into a weapon for attack on themselves: "nec tantum refutabo quae nobis obiiciuntur, sed etiam in ipsos retorquebo, qui obiiciunt"[1] – and all the resources of sarcasm, epigram and balanced argument are employed with telling and deadly effect. The intricacy of cross-examination is applied to opponents, who can neither answer nor state their own objections in their own way; the force of the apology is irresistible. There is an example of clever argument in the very first chapter, where Tertullian is attacking ignorant pagan condemnation of Christians. "Quid enim iniquius quam ut oderint homines quod ignorant?... testimonium ignorantiae est... cum omnes qui retro oderant, quia ignorabant quale sit quod oderant, simul desinunt ignorare, cessant et odisse, ex his fiunt Christiani, utique de comperto et incipiunt odisse quod fuerant, et profiteri quod oderant, et sunt tanti quanti et denotamur. Obsessam vociferantur civitatem; in agris, in castellis, in insulis Christianos; omnem sexum, aetatem, condicionem, etiam dignitatem transgredi ad hoc nomen quasi detrimento maerent, nec tamen hoc modo ad aestimationem alicuius latentis boni promovent animos."[2] The argument is always pushed home till the

---

[1] ib. IV. ["I will… not only refute the charges which are brought against us, but even retort them upon the very men who bring them." ibid. p.10.]

[2] ib. I. ["For what more unjust than that men should hate that of which they know nothing… It is an evidence of that ignorance… when all, who aforetime hated because they were ignorant what it was which they hated, as soon as they cease to be ignorant, cease also to hate. From being such, they become Christians, to wit from conviction, and begin to hate what they were, and to profess what they hated, and are as numerous as indeed we are publicly declared to be. Men cry out that the state is beset, that the Christians are in their fields, in their forts, in their islands (perhaps = apartment blocks). They mourn, as for a loss, that every sex,

enemy is placed hopelessly and completely in the wrong. Here is another example. "Deos vestros colere desinimus ex quo illos non esse cognoscimus. Hoc igitur exigere debetis, uti probemus non esse illos deos, et idcirco non colendos, quia tunc demum coli debuissent, si dei fuissent, tunc et Christiani puniendi, et quos non colerent, quia putarent non esse, constaret illos deos esse. Sed nobis, inquitis, dei sunt. Appellamus et provocamus a vobis ad conscientiam vestram. Illa nos indicet illa nos damnet, si poterit negare omnes istos deos vestros homines fuisse."[1]

The statements are short and precise, but they are filled with vigour and the fire of hand-to-hand conflict. Tertullian delights in chiasmus and balanced phrases, in which the same words are repeated again and again. "Cogis negare, ut absolvas, quem non poteris absolvere, nisi negaverit."[2] "Quodsi, quia non debet, ideo non vultis licere, sine dubio id non debet licere quod male fit, et utique hoc ipso

---

age, condition and now even rank is going over to this sect. And yet they do not by this very means advance their minds to the idea of some good therein hidden." ib. pp.2-3]

[1] ib. 10 ["We cease to worship your gods from the time when we discover that they are no gods. This therefore ye ought to require, that we prove that they be no gods, and therefore not to be worshipped, because then only ought they to have been worshipped, if they had been gods. Then also ought the Christians to be punished, if it were proved that those are gods, whom they worshipped not, because they thought them not to be so. 'But to us,' ye say, 'they are gods.' We challenge this and appeal from yourselves to your conscience. Let that judge us; let that condemn us, if it shall be able to deny that all these gods of yours were men." ibid. p.25.]

[2] ib. II ["Thou compellest to deny that thou mayest acquit, whom thou wilt not be able to acquit, unless he deny." ibid. p.7]

praeiudicatur licere quod bene fit."[1] "Per quod ostenditur, dum a bonis maiorum institutis deceditis, ea vos retinere et custodire quae non debuistis, cum quae debuistis non custodistis."[2] "Ergo aut eruite, si creditis, aut nolite credere, qui non eruistis"[3] "Ex eo enim quod aliud a se coli decet quam colit, negat quod colit, et culturam et honorem in alterum transfert, et transferendo iam non colit quod negavit."[4] Even in the word-jingles there is the sensation of a hail of blows. The orator's gift of epigram is added to the arts of the lawyer, and such phrases as the following constantly give brief and vivid expression to Tertullian's thought. "Laudatis semper antiquitatem, et nove de die vivitis;"[5] "fiunt, non nascuntur Christiani"[6]; "tot igitur sacrilegia Romanorum quot tropaea"[7]; "cum damnamur a

---

[1] ib. IV. ["But if, because it ought not to be, therefore ye will not have it lawful, doubtless that ought not to be lawful, which is ill done, and surely it is, even hereby, already determined that what is well done is lawful." ibid. p.11.]

[2] ib. VI. ["By which it is manifest, that, while ye fall back from the good customs of your ancestors, ye retain and guard those things which ye ought not, while ye guard not those which ye ought." ibid. pp.16-17]

[3] ib. VII ["Wherefore either expose it, if ye believe it, or be unwilling to believe it, seeing ye have not exposed it." ibid. p.17.]

[4] ib. XXI cf. VIII (last sentence), X (hoc igitur exigere…) XXIV (end of sentence beginning "videte enim") ["For in that he saith that aught else is worshipped by him than that which he doth worship, he denieth that which he worshippeth, and transferreth his worship to another, and, in transferring it, he already ceaseth to worship that, which he hath denied." ibid. p.52.]

[5] ib. VI. ["Ye are ever lauding the ancients, yet fashioning your lives anew every day." ibid. p.16.]

[6] ib. XVIII ["Christians are made, not born such." ibid. p.41.]

[7] ib. XXV. ["As many therefore as are the trophies of the Romans, so many are their acts of sacrilege." ibid. p.65.]

vobis, a Deo absolvimur".[1] Latin in Tertullian's hands was moulded into an instrument for the mediaeval Church to use in worship as well as in controversy; yet, while he enriched it with new words and filled old words with a new meaning, he took from Latin none of the strength and dignity which had been its chief quality as long as there had been literature in Rome. The chapter, in which he speaks of Roman religion, is alone a sufficient proof. "Videte igitur, ne ille regna dispenset cuius est et orbis qui regnatur et homo ipse qui regnat, ne ille vices dominationum ipsis temporibus in saeculo ordinarit qui ante omne tempus fuit et saeculum corpus temporum fecit, ne ille civitates extollat aut deprimat sub quo fuit sine civitatibus aliquando gens hominum. Quod erratis? prior est quibusdam deis suis silvestris Roma, ante regnavit quam tantum ambitum capitolii extrueret. Regnaverant et Babylonii ante Pontifices, et Medi ante Quindecimviros, et Aegyptii ante Salios, at Assyrii ante Lupercos, et Amazones ante Virgines Vestales. Postremo si Romanae religiones regna praestant, nunquam retro Judaea regnasset despectrix communium istarum divinitatum, cuius et deum victimis et templum donis et gentem foederibus aliquamdiu Romani honorastis, nunquam dominaturi eius, si deo non deliquisset ultimo in Christum."[2] Although

---

[1] ib. L. ["When we are condemned by you, we are absolved by God." ibid. p.106.]

[2] ib. XXVI. ["See then whether He be not the Disposer of kingdoms, Whose is both the world which is ruled, and man himself who ruleth; whether He have not ordered the changes of dominions with their times, in the course of the world, Who was before all time, and made that world, the universe of times. See whether it be not he Who exalteth and putteth down states, under Whom the race of men once lived without states. Why do ye err? Rome in her rude state is more ancient than certain of her own gods; she reigned before so large a compass of Capitol

Tertullian complains of being allowed to defend his Faith only by the "occulta via tacitarum litterarum,"[1] the limitations of the written word are almost entirely transcended in his book. So much is the personality of the man and the orator flung into the words that we can almost see his gestures and hear his vehement appeal. The absolute conviction, which possesses him, makes his attack fierce and intolerant, but it is the fierceness which comes from the defence of a passionate love. It is always there, mercilessly driving home the point of an argument or adding strength to the declaration of what the faith really is. It flashes out sharp sarcasms, such as "hic tantum humana curiositas torpescit;"[2] "plane olim, id est semper, veritas odio est;"[3] it rages triumphantly through the indictment of heathen gods[4] and the Roman desertion of ancient laws;[5] it reaches the height of its power in the last chapter, when the victory of martyrdom is crowned with glory and eternal defiance is flung in the faces of these who persecute the pardoned of God.[6]

---

was erected. The Babylonians too reigned before the High Priests, and the Medes before the Fifteen, and the Egyptians before the Salii, and the Assyrians before the Luperci, and the Amazons before the Vestal Virgins. Finally, if the religious rites of Rome procure kingdoms, never would Judaea have reigned aforetime, that despiser of those common deities, whose God too ye Romans for some time honoured with sacrifices, and her temple with offerings, and her people with treaties: nor would ye ever have ruled over her, had she not at the last sinned against Christ." ibid., p.66]

[1] ib. I ["The secret way of silent writings" ibid. p.1]

[2] ib. I. ["Here alone is the curiosity of man dull" ibid. p.3]

[3] ib. XIV ["Verily, of old time, indeed at all times, truth is hated." ib. p.34.]

[4] ib. XIII.

[5] ib. VI.

[6] ib. L.

In the end, however, it is neither Tertullian's smashing rhetoric nor his vehemence of appeal, which gives life and lasting value to his apology; it is his own sincere and unwavering faith in Christ, his utter devotion to His service through and beyond death. He is full of the zeal of one, who has been in error and at last found the truth. "haec et nos risimus aliquando. de vestris sumus. fiunt, non nascuntur Christiani."[1] The spirit of his personal religion is the spirit of a soldier: "illos nunquam magis detriumphamus quam cum pro fidei obstinatione damnamus."[2] His confession of faith is final, and it shows how he was forced to be intolerant by the very greatness of the possession he had found in Christ. "Dicimus, et palam dicimis, et vobis torquentibus lacerati et cruenti vociferamur: 'Deum colimus per Christum.' illum hominem putate, per eum et in eo se cognosci et coli deus vult. Ut Judaeis respondeamus, et ipsi dominum per hominem Moysen colere didicerunt: ut Graecis occurram, Orpheus Pieriae Musaeus Athenis, Melampus Argis, Trophonius Boeotiae initiationibus homines obligaverunt: ut ad vos quoque dominatores gentium adspiciam, homo fuit Pompilius Numa qui Romanos operosissimis superstitionibus oneravit. Licuerit et Christo commentari divinitatem, rem propriam, non qua rupices et adhuc feros homines multitudini tot numinum demerendorum attonitos efficiendo ad humanitatem temperaret, quod Numa, sed qui iam expolitos et ipsa urbanitate deceptos in agnitionem veritatis ocularet. quaerite igitur si vera est ista divinitas Christi, si ea est qua cognita ad bonum quis reformatiur,

[1] ib. XVIII. ["These things we once laughed to scorn. We were of you. Christians are made, not born such." ibid. p.41.]

[2] ib. XXVII. ["Never do we triumph over them more, than when we are condemned for steadfastness in our faith." ibid. p.68.]

sequitur ut falsae renuntietur, comperta inprimis illa omni ratione quae delitiscens sub nominibus et imaginibus mortuorum quibusdam signis et miraculis et oraculis fidem divinitatis operatur."[1]

In the history of Christian apologetic both Tertullian and Origen can claim a distinguished place, but their contributions are as different in form and character as their own personalities and surroundings. Tertullian is ardent and intolerant, a Roman, a lawyer and a soldier; Origen is possessed of wide sympathy and intellectual understanding – a teacher, a scholar and a Greek. This is plain in their apologetic work; yet they are alike in that their apology is based on fundamental facts. "In both" says Pressensé, at the end of his vivid comparison of the two men, "we find perfect

[1] ib. XXI. ["We say, and we say openly, and while ye torture us, mangled and gory we cry out, 'We worship God through Christ:' believe Him a man: it is through Him and in Him that God willeth Himself to be known and worshipped. To answer the Jews, they themselves also learned to worship God through the man Moses: to meet the Greeks, Orpheus in Pieria, Musaeus at Athens, Melampus at Argos, Trophonius in Boeotia, bound mankind by their rites: to look to you also, the masters of the world, Numa Pompilius was a man, who loaded the Romans with the most burthensome superstitions. Let Christ also be permitted to pretend to the divine nature, as a thing proper to Himself, Who did not, as Numa, soften to a state of gentler culture rude and as yet barbarous men, by confounding them with so great a multitude of gods to be propitiated; but Who opened to a knowledge of the truth the eyes of men already polished, and blinded through their very refinement. See then whether this Divine Nature of Christ be real: if it be such that by the knowledge of it any one be changed unto that which is good, it followeth that any other, which is found to be contrary to it, must be pronounced false; specially that, by all means, which, hiding itself under the names and images of the dead, doth by certain signs, and miracles, and oracles, work out the proof of a divine character." ibid. pp.52-3.]

sincerity and an equal love to Christ and to truth. Hence their great influence in the Church."[1] Tertullian stands for the uncompromising puritan attitude towards paganism, and he left a brilliant expression of it in this apology.

Although the Protrepticus of Clement of Alexandria can hardly be called an apology, it has much in common with the apologists, and Clement's work and influence in themselves place him in the line of apologetic development. As head of the Catechetical School in Alexandria at the end of the second century, in lectures and in private discourse, he was not only defending but actively preaching the Gospel to educated and intellectual hearers. He carried on the work which Pantaenus, his master had begun; and to which Origen, his own pupil, added even greater fame.[2] A Greek himself, he knew Hellenism from the inside, and he had sympathy with men of Hellenic outlook and education, which gave him a special faculty for dealing with the perplexed of eclectic Alexandria. His own experience of paganism, followed by his conversion to Christianity, was the guide of many others, whose thought and education had run on similar lines; and who could lay hold on the Christian Gospel, when it was set forth by Clement. "Clement cannot have worked for long in Alexandria without being conscious that he might be of special service to men and women of a particular type... persons of Greek culture who were not wholly satisfied with paganism. They felt the claim and the hold of the ancient traditions. They were not unconscious that both from philosophy and from the mysteries a large

[1] Pressensé. *The Early Years of Christianity* (tr. Harwood) Vol. II pp.413-14. cf. Farrar. *Lives of the Fathers,* Vol. I. p.246.

[2] cf. Fairweather *Origen and Greek Patristic Theology* Chap. I, p.12. "It fairly harnessed secular science to the chariot of Christian apologetics."

measure of guidance and spiritual assurance might be gained. They were sufficiently sincere to be troubled rather than amused, by the abundant ridicule that had been poured upon the old mythology. But they were at rest neither in mind nor soul. They passed from one lecture room to another, as Justin had done, with a growing dissatisfaction, welcoming and debating each fresh theory of life they heard propounded, but adopting and retaining none. They had not infrequently come into contact with Christians. They had heard undoubtedly strange tales of this remarkable people. Sometimes they felt at a distance the beauty and attraction of the new religion, much as Pater's Marius felt them, with the difference that they were Greeks and he a Roman. But they only knew vaguely and indistinctly what Christianity had to offer, and no sufficient reason had yet been given them for leaving the old ways and committing themselves to this obscure track, which hitherto had been commonly avoided by the educated... It is to them that Clement's Protrepticus is addressed... It would hardly have converted a convinced pagan of the type of Celsus or Caecilius, but it may well have enabled many of the unsettled to take the decisive step."[1]

Clement won his converts not by answering objections so much as by a positive presentation of Christianity: the λογὸς προτρέπτικος πρὸς Ἕλληνας[2] is a book of this type with a definite missionary spirit. It opens with a typical preface, which tells of Amphion and other famous pagan minstrels, whose stories are only fables. "But let us bring down out of heaven above truth and fairest wisdom, and lead

[1] Tollington *Clement of Alexandria* Chap. VII. pp.210-11.

[2] ["Exhortation (Protrepticus) to the Greeks" – GPB]

them to the holy mount of God and to the holy choir of the prophets. And let truth, shedding abroad her light which shines afar, pour a flood of radiance on all, who everywhere are wallowing in darkness, and set men free from error, stretching forth her mighty hand, even the insight of wisdom, to save them. Let them bow the head and worship, let them leave Helicon and Cithaeron desolate and dwell in Sion – "for from Sion shall come out a law and a word of the Lord from Jerusalem" – a heavenly word, the true athlete, crowned in the amphitheatre of the whole universe. My Eunomus sings too, not the tune of Terpander... but the undying tune of the new harmony, whose name is the name of God."[1] Orpheus and all the others were deceivers and they led men to idols. "But my song is not like that[2]... Behold the mighty strength of the new song; out of stones, out of wild beasts it has made men."[3] By the Holy Spirit God set in tune the universe and especially man. "The instrument of God is full of love for man."[4] God saves us of His "Super-abundant goodness".[5] This purpose and new song of His were from the beginning; but though we erred, He saves us. Let us run to Him. "Yes, the Saviour has many voices and many ways for the saving of men."[6] Surely it is incredible that we should spurn the goodness of God, who is always appealing to us. Nothing is given to the unbelieving. First we must accept

[1] Clement, Protrepticus I. § 49-53.
[2] ib. I. §59.
[3] ib. I. § 63
[4] ib. I § 77 φιλάνθρωπον τὸ ὄργανον τοῦ θεοῦ.
[5] ib. I. § 77 ἐκ περιουσίας.
[6] ib. I § 89 πολύφονός γε ὁ Σωτὴρ καὶ πολύ τροπος εἰς ἀνθρωπων σωτηρίαν.

Christ, and He who has opened the shut door will reveal afterwards what is inside.

There is Clement's appeal that Christ should be put to the test; it is made in a Greek setting of music and choirs and victorious athletes, with a summons to the light of perfect truth; it is the appeal of Hellene to Hellene, but it ends in Christ. Next follows a long and fierce attack on the stories of heathen gods, showing their impiety, indecency and foolishness, and denouncing the power of daemons. Sacrifices to the gods are condemned as cruel; worship of tombs images and demons is only superstition "νυκτὶ μὲν ὑμῶν, εἰλύαται κεφαλαὶ..."[1] Images are ridiculous and impious, let no one worship the sun, but let him turn rather to the Maker of the sun. In these three chapters Clement sums up that part of paganism which must be utterly cast aside; next he turns to the philosophers and poets to show how to them was given "some dream of truth", but points on past them to the Hebrew prophets for right ideas of God. Philosophers make an idol of matter, but we can show that philosophy, in spite of deifying demons, "is dreaming of the truth."[2] Sometimes Plato and others hit the truth "by the inbreathing of God's spirit."[3] "And I pray thee, O philosophy; hasten to produce not only the one – Plato – but many others to confess the one God, who alone is really God, by His own Spirit, if they could lay hold on the truth."[4] The poets also – Aratus, Hesiod, Euripides, Sophocles, Orpheus – are witnesses of the truth, for they held right ideas

---

[1] Homer Od. XX. 351. ["From head to toe you are shrouded in darkness" – GPB]

[2] Clement, Protrept. V. § 29.

[3] ib. VI. § 75.

[4] ib. VI § 75.

of God and criticised mythology. "Euripides is indeed worthy to belong to the Socratic school, for he took his eyes off the theatre audience and fixed them upon truth."[1] "γραφὰι δὲ αἱ θεῖαι καὶ πολιτεῖαι σώφρονες σύντομοι σωτηρίας ὁδοί· γυμναὶ... τῆς ἐκτὸς καλλιφωνίας... ἀνιστῶσιν ἀγχόμενον ὑπὸ κακίας τὸν ἄνθρωπον, ὑπεριδοῦσαι τὸν ὄλισθον τὸν βιωτικὸν."[2] Then follow quotations from the prophets, declaring the true nature of God. "Sons of men how long will ye be slow of heart? Why do you love vanity and seek after a lie?"[3] Let us hasten to such a God as ours. ὤ τῆς ὑπερβαλλούσης φιλανθρωπίαις.[4] Not as a teacher to pupils, not as a master to servants, not as God to men, but like a father the Lord gently appeals to His sons "ἥκετε, ἥκετε, ὤ νεολαία ἡ ἐμη."[5] God is calling us always, for the grace of His promise is great, if "today we hear His voice". "And 'today' He shall increase day by day, until each day be called 'today'. And until we are complete and perfect, 'today' remains and the chance of learning: and then the real 'today' the eternal day of God, lasts on from age to age."[6] So let us hasten to salvation, so that we may come near to one another in one love. So the many, united in one, become one symphony following one choir-leader and teacher, the Word, resting in

---

[1] ib. VII § 27.
[2] ib. VIII § 37 ["The divine Scriptures and institutions of wisdom form the short road to salvation; devoid of… beauty of diction… they raise up humanity strangled by wickedness, teaching men to despise the casualties of life" – GPB]
[3] Ps. 4.3
[4] Clement Protrept. IX. § 59 ["O surpassing love for man!" – GPB]
[5] ib. IX § 60. ["Come, come, O my young people!" – GPB]
[6] ib. IX § 74

the same truth and crying "Abba Father." "This cry, if it be real and true God loves – His first reward of love from His sons."[1]

Such is the beautiful and touching appeal which Clement makes for the God and Father of all; and then he imagines his pagan friends objecting that, although this is a worthy philosophy, ancestral customs are strong and venerable too; can it be right to desert them? To this he answers by declaring with all the force and persuasiveness of which he is capable, the supreme value of God and of what Christ gives to men, ending with a challenge to choice and decision.

Custom makes you blind and deaf to the goodness of God, who of His great love comes to help man, like a mother-bird to a young one, who has fallen out of the nest. Who that may be a son of God prefers slavery? "It is a glorious risk to desert to the side of God."[2] Why do you hesitate? Leave your old ideas of darkness and superstition. "Nothing stands in the way of him who is eager for the knowledge of God... Christ can save everywhere."[3] Seek God and your souls shall live. "God looks on you as innocent children."[4] Keep His law and His power will work in you as He worked in Christ. Remember what God has given to us in Christ, light, life and wisdom to men in darkness and death. Let us look up to God in this hymn of praise: "Hail, O Light! For to us buried in darkness, locked up in the shadow of death, light has shone forth from heaven, purer than the sun, sweeter than our life here. That light is life everlasting;

---

[1] ib. IX § 94.

[2] ib. X § 18. Καλὸς ὁ κίνδυνος αὐτομολεῖν πρὸς θεὸν.

[3] In. X § 85-6 ἐμπόδων γὰρ ἵσταται οὐδὲν τῷ σπεύδοντι πρὸς γνῶσιν θεοῦ... ὁ Χριστός ἐστι πανταχοῦ σωτήριος.

[4] ib. X § 4.

whatever has partaken of it, lives. But night fears the light, and sinking down into terror, makes way for the day of the Lord. All has now become sleepless light and the setting of the sun has put trust in the rising. For this was the meaning of the 'new creation'. For the 'sun of righteousness', who drives His chariot over all, is present with all men equally, like His Father, who makes His sun rise on all and drops on them the dew of truth. He has changed sunset into sunrise, and through the cross turned death into life; having snatched man from destruction, he raised him to the skies, transplanting mortality into immortality, and translating earth to heaven – He, the husbandman of God,

Pointing out the favourable signs and
rousing the nations
To good works, putting them in mind
of the true livelihood,

giving us the truly great, divine and inalienable gift – the inheritance of the Father – deifying men by heavenly teaching, placing laws in their minds and writing them on their hearts. What laws does He write? 'That all shall know God from small to great', and 'I will be kindly to them' says God, 'and will not remember their sins.' Let us accept the laws of life, let us listen to God, when He calls to us; let us learn to know him that He may be gracious. And, though He needs it not, let as render to Him the recompense of thanksgiving... a kind of house-rent for our dwelling here."[1] Let the light shine in your hearts. The trumpet collects soldiers for war. Shall not Christ gather together His own soldiers, the soldiers of Peace? "The trumpet of Christ is the Good News of Him: He has sounded His trumpet, we have

[1] ib. XI § 35-41.

heard[1]... O What holy and happy power is this, whereby God lives with men[2]... Ah, how can I stir your hearts? I long for you to be saved. Christ desires it: in one word, He offers you a free gift of life."[3] Who is He? I will tell you briefly – Logos of Truth, Logos of incorruption, who regenerates man and brings him back to truth, the goad of salvation, who drives away destruction, who pursues death, who builds in men the temple of God that He may in men establish God. Therefore, cast aside your old errors and exert your will. Be initiated into the mysteries of heaven – join the choir of angels. Listen to Jesus, calling to everyone, Greeks and barbarians, to join the great harmony of the universe and take His easy yoke. Let us hasten, let us run, let us become lovers of God and win – God and life.

As are men's wishes, so are their words;
As are their words, so are their deeds;
And as their works, such is their life.

"Best in every way is the life of men, who know Christ."[4] Choose.

The very words of the Protrepticus are full of light and music – the light of perfect truth and the music of perfect harmony; to these Clement summons men, pointing to their source in the goodness and love of God. He is sure that the knowledge of God means life, separation from Him, death. Men who have strayed from Him are in darkness or are out of tune. Now God by His Logos has told men clearly that

---

[1] ib. XI. § 46. Σάλπινξ ἐστὶ Χριστοῦ τὸ Εὐαγγέλιον αὐτοῦ ὅ μὲν ἐπάλπισεν, ἡμεῖς δὲ ἠκούσαμεν.
[2] ib. XI. § 46.
[3] ib. XI. § 50.
[4] ib. XII. 90 Χριστὸς ὁ σύμπας ἀνθρώποις βίος τῶν Χριστὸν ἐγνωκότων.

"the music of God is love for men"[1] and "all has now become sleepless light."[2] The "Good News of Christ" is that "God lives with men".[3] There is no argument in the Protrepticus, nor did Clement intend any; his main purpose was to conquer indecision by showing the riches of God in Christ; he gave his own experience, graciously expressed and with all its gentleness, strong in a force driving to decision; for Clement is certain of his faith as Tertullian and the others are certain, even though he can see truth in paganism and had found it "a risk to desert to God."[4] He is sure there are "many ways"[5] to Christ, but the Christ to whom they lead is supreme; he finds truth in philosophy but only when it led men to the true God. Perhaps the greatest contribution he made to apologetic was his catholic outlook – his real belief in Christ as the complete fulfilment of the whole life of every man, and his consciousness of the harmony between God, the Universe and man "in the unity of the Spirit and the bond of peace", which rests in the unfathomable love of God. This is the thought of his "Hymn to Christ the Saviour", the last verse of which runs:–

> The Christ-born, the choir of peace,
> We, the people of His love,
> Let us sing, nor ever cease,
> To the God of peace above.[6]

So far then had the Church advanced in the realm of apologetic when Origen wrote his book: it now remains only

[1] ib. I § 77.
[2] ib. XI. § 35.
[3] ib. XI. § 46.
[4] ib. X. § 18.
[5] ib. I. § 89.
[6] Trans. Wilson

to estimate his own contribution, and, in doing so, it is necessary he remember that his world was the world of Clement and that the influence of the Catechetical School was strong.

CHAPTER VI
ORIGEN AS APOLOGIST

The first test to be applied to the work of any apologist is a simple and a fair one: did he answer the questions which were put to him, and is his answer satisfactory? This test, when applied to Origen, becomes complicated, because he is not arguing with Celsus face to face, but refuting him for men whose minds were accustomed to a milieu rather different from that of this patriotic Roman of the last century. It is not a large point, but it is worth remembering in any criticism of Origen's work: it is often the exigencies of polemic which are responsible for confused or exaggerated statements. There were many danger-points, open to attack, in ancient Alexandria, and Origen was sometimes forced into extremes, in order to win bare acceptation of a vital fact; it was an age too, when the exact meaning of terms was undefined and the expressions of theology were tentative rather than final. Equally, of course, some reasoning, which satisfied a third-century Alexandrian, is insufficient for the mind of a later age. Origen may be criticized in two ways in his apology – either in certain general principles or in certain definite answers.

The greatest cause of stumbling is probably his allegorical treatment of Scripture; he applies it on one occasion even to Plato,[1] identifying his meaning with a purely Christian interpretation after the manner of Philo himself.[2] It is hard to know how far figurative interpretation was satisfying to

---

[1] VI. 9.

[2] cf. VI. 21.

Origen's audience; he certainly carried it to an unnecessary extreme and allegorized where there was no need.[1] Probably, however, Alexandria would not criticize him for this; he is more open to blame, when he replies to Celsus' charge that the Old Testament stories are disgraceful and the allegories made to explain them even worse, by retorting that heathen mythology and its explanations are worse still.[2] The "Tu quoque"[3] argument is no more than a momentary silencing of an opponent, even if it is that. There is a similar weakness in the evasion of reply to Celsus' attack on Moses; I think Moses knew more of God than Plato, affirms Origen, but if Celsus ask me for my reasons I shall first demand that he give proofs for his unsupported assertions.[4] Again, throughout his refutation of that part of the treatise in which Celsus speaks in the person of a Jew, Origen seems to avail himself almost excessively of arguments, which would be fully convincing only to a believing Jew;[5] at the same time, he loses no opportunity of pointing out that the Jew of Celsus is not true to life, either in opinions or statements, which is practically an admission that Celsus himself is behind the Jew's arguments – unanswered. It may be urged that Celsus in using the literary device of the Jew laid himself open to attack on the ground whither he had ventured, so that in the interests of polemic Origen's treatment of that section of the book may be justified.

Sometimes Origen's eagerness to speak to Hellenes as a Hellene leads him into arguments which are at variance with

---

[1] e.g. IV. 40-51, 87. VI. 21.
[2] IV. 48.
[3] ["you are just as bad" – GPB]
[4] I. 19 (ad. fin.)
[5] e.g. I. 43, II. 54.

or at least weaken other statements. He quotes the myth of Er from Plato[1] and gives other examples of pagan heroes, who are said to have come back to life, as parallels to the story of Christ's resurrection; yet elsewhere he affirms the far stronger defence that Christ's death and resurrection are unique both in history and in moral influence.[2] The defence of the Virgin birth to Greeks who do not accept Jewish prophecy, is based on similarly dangerous ground.[3]

In a treatise composed on this principle of question and answer without any summing up or systematic presentation of teaching, it was easy for Origen to use arguments and terms in one place, which do not entirely accord with his statements in others – especially as theological language was at the time so undetermined. When he is replying to the charge of Celsus that Christians worship two Gods and exalt Jesus above the Father, he declares that he does not agree with those[4] who say with headlong rashness that the Saviour is the most High God, and quotes Jesus' words, "The Father who sent me is greater than I":[5] herein he seems to lay himself open to the accusation of subordinating one Person of the Trinity to another, but he has stated quite clearly, only two chapters before, the relationship of the Son to the Father in terms which cannot admit question. He quotes "I and my Father are one,"[6] continuing "if anyone shall be disturbed by these words, thinking I am deserting to those who deny that the Father and Son are two persons, let him consider the

[1] II. 16.
[2] II. 56.
[3] I. 37.
[4] VIII. 14.
[5] John 14.28.
[6] John 10.30.

words ‘and the multitude of them that believed were of one heart and of one soul’,[1] that he may grasp the meaning of ‘I and my Father are One’. One God then we worship – the Father and the Son.”[2]

There is sometimes an ambiguity in Origen’s language about the Incarnation, which almost implies a manifestation of God in man, which was not actual but dynamic; there is the kind of haziness which was liable to creep into a philosophy surrounded by docetic theories. On the other hand, his main belief and statement is quite definite:[3] God in Jesus really shared human life, and Jesus was perfectly man[4] as well as the Logos and Truth of the Father. Origen will not let go of the facts, though he cannot always give a satisfying philosophical explanation to Celsus.[5]

There are some passages where the answer seems confused or inadequate whereas a clear and sufficient answer is given later in another connection. In one chapter there seems very little answer to Celsus’ confusion of the power of Jesus with the power of daemons,[6] but there is no lack of decision in the defence given in the next book:[7] the same applies to Celsus’ question about the comparative lateness of

---

[1] Acts 4.32.

[2] VIII. 12. cf. Prat. Op. cit. Liv.I. Chap. 2 p.28. “la réfutation des unitaires lui fit donner tant de relief à la distinction des Personnes divines qu’il parut parfois les diviser ou ne les unir qu’en les subordonnant.” [“(The need) to refute Unitarians caused him to place such emphasis on the difference between the divine Persons that he sometimes appears to divide them – or to unite them only by subordinating them.” – GPB]

[3] IV. 18.

[4] VII. 16.

[5] VII. 13.

[6] I. 6.

[7] II. 49-51.

the Incarnation.[1] There are occasions also, when Origen gives at length theories about the nature of names[2] or the distribution of lands,[3] which are partially based on interpretation of the Bible and would not have commended themselves to Celsus; they seem sometimes obscure and irrelevant to the matter in hand, but this, as it has been suggested, is probably the mark of the teacher who has in his mind a special audience of students.

If we admit that Origen did not answer all the statements in Celsus' treatise, we are only admitting that he was a man and not an automatic machine; if we accuse him of ambiguous language and conflicting ideas, we are only showing once again that he lived not only in an age of eclecticism and confusion, but of life, combat and growth. The apology of Origen is so adequate and so great that criticism of points in it seems almost an impertinence, but the fact that small parts are ineffective cannot loosen the sure foundations of the whole. In the last chapter Origen does not claim to have answered all the questions completely; he has said as much as he can, and now let the reader judge between him and Celsus and say which of them breathes most of the spirit of the true God, of the way to worship Him and of truth.[4] There are a number of questions to which no final and complete answer can be given; when the apologist is met by those questions, his only honest course is to admit their difficulty and help the puzzled to face them with a larger outlook and deeper knowledge, by giving them a wider and greater understanding of the ways and character of God. This

[1] IV. 8-9 cf. VI. 78.
[2] I. 24-5, IV. 33-5, V. 45-6.
[3] V. 29-32.
[4] VIII. 76.

is the path which Origen follows, when he deals with the problem of evil; he points out the superhuman difficulties in the way, but also he makes it clear that there are facts about God, which lift man to a secure position, wherein he may live facing this and other questions, though he cannot give a complete philosophical explanation of them.[1] There are two words, frequently recurring all through the Reply to Celsus, which sum up in themselves Origen's attitude on this point – οἰκονομία and φιλανθρωπία;[2] they are the essence of his belief about the universe and God; they combine belief in the all-wise power and will, which control and guide all things, with certainty of the character of this power – love to man; the Universe is not a fixed, unchanging system: but is full of the boundless possibilities of "the will that can";[3] God cares always for rational beings and the Universe is governed with allowance for their free-will. Augustine's words "natura rerum, voluntas Dei"[4] are joined with "God so loved the world that He gave His only Son". Origen, therefore, answered questions when there was an answer; but above and beyond his answers he led the perplexed up to a sure stronghold whence they could contemplate even the maze of Alexandrian thought unafraid, and fight with fresh strength the difficulties which beset them.

The positive side of Origen's apologetic is even more important than his defence pure and simple; for, by his attitude and qualities he made a new and lasting contribution

---

[1] cf. Carnegie Simpson, *The Facts of Life* p.91. "While a final philosophy of sin, from its very terms, is impossible, a theodicy in face of sin may be possible; and it is this which faith is entitled to require."

[2] [i.e. "arrangement" ('economy'); "love of humankind" – GPB]

[3] cf. IV. 64, 99, V. 21, 23-4, VI. 78-9, VII. 26.

[4] ["God's will constitutes the nature of things" – GPB]

to the Christian Church. The permanent significance of Origen's work is seen to be the more remarkable in the present century because of conditions which prevail both in the East and the West, combining to produce an extraordinary resemblance to the first few centuries of the Christian era. It is not a repetition of history, for there are countless fresh forces at work and streams of fresh knowledge flowing, which place the twentieth century at its full distance from the third; it is a renewing of the story of man's experience of life and of his search for God through ages of ebbing and flowing civilisation; a renewing also of the upheaval which comes when ancient civilisation meets the Christian Gospel, which in spite of the centuries, merits the word given by Plutarch to the Acropolis sculpture – "a soul that knows not age."

It is in the East and especially in India that this parallel to ancient Alexandria is so apparent. It is a parallel which can be drawn in great detail, but only a few outstanding characteristics are relevant here. What links can there be between the Alexandrian Origen and the modern Indian? Both possess the inheritance of a long and composite religious development, holding within its bounds the heights of philosophic speculation, the raptures of mysticism and the sternness of asceticism, yet reaching down also to depths of idolatry, daemon-worship and degrading superstition. To both comes the Gospel of Jesus Christ, and there follows revolution and the whirl of a struggle for re-adjustment. It was amid this struggle that Origen lived; Indians are living in it now. In both centuries the preaching of Christianity has had the same result – a two-fold result, for it has aroused both sympathy and antagonism, though even in opposition the influence of the Personality of Jesus is evident. When men's eyes are turned to Him, He becomes (sometimes almost without their acknowledgment} their standard, if not their ideal, and by Him they test their religious, moral and social life.[1] So when ancient paganism and modern Hinduism came under that searchlight, the first instinct was an instinct for reform, reform both of social customs and idolatrous worship. The reform took two lines: on one side the reformers adopted much of the teaching of Jesus, reverencing Him as a great Master; on the other, there was definite hostility, though the principles of reform showed the influence of Christianity. Even if Jesus was revered as an ethical example, philosophy, whether Platonist or Brahman, refused to accept the story of the Cross; it is incredible to Eastern as it was to Hellenic speculation that God should really share the suffering life of man. Therefore, as eclecticism was the mark of philosophy in the third century and as it has always marked the history of Hinduism, as eclecticism was applied to the Christian Faith, and such parts only as fitted in with preconceived ideals were accepted and adapted: its absolute claim made enemies of its adherents even where some of their teaching was approved.

In Alexandria there arose Gnosticism, in some of its forms oriental, in some Hellenic, sometimes very near to Christianity, sometimes with the Christian element almost entirely lost, perplexed with the problem of dualism, concerned with philosophy rather than religion, and running riot in strange and wild cosmogonies, which have an affinity with the Puranas of Hinduism. In Alexandria too arose neo-

---

[1] cf. "Keshub Chunder opened his heart to the Christian spirit, and it begat a sense of sin and the spirit of earnest prayer." *History of the Brahma Samaj* by Siva Nath Sastri, I. 133. Quoted by Farquhar, *Modern Religious Movements in India,* p.60.

Platonism, “the summary or concentrated expression”,[1] as Caird calls it, of Hellenic philosophy, influenced by Philo and his school and the very crown of eclecticism. There was a good deal of common ground between neo-Platonism and Christianity – so much that Porphyry finally wrote a book to show Christianity, as he accepted it and as he vehemently wished it to be understood. Yet, in spite of the great agreement, the dividing line was definite.[2] Augustine put it simply and conclusively. “For that before all time and above all time Thy only-begotten Son abideth unchangeable and co-eternal with Thee, and that of His fulness all souls receive, in that they may be blessed, and that by participation of Thy eternal wisdom they may be renewed in order that they may be wise – this is there. But that in due time He died for the ungodly; that Thou sparedst not Thy only Son, but delivered Him up for all – this is not there.”[3] Further, the doctrines of neo-Platonism appealed only to the philosopher; he and he only could reach the highest good; Christianity is the Gospel for every man. In spite of its lofty idea of one God, the revival of all the spiritual force in paganism could only explain and justify the polytheism of the multitude, and it found a place also for magic and all kinds of occult superstition. The longing of men for an incarnate life, who should reveal to them God, was answered by the neo-Platonists in the deification of Apollonius of Tyana, whose history is often described as the Gospel story revised to suit neo-Platonists; but the revised Gospel did not satisfy wholly, because the facts which it omitted are true facts of human

[1] Caird, *The Evolution of Theology in the Greek Philosophers*, Lecture, 23.

[2] Elsee. *Neo-Platonism in relation to Christianity.* pp.91ff.

[3] Aug. Conf. VII. 9.

experience. The pagan or semi-pagan revival of religion in the early centuries could not live long, for it was stimulated by life borrowed from its new foe.

In India throughout the nineteenth century there has been a similar revival of ancient religion and reform of ancient customs, extending through many sects and varieties of Hinduism and Mohammedanism. The first movement came from the influence of Christianity and western education. Ram Mohan Ray, "the pioneer of all living advance, religious, social and educational, in the Hindu community during the nineteenth century,"[1] founded the Brahma Samaj, a society which has vigorously attacked idolatry and caste and stood for a radical policy of social reform. Other societies and groups have sprung from this movement, but they have all been imbued with the same spirit – the most progressive movements in India. It is notable that Ram Mohan Ray[2] and other later leaders[3] were strongly influenced by the teaching and personality of Christ. Once again there is eclecticism; it is His ethics and His example

[1] Farquhar, op. cit. p.29.

[2] "The consequences of my long and uninterrupted researches into religious truth has been that I have found the doctrines of Christ more conducive to moral principles, and better adapted for the use of rational beings, than any other which have come to my knowledge." Quoted by Farquhar. op. cit. p.32.

[3] "Christ has been my study for a quarter of a century. That God-Man – they say half God and half man – walks daily all over this vast peninsula, from the Himalayas to Cape Comorin, enlightening and sanctifying its teeming millions. He is a mighty reality in Indian history. He is to us a living and moving spirit. We see him and commune with him. He permeates society as a vital force, and imbues our daily life, and is mixed with our thoughts, speculations and pursuits." Keshab Chandra Sen [=Keshub Chunder Sen; both spellings are recognized – GPB]. Lectures in India, 330. Quoted by Farquhar, op. cit. p.61.

that are adopted. This vigorous spirit of reform provoked a reaction in orthodox Hinduism, and many movements have arisen to defend either partially (like the Arya Samaj), or completely (like Ramakrishna Paramahamsa and the Theosophists) the whole system of ancient Hindu religion. Ramakrishna held Celsus' doctrine that a man should follow the religion wherein he was born, whence he advanced to the position that all religions are essentially the same.[1] His disciple, Svami Vivekananda, taught the duty of devoted service of India, but the general effect of defence of the old faith is not the arousing of enthusiastic self-sacrifice and devotion. The extraordinary mixture of occultism, magic, fraud and religious syncretism found in the Theosophical movement, which stands for modern education and yet defends the most degrading forms of animism, only finds its parallel in the varied beliefs and cults of the first few centuries after Christ. There is esoteric teaching, corresponding to the mysticism of neo-Platonists, limited only to the elect; there is the Theosophical expectation of a new Incarnation, and there is the old docetist belief that Christ only dwelt in semblance in the human body of Jesus. Even more strong than any of these definite attempts to rehabilitate Hinduism is the vigorous Spirit of Nationalism, which is ever growing, especially among the educated, throughout India. This newly-awakened self-consciousness and desire for unity shows itself in a longing to serve India and a passion for all things Indian. So Christianity is called a foreign faith, and even as the Greeks quoted Plato of old, so the Hindu sages are quoted to show that all Christ's teaching is really Indian.

[1] cf. Farquhar. op. cit. p.198.

It is impossible in this space to make the picture more than sketchy, but detail only elaborates still further the main facts. There are in India, students like the students who filled the University of Alexandria, students who wander as Justin and Tatian, as Clement and Porphyry and as the founder of the Arya Samaj himself wandered, seeking for a teacher, who could help them and finding none. Round them is an atmosphere no less perplexing than that of the third century, and indeed for them the path has become even more difficult and complex, because the centuries have awakened them with a crash of new knowledge, and modern science and materialism have struck them with overwhelming force. The way to Christ is made hard for them (as it was not made hard in the third century) by the inconsistent lives of so-called Christians and the failure of so-called Christian civilisation. Finally their own seeking spirits and the spirits of many outside the student community, are quickened into a still deeper sense of need, when they look at India and her need of their service. Their mind is reflected in these words of a non-Christian Indian, a leading thinker, who says, "We are all feeling now the need of a new religious impulse, if the national movement is to go forward. The heart of India is eternally religious and cannot understand anything unless it is stated in religious terms... But what this new religion will be, which will hold India together, we cannot even imagine. Hinduism can never do it. Islam cannot either. No mere eclectic religions, such as Theosophy, can help us. You will probably say that Christianity is the supreme religion of the future, and we in India are looking anxiously towards it as they are also in Japan. But the Christian religion in its present outward aspect does not greatly attract us; though its teaching as seen in the Sermon on the Mount is very beautiful and thoroughly 'Indian'. We are really waiting, expecting, hoping, for the new religious impulse to come."[1] Here is the modern ache of ancient Alexandria, and the search for a power which can give spiritual impulse to a nation is true also of China and Japan.[2]

When we turn from the East to the West, there seems at first sight to be not even a fanciful connection between modern Europe and the days of Origen. Yet what is true of the East is true also, of the West, though there is no such obvious parallelism of conditions and thought. It manifests itself in the seeking for a fuller life, for a power which will endure and can control the vast, unmanageable forces of material civilisation; it manifests itself also, not only in a seeking – which is fundamentally the longing for the eternal, but also in an attitude to Christianity, which is a mixture of reverence for its Founder, dislike of its forms and recognition of its ethics as supreme. There is the same eclectic tendency abroad; people (to use their own words) "honour Christ's teaching, but cannot accept the Christian dogmas" and frequently these are people with a great passion for social reform and a spirit of self-sacrifice. So far there is a life running through and uniting the ages. What is the value of Origen's defence? Has he anything in common with the

[1] Quoted by C.F.Andrews – *The Renaissance of India,* pp.22-3.

[2] "The fatal defect of the teaching of the great sages of Japan and China is that while they deal with virtue and morals they do not sufficiently dwell on the spiritual nature of man, and a nation that neglects the spiritual, though it may flourish for a time, must eventually decay. The origin of modern civilisation is to be found in the teachings of the sage of Judaea, by whom alone the necessary moral dynamic is supplied." Count Okuma - Japanese Premier.

modern apologist, be he Indian or Western? There are here and there in the Reply to Celsus phrases which might almost have come from a man facing Asia or Europe in this century; "I see that much of my teaching about a sound life the enemies of the faith teach also", or in the chapter where he points to the unifying influence of the Roman Empire as the very call for a universal Gospel, in tones which have the same ring as the modern challenge of a world united by Marconi and commerce. It is not however on chance phrases that Origen's significance as apologist is based.

The first element of his efficiency is the fact that he united with personal experience of Christianity, the conviction of the necessity of hard and deep thinking; he knew that no student could attempt to give reasons for his faith, unless he gave the best of his energy and thought to its service. It counted greatly towards Origen's value as apologist that he was also a strenuous theologian. Not only did he affirm his own personal faith,[1] not only did he identify himself with his audience ("we who have been converted from paganism")[2], but also he reminded them to use their minds. "But if some people are lazy and do not train themselves to concentrate on the reading of God's books and to 'search the scriptures', and according to Jesus' command, to seek the meaning of the Scriptures and to ask God about them, and to keep on knocking at the parts of them which are shut, the Word is not therefore void of Wisdom."[3] The study of the Bible was the main instruction given at the Catechetical School, whose principles were the source of all Origen's apologetic work, and he took this as the central

---

[1] II. 8, 42.
[2] II. 1.
[3] VI. 7.

point, alike for faith and wisdom. The tradition of the School and his own personality and gifts formed Origen into as strong an apologist as occasion could demand.

The characteristics of his apologetic are two-fold, and may be summed up in a phrase which he applied to the Church – καθολίκη καὶ ἀποστολίκη [1] – a phrase which has lost the striking contrast of its wide claim through its constant verbal repetition.[2] The catholic claim of Jesus Christ – His universal significance for man in every branch of life, His vital relation to the cosmos throughout and before history – found its expression to Greek minds in the doctrine of the Logos, the Mind and Rational Principle inseparable from the Word of God. It was an affirmation of the universal supremacy of Christ, like Paul's words in the Colossians,[3] wherein he calls Him the "first-born" of all creation, centring in His personality the life and existence of all things; the passage rings with the emphasis on the word "αὐτος"[4] and sweeps on to the saving work of Christ on the Cross and in the Resurrection. He who is the reason of the Universe, is also the Saviour of all men. Origen held this "catholic" view of the Gospel with remarkable clearness, without restricting the power and work of Jesus to a narrow idea of the word Logos. He calls the Son of God, Who became incarnate,

---

[1] ["catholic and apostolic" – GPB]

[2] Migne P.G. and DXVII col. 225, cf. Prat. Op. cit. Bk.I, chap. 2 p.22. "expression heureuse que le symbole de Nicée consacre en l'adoptant." ["a happy expression which the Creed of Nicaea hallowed by adopting it".– GPB]

[3] Col. 1.15-18.

[4] ["He" – the pronoun is not always necessary in Greek, and may be emphatic when expressed – GPB]

"πρεσβύτατον πάντων τῶν δημιουργημάτων;"[1] he says that Jesus is absolute reason, absolute wisdom, absolute righteousness, absolute truth,[2] God the Logos, who reveals the Father,[3] and the Logos is ruler of the universe,[4] in Christ is found the sum of the life of the universe as well as the life of man.

He "Is of all things fair
That shall be and that were
The sum and very truth".

Therefore Origen looks with wide appreciation on wisdom, truth and holiness wherever they are found; God's Logos in every generation is in pure souls, whatever their nation or religion.[5] "God has written on the hearts of men their sense of duty."[6] Since he was a Hellene and speaking to Hellenes, his appreciation is expressed chiefly of the writings of the philosophers, and above all of Plato. Gregory has recorded his wide, unbiased reading of all philosophy,[7] and Origen himself says that there is harmony to a certain extent between Christianity and philosophy,[8] and that if teaching is true and sound, it matters not to whom it is given, Greek, Jew or Christian.[9] He approves of Plato and other Greeks, bearing witness of certain Greek philosophers that they knew God.[10]

---

[1] V. 37. ["the most ancient of all the works of creation" – GPB]
[2] V. 39, cf. III. 81. VIII.9.
[3] VII. 41-2.
[4] VIII. 33-4.
[5] IV. 3-4.
[6] I. 4-5.
[7] Gregory Sec. XIII.
[8] VII. 59.
[9] IV. 81.
[10] IV. 30, 48, V. 15, VI. 3-4, cf. VII. 46-7.

This recognition of "the light that lighteneth every man" leads Origen to find in the ideas of pagan religion the hope of their fulfilment in Christ. Pagans have believed in immortality,[1] and certain heathen nations have recognised a virtue in the death of one who died voluntarily for all.[2] This thought has been nourished to a stronger growth by modern research into the history of religions. The Catholic Christ in whom Origen found the crown of Hellenism, centuries later is claimed as the fulfilment of Hinduism. "He comes to fulfil and perfect that religion of communion for which India has been panting, as the hart panteth after the water-brooks. Yea, after long centuries shall this communion be perfected through Christ."[3] In the epistle to the Colossians Paul passes on from the relation of Christ to the cosmos to the relation of Christ to men, which leads him at once to exclaim that in Him there is neither Greek nor Jew, barbarian nor Scythian;[4] and it is true that the Epistle to the Ephesians, which is full also of the catholic view of Christ, is the great epistle of the church universal, wherein all though diverse are made one. So we find in Origen also a vision of the Church and the Kingdom of God, which reaches to the ends of the earth. The "many nations" come to the light, which has shone forth in

---

[1] III. 81.
[2] I. 31.
[3] Kashab Chandra Sen *Lectures in India* 258 – quoted by Farquhar op. cit. p. 62. cf. Rudra - *Christ and modern India*, "If Christ becomes the object of the contemplation and love of India, who can place any limit to the assimilation of His Life and Spirit... To India would come at last in Christ that centre of unity which it so surely needs. India's children would gain in Christ the full fruition of their new-found national consciousness. A great Indian church would become possible; and therefore a great Indian Nation."
[4] Col. 3.11.

the last days in Jesus Christ;[1] God is "lord of all the languages of the earth;"[2] His word shall spread forth from Judaea through all the world;[3] All the barbarians shall obey it; every other religion shall perish and the religion of Christians alone shall prevail.[4] Origen's universal vision finds its reflection in the thought of many modern minds, as it is expressed by a modern apologist:– "The revival awaiting the Church may be one in which men shall turn again to Christ, saying not only – though this will ever be with the other – that He and He only is the Saviour of their souls, but that He and He only is the Saviour of the world."[5]

That is one aspect of Origen's apologetic – its "catholic" aspect: but the faith he defended was not only catholic but apostolic, and it was in the preaching of the apostles that the Greeks found "foolishness". Origen's apologetic has also its "apostolic" side, and on it he lays the utmost emphasis. He stood firmly by two claims which are interdependent – no man can be eclectic with Christianity; the Christian Gospel is unique, final and complete. In spite of his broad mind and appreciation of truth wherever he found it, he would make no compromise with paganism nor abate at all the claim of the Christian Gospel. The crux of the matter lay in the question as to what that Gospel was; it was not a system of ethics or of speculative philosophy, not primarily even a religion of high ideals. After Pentecost when the apostles began to tell the "good news", their first preaching was not the Sermon on the Mount nor any of the precepts of Jesus;

---

[1] V. 33.
[2] VIII. 37.
[3] V. 50, cf. II. 13.
[4] VIII. 68.
[5] Carnegie Simpson op. cit. p.268.

they told the story of His life among them, of His crucifixion and of how God raised Him up and through Him "loosed their sins". They preached the life of God incarnate in a Person, and the account of the early days given in the Acts shows plainly that the theological doctrines of later years are rooted firm in the central experience of the apostles. Therefore, with all his love of Plato, Origen would not give way one inch to alterations of the Gospel made to suit Hellenic ideas.[1] Christ must be supreme even over ancestral law and custom; if the law of a man's city conflicts with the standard of God's righteousness, he must abandon it, even though the cost be death and dishonour.[2] Origen knew how hard it was for a pagan to cut himself free from the worship of daemons, just as it is hard for the Hindu to abandon idolatry and caste; but he refused any compromise with eclecticism.

The claim that Christ must be all in all is finally based on His uniqueness; "Jesus Christ is the only Son of God who visited the human race."[3] Celsus points to poets and philosophers; can he show anyone to compare with Jesus?[4] He is unparalleled in human history and human experience.[5] So Tertullian's firm hold on the Gospel and Clement's catholic view of the Saviour with many voices and many ways, Origen united in apologetic which was strong by the very contrast of its twofold character.

---

[1] cf. Lawson *Modern Greek Folk Lore and Ancient Greek Religion* introd. for the compromise which Christianity actually made in Greece.
[2] V. 37.
[3] VI. 11.
[4] VII. 41.
[5] I. 29, cf. III. 81.

ORIGEN AS APOLOGIST

Origen is remarkable both for the breadth of view and sound basis of his apology proper, but his constructive teaching is an even greater contribution to the history of Christianity.[1] The surest test of his work is his fulfilment of the obligation which lies on every Christian apologist, to remove all obstacles which enemies and friends alike set up to block their knowledge and understanding of Christ. No man of any nation has yet been able fully to express Christ; He has risen above and beyond them all; but a man is able to make the road to Him clear, that He may be found even of them that sought Him not, and that all, whether friend or foe, may face squarely the question "What think ye of Christ? Whose Son is He?" The most permanent value of Origen's apology endures in his simple words; "Go back now with your mind to Jesus;"[2] and in this age so strangely like Origen's own there comes a confirming comment alike from the East and the West. "In Him the Living Person, and not in writings, however sacred; in Him, the Living Person, and not in any philosophy or system, lies the key to India's future."[3] "If an agnostic would be honest, he must spend some serious days at Caesarea Philippi; after that, he may be an agnostic – if he can."[4]

---

[1] IV. 1. VIII. 1.

[2] II. 13.

[3] Rudra, *Christ and Modern India.*

[4] Carnegie Simpson *The Fact of Christ,* p.14.

BIBLIOGRAPHY[1]

Schwartz und Mommsen	Eusebius Werke
Trollope	Justini Apologia prima and Justini Dialogus cum Tryphone
Vopiscus	Vita Saturnini.
Walford	Epistle to Diognetus.

Ante-Nicene Christian library (Translations of the Fathers – ed. Roberts and Donaldson)

Justin Martyr and Athenagoras.
Tatian.
Theophilus.
Clement of Alexandria
Origen
Tertullian

Select Library of Nicene and Post-Nicene Fathers (ed. Wace and Schaff).

Vol. I Eusebius

II . General.

Andrews	The Renaissance in India
Aubé	Histoire des persécutions de l'église
Avesque	Origène envisagé comme apologète
Bardenhewer	Geschichte der Altkirchlichen Literatur
Bevan	Indian Nationalism.
Bigg	The Christian Platonist of Alexandria. Neo-platonism.

[1] *Note: The typescript of Mrs Pym's thesis was somewhat damaged at this point, and one or more pages of bibliography are missing.*

The Church's task in the Roman Empire.

Buhl — La polémique de Celse contre le Christianisme

Caird — The Evolution of Theology in the Greek Philosophers.

Cairns — Christianity in the modern World.

Capes — University life in Ancient Athens.

Croiset — Histoire de la littérature grecque, Vol. V.

Cruttwell — A Literary History of early Christianity. Vols I and II.

Cumont — Les Religions Orientales.

Denis — De la philosophie d'Origène

Dill — Roman society from Nero to Marcus Aurelius

Donaldson — Church Life and Thought in N. Africa.

Drummond — Philo Judaeus.

Elsee — Neoplatonism in relation to Christianity.

Fairweather — Origen and Greek Patristic Theology.

Farquhar — The Crown of Hinduism.
Modern religious movements in India.

Farrar — Lives of the Fathers.

Foakes-Jackson — Christian Difficulties in the Second and Twentieth Centuries.

Gibbon — The Decline and Fall of the Roman Empire. (ed. Bury) Vols I and II.

Glover — The conflict of Religions in the early Roman Empire.

Gwatkin — Early Church History.
The Church Past and Present.

Hatch — The Influence of Greek Ideas and Usages upon the Christian Church (Hibbert Lectures 1888).

BIBLIOGRAPHY

Harnack	The Expansion of Early Christianity.
	History of Dogma Vols I and II.
Hastings	Encyclopaedia of Religion and Ethics. Art. *Demons*.
Kayser	La philosophie di Celse
Keim	Celsus Wahres Wort.
Kingsley	Historical Lectures and Essays
Lehmann	Die Katechenschule zu Alexandria.
Mahaffy	The Greek world under Roman Sway.
Mansel	Gnostics
Merivale	History of the Romans under the Empire.
Milne	A History of Egypt. Vol.V.
Mommsen	The Provinces of the Roman Empire Vol II
Patrick	The Apology of Origen.
Pélagaud	Étude sur Celse.
Petrie	Personal Religion in Egypt before Christ.
Prat	Origène, le Théologien et l'Exegète.
Preseensé	The early years of Christianity.
Redepenning	Origenes.
Sayce	The Religion of Ancient Egypt.
Scott Moncrieff	Paganism and Christianity in Egypt.
Tollinton	Clement of Alexandria.
Westcott	Essays in the History of Religious Thought in the West.

Dictionary of Christian Biography Art. "Origen"